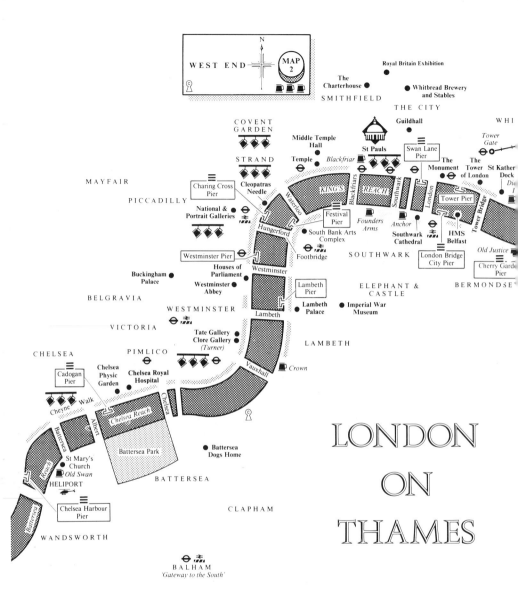

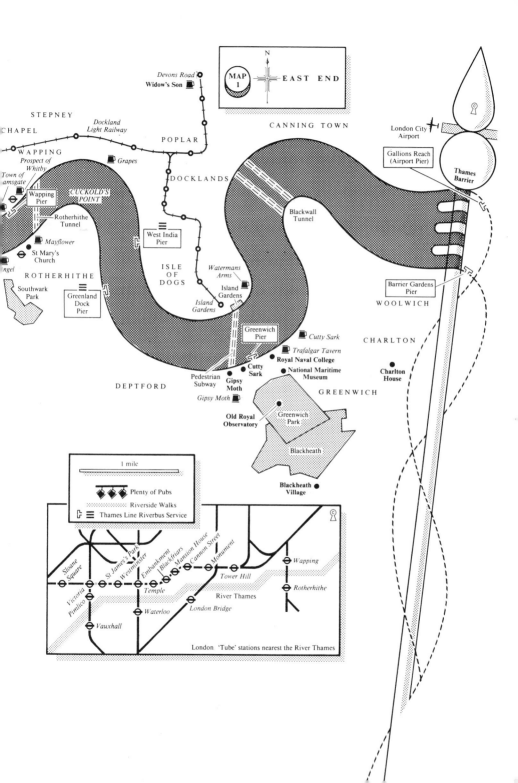

MAP 1 — EAST END

N

Devons Road
Widow's Son

STEPNEY
CHAPEL

Dockland
Light Railway

POPLAR

WAPPING
Prospect of
Whitby
Town of
Ramsgate

Grapes

DOCKLANDS

CANNING TOWN

London City
Airport

Gallions Reach
(Airport Pier)

Thames
Barrier

Wapping Pier

CUCKOLD'S
POINT

Rotherhithe
Tunnel

Mayflower
St Mary's
Church

Angel

ROTHERHITHE

Southwark
Park

West India
Pier

ISLE
OF
DOGS

Watermans
Arms

Island
Gardens

Island
Gardens

Blackwall
Tunnel

Barrier Gardens
Pier

WOOLWICH

Greenland
Dock Pier

Greenwich
Pier

Cutty Sark

Trafalgar Tavern

Royal Naval College

National Maritime
Museum

CHARLTON

Charlton
House

Pedestrian
Subway

Cutty
Sark

Gipsy
Moth

Gipsy Moth

Old Royal
Observatory

Greenwich
Park

GREENWICH

DEPTFORD

Blackheath

Blackheath
Village

1 mile

Plenty of Pubs

Riverside Walks

Thames Line Riverbus Service

Sloane
Square

St James's Park

Westminster

Embankment

Blackfriars

Mansion House

Cannon Street

Monument

Wapping

Victoria

Pimlico

Temple

Tower Hill

River Thames

Rotherhithe

Waterloo

London Bridge

Vauxhall

London 'Tube' stations nearest the River Thames

LONDON ON THAMES

AN ENGLISH HERITAGE
UPSTREAM

– from WESTMINSTER to WINDSOR –

(to say nothing of the bridges in between)

WRITTEN AND ILLUSTRATED

BY

TIMOTHY TYNDALE DANIELL

GRACED WITH

A FOREWORD BY

Sir Christopher Leaver, G.B.E.
J.P., K.St.J., D.Mus.(Hon),
F.C.I.T., F.R.S.A., Order of Oman II.

Third Millennium Leisure Limited
MCMLXXXVIII

LONDON ON THAMES – UPSTREAM – First Edition 1988

British Library Cataloguing in Publication Data

Daniell, Timothy Tyndale
London On Thames : upstream.
1. London – Visitors' guides
I. Title
914.21'04858

ISBN 0–9512448–0–9
ISSN 0954–6758

Published by
THIRD MILLENNIUM LEISURE LIMITED
(registered office) The Courtyard, Chobham High Street, Surrey, England GU24 8AF

Considerable care has been exercised throughout this book to be accurate but the publishers cannot accept any responsibility for any errors which appear, or, their consequences.

— Principally set in Bembo Bold type (and Baskerville Roman see) —
227
Type set, printed and bound by
The Bocardo Press Limited, Didcot, England OX11 7EN

DEDICATION

In esteem of my parents, Ralph and Diana –
for the opportunity of *and in* life!

CONTENTS PAGE

PRINCIPAL LIST OF ILLUSTRATIONS

Sir Christopher Leaver G.B.E.
Chairman – London Tourist Board Ltd.
Chairman – Thames Line PLC.
Chairman – Russell and McIver Ltd.
Deputy Chairman – Thames Water Authority
Lord Mayor of London (1981–82)
Master of The Worshipful Company of Carmen (1987–88)
Freeman of The Company of Watermen and Lightermen;
Hon. Liveryman of The Worshipful Company of Farmers, and,
The Worshipful Company of Environmental Cleaners.

FOREWORD

AS ONE WHO HAS SPENT MANY YEARS committed to the revitalisation of our capital's great river, I can only most warmly welcome anything that helps anyone enjoy our Thames heritage. This book does. Especially so, as LONDON ON THAMES is being launched at a time when the river is, once again, coming to life after the years of decline following the closure of the London docks and abandonment of the wharves and basins. The past two decades have seen, therefore, both a death and a renaissance. This book can play an important part in the rebirth of the Thames.

Londoners and visitors alike, in their hundreds of thousands, enjoy river trips and that different view of London which the river furnishes. The new architectural adventures along the reaches above and below Westminster provide all that one could ask by way of proof that the Thames river frontage is once again alive and well. This vitality has its historical origins in the organic growth of our national life along so much of the Thames, London's Great Highway. It is increasingly reflected in a new liveliness of river usage for travellers, tourists, and leisure purposes, alike.

The glories of the Thames, its Valley and the historic buildings which line it, provide a rich experience for tourists from all over the world. LONDON ON THAMES will help their enjoyment and by doing so will serve both the reputation of our City and our Nation.

NOËL PICARDA KEMP, M.A. [Oxon.]
P.G.C.E. [London].

INTRODUCTION

LONDON ON THAMES is exactly the sort of book one is delighted to give, or, better still, to receive as a present. Written for the traveller who has 'done' the 'sights' of London on previous visits, this excellent book, with its charming illustrations by the author, leads the visitor (and native alike) on a superbly researched series of river safaris.

At last one can, in one book, find accurate sailing times and overland travel advice that enables one to visit some of the splendid houses and locations in and around London, without wasting hours. We are wisely advised when a river trip is rewarding or when it would be better to save time and boredom with an Underground or British Railway dash.

LONDON ON THAMES – UPSTREAM – generously occupies itself with the stretch of river between Westminster and Windsor thus focussing on as rich a stretch of scenery and history as any to be found in the world: packed with useful information, timetables, maps, and description.

To visit some of the great riverside houses of London and the river with this book as a companion is like going out on a treat with an amusing, unstuffy and very knowledgeable friend.

Timothy Tyndale Daniell writes with the relish of an Edwardian traveller but with the precise curiosity and exactitude of observation of a Georgian *grand touriste*. No mean artist himself (the book may well become a collector's item for his delicious sepia evocations of the Thames-side scenery alone), his descriptions of, for example, Southside House and the history of the resident family, the Pennington-Kemys-Wharton-Tynte-Vaughan-Mellor-Munthes, owe as much to Alexandre Dumas as to Osbert Lancaster.

As well as introducing the visitor to, and reminding the Londoner of, the delights of places like Kew Gardens and Hampton Court, T.D. has taken care that the body of the dedicated user of his book is as well nourished, as is the mind. Here is an excellent *vade mecum* for good pubs and restaurants in the Lower Thames Valley.

Like a good recipe book, good travel writing can become an end for the reader in itself. The meal may be enjoyed as well in the mind as in the preparation and eating of it. Such a delightful travel book as this, runs the risk of relieving the traveller of the need to venture out and about.

A quick dip into the contents of this book will kindle feelings of guilt in Londoners that they so often neglect the glories around them; for the visitor, perhaps, envy for the Londoner; and certainly a determination to see with their own eyes the splendours of the English heritage so ably depicted here by pen and brush.

It may well be that better books become available to introduce readers to the treasures to be found in and around a capital city. When such books are written, it is most unlikely that they will be by anyone but the author and illustrator of LONDON ON THAMES.

THE MOST STRIKING IMAGES OF LONDON may be had by those who venture on the water. Add to those the intrinsic attraction of a slow-moving panorama of sights – often with an informative commentary from a member of the crew – and the benefits of a voyage afloat become obvious.

Besides, the river offers an escape from traffic; noise; fumes.

Scheduled river services cater for excursionary trips on the tidal section of the river, from Westminster to new Thames Barrier at Woolwich, (beyond Greenwich and the Tower), and all the way to Hampton Court, (beyond Chelsea, Richmond and Kingston), some twenty miles further inland.

A handy passenger service is now available to Londoners and visitors, launched by *Thames Line Plc* (1988), providing a fast and easy access to places of interest along the river Thames between Chelsea Reach (upstream) and Gallion's Reach (downstream).

ONE WAY TO DISCOVER LONDON is to ask a policeman:

The party was to meet at the pier of the House of Commons, and go up the river in two steamers. As we did not know precisely where the pier was, we stopped outside the House of Lords to ask a policeman.

Dialogue:

I. 'Can you tell me where I shall find the pier of the House of Commons?'

Policeman. 'No, sir, indeed, we have plenty of peers in the House of Lords, but I have never yet heard of a peer of the House of Commons.'

Wilfred Scawen Blunt: [Diary, 17 June, 1893.]

THE MOST ATTRACTIVE WAY, however, is to take to the river. Not only are the prime sights seen to such advantage from the river (weather permitting, of course) but the Thames is a living link to two thousand years of history –

I have seen the Mississippi. That is muddy water. I have seen the St. Lawrence. That is crystal water. But every drop of the Thames is liquid 'istory.

John Burns: Remark to Transatlantic visitors; attrib. by Sir Frederick Whyte. [19thC.]

Sacred is the name of *olde* Father Thames, to Londoners and to men of every age. Writers, from Chaucer and Shakespeare to modern day poets, invariably acknowledge their kinship to the River and many have drawn inspiration from it. Artists, too, have responded to the beauty of the Thames and have left their paintings of the River as their testaments. A sensual pleasure awaits all those who venture *to the visual galleries* upstream, such as at the superb water-palace of Hampton Court, the Royal Botanic gardens at Kew, or the graceful settings that abound at Richmond and Twickenham – where respectively Reynolds and Turner lived.

To reach the aspects of the River that are highlighted in the many excursions that follow, a combined use of road, rail and water transport is recommended. To embark by river from Westminster for locations upstream can involve a considerable journey-time, which may be circumvented by travelling on London's fast Underground system or by British Rail. Such time saved can be better devoted to exploring the localities, which are set amidst some of the most delightful stretches of the river.

With so much history on offer, it is easy enough to become awash with dates and details, names and more names – titles galore! – which can blur the senses and dull the mind. If only history was a little shorter, would it not make the difference to a better recollection of all those events that stride down the centuries? Every now and then, however, some special piece of information comes forward which renders all that time spent listening to historical patter worth the effort; some special feature of the umpteenth historic outing justifies the discomfort of stifling crowds and aching feet.

And all those kings of England, jostling for attention amidst their muddlesome sons and heirs and grandfathers before them. Should they not have realised that their numbered namesakes would lead to a chronology of confusion? Their subjects are not as well versed as are professors of history or royal genealogists.

The pages ahead should help the traveller to combine the pleasures of their visit with an enhanced appreciation of the past.

Welcome aboard!

This book presents a series of riverside excursions along the river Thames from Westminister, westwards, up to Windsor – where so many of London's interesting and picturesque sights exist – based on the common historical link of the river.

The pier near the House of Commons

The starting point is at Westminster or Charing Cross (Piers) and a progression sketched upstream to where the beauties of the river are later featured in individual excursions. A logical progression to Windsor, one of the furthest points upriver, follows the excursions to famous beauty-spots – Hampton Court, Richmond, Kew – which are taken in sequence, together with less well-known but equally appealing locations – Twickenham, Ham, Petersham – after the better known 'reaches' downstream, such as at Chelsea and Westminster.

In all, the river offers everyone something, whichever course is decided. Before that choice is made, a word or two must be addressed in homage to the Great Highway of London itself, Father Thames.

Because Lambeth Bridge was not built until 1862, William Wordsworth had to make do – which he did pretty well – with the view from another one –

Earth has not any thing to show more fair:
Dull would he be of soul who could pass by
A sight so touching in its majesty:

This City now doth, like a garment wear
The beauty of the morning; silent, bare,

Ships, towers, domes, theatres, and temples lie
Open unto the fields, and to the sky;
All bright and glittering in the smokeless air.
Never did sun more beautifully steep
In his first splendour, valley, rock, or hill;
Ne'er saw I, never felt, a calm so deep!
The river glideth at his own sweet will:

Dear God! the very houses seem asleep;
And all that mighty heart is lying still!
Composed upon Westminster Bridge September 3, [1802].

The Great Highway of London

. . . The Knight in the triumph of his heart made several reflections on the greatness of the *British* nation; as that one *Englishman* could beat three *Frenchmen*; that we cou'd never be in danger of Popery so long as we took care of our fleet; that the *Thames* was the noblest river in *Europe*; that *London Bridge* was a greater piece of work than any of the Seven Wonders of the *World*; with many other honest prejudices which naturally cleave to the heart of a true Englishman.

Joseph Addison: The Spectator, no.383. [c.1712.]

IF GOD'S GIFT were an Englishman then his Greatest Blessing must be the Thames. Englishmen of every hue, and Londoners particularly, think so of their very fine river which has provided much of their good fortune in this world.

Blessed foreigners agreed about the Thames

It did not take long for others to agree, the Vikings, the Romans and even the French. From the cornerstones of the Norman Conquest at the great garrisons of Windsor and the Tower, the ebb and flow of British history has been borne on the Thames's tides: from Runnymede where the City Fathers and the Barons checked the conscience of King John, to downstream Guildhall, hardby London Bridge, where England's civil liberties were hatched and zealously upheld, then enshrined at Westminster, and later transposed overseas.

' . . . every drop of the Thames is liquid 'istory'

These, and the many subsequent events that have enlivened English history, took place on the riverbank, where once the Viking longships and the Roman galleys were first sighted by the heathen ancestors of Englishmen good and true.

Until the advent of horse-drawn transport the river was Man's primary means of travel as well as transportation of his goods in

1

the southern region of England. Traders and travellers journeyed via the Thames valley and:

> In this connection the Thames is of an especial interest, for it had, in proportion to its length, the greatest section of navigable non-tidal water of any of the shorter rivers in Europe . . .
>
> This exceptional sector of non-tidal *navigable* water cutting right across England from east to west, and that in what used to be the most productive and is still the most fertile portion of the island, is the chief factor in the historic importance of the Thames.
>
> *Hilaire Belloc: The Historic Thames [1915]*

Provided a vessel or craft bore a light draught of less than a metre, it could run between Oxford and London Bridge, propelled by a twice-daily tidal current through the many upstream reaches of the river. Traders and journeymen plied the *Great Highway*, as it came to be known, and the river duly acted as the prime focal point for the early settlements in southern England.

Tons of 'tons'- 'dons'- 'fords'- and 'hythes'

From the estuary to the head of the river at Lechlade, countless communities settled on its banks, today's names for them still abounding with the vestiges of old Saxon or Teutonic syllables – the '-tons' and '-dons', the '-fords' and '-hythes' – the placenames stand out as much older than the Norman or Roman invasions. Because of the self-sufficiency that an inland waterway provided for these communities, the Thames valley became a populous region from earliest times (as is shown by the great number of archaeological sites of interest today) and has so remained to this day. In time, when water could be tapped and harnessed to supply the essential needs of man far removed from its source of extraction, the hinterland developed, and with it the trade on which Thames-side communities prospered. Londoners did best of all and benefitted from the good fortune of their location, at the crossways of water and overland routes of communication.

Pepys makes the point

If London's history is the story of its river as is commonly said, so also does her prosperity stem from the same source. The Great Highway, London's Great Highway, served the city which was built on, rather than beside, her waters. A great proportion of the trade and merchandise passing through was also borne by water. And so were her inhabitants: Pepys, for example, took pains to record in his Diary *the point when he travelled to a place by land.* So

frequent and commonplace was his use of the river, that it barely
rated mention, in the absence of an unusual occurrence (or a
catastrophe, such as in the fateful passage of his cheeses on the
water to which he abandoned them in the hope of preserving
them from the peril of the Great Fire).

Only one London Bridge

It will be recalled that in Pepys's day there was only London
Bridge, spanning the river. A second bridge, at Westminster, was
built in 1751 – comparatively late when considering the require-
ments of traffic passing between the two riverbanks. Pepys was
born at the time when Hackney coaches were introduced to
London. Cost denied this means of conveyance to the majority,
and while those who could afford the use of a mule or horse did so
(in spite of the notorious risks and discomfort on the by-ways),
the most expeditious means of travel across London was by water.
This involved a certain degree of trust in the proficiency of the
licensed carriers, the Watermen and Lightermen, a breed whose
language – or 'riverwit' – was quite as lively as their thirst. They
stroked their oars in time to songs, with versions which most of
their passengers would scarcely be likely to hear on dry land, let
alone repeat.

My wife and I by water, with my brother, as high as Fulham, talking
and singing and playing the rogue with the western bargemen, about
the women of Woolwich which mads them.

Pepys: Diary. [14 May, 1669]

To the knight's great surprise, as he [Sir Roger de Coverley] gave
the good night to two or three young fellows a little before our
landing, one of them instead of returning the civility, asked us what
green old Put we had in the boat, and whether he was not ashamed to
go a wenching at his years & with a great deal of the like Thames
ribaldry.

Addison: The Spectator, no.383.

There's no talking to these watermen, they will have the last word.

Ben Jonson's Leatherhead.

In the rich Company of Watermen

The Guild of Watermen and Lightermen of the River Thames was
first regulated in 1555 and has long been a colourful feature of the
city. Their number 'by the only labour of oar and the scull' was
estimated 'betwixt the bridge of Windsor and Gravesend' as
'could not be fewer than 40,000'. They also provided, on occasion,
'upwards of 20,000 men for the fleet', in the days when the Navy
was supplied of men through impressment. Their traditions are
still fostered in an annual contest, the Doggett's Coat and Badge,

named after Thomas Doggett, the sponsor of a prize – a Badge and livery – for winning a race between six post-apprentices conducted from the *Swan* at London Bridge to the *Swan* at Chelsea, since 1715.

For those who disdained the above company, or such means of travel, there was always an alternative, which may be preferred, more *even* today –

> *Let others in the jolting coach confide,*
> *Or in the leaky boat the Thames divide,*
> *. . . Still let me walk.*
>   John Gay [1715].

Of the many other forms of life that existed on the banks of Father Thames down the centuries but which are no more, there was one particular institution which, greater by far than all others combined, has left its imprint in a legacy still visible to this day: it was the era of monastic influence – brought by the monks to the Thames valley in the 7thC – through which the cultural heritage of the kingdom was evolved until suppressed, abruptly in the 16thC.

The Habit of Residence in the Thames Valley

The three great foundations on the River Thames were established by the followers of St. Benedict, according to tradition. These monasteries were at Westminster, Chertsey and Abingdon. The Benedictine Order returned the British Isles to mainstream European culture in the wake of St. Augustine's mission, when its civilising influence helped sweep away the Dark Age which had descended on a mainland abandoned by the Roman legions.

The monastic era was greatly advanced by the invading Normans, themselves schooled in the grand monastic houses of northern France. It was at about this time that the Cluniac and Carthusian monasteries, of Reading and Sheen, were instituted.

Thus, the *habit of residence* in the Thames valley followed on from the monastic presence of the great religious houses that held sway in the communal existence of the river. In the monastic tradition of receivers of wealth, the prosperity of the Thames valley was cultivated. Our mediaeval forbears needed no schooling in a monk's calling – the quest of Truth – to comprehend the homely truth of the monastic institutions that became thus enriched:

Money begets money.

The Great Monastic Orders

For these religious houses, with their monopoly of learning, their
lands and their treasured possessions, fulfilled the functions of a
local exchange and mart. As their revenues increased, so their
influence stretched broader and deeper through the Thames
valley. They tempered their worldly values with charity; providing transient hospitality and alms to the poor, relief and
medicaments to the sick and suffering and tended the common
land of the neighbouring parishes as good husbandmen.

Father Thames enjoyed a staggering number of these communi-
ties which lined the river banks in profusion. The Augustinians,
Benedictines, Carthusians, to name the great Orders, with their
Abbeys, Priories, cells and other foundations in scores of greater
and lesser degree, they, together with the Nunneries and their
Schools, represented a formidable riparian presence.

Henry Tudor's monastic plunder

Tudor avarice, as every schoolboy knows, replaced the abbot with
the squire. A whole economic power system was transformed,
with consequences that were to be felt by all succeeding
generations and which are still visible in the social fabric of
England. In the century following the monks' obliteration,
profound changes occurred in the English way of life. Village life
for the common man fell under the autocracy of the private
landlord – the 'squirearchy' – who extinguished villagers' ancient
rights to common land and appropriated the land to their estates.
What had begun as a measure to bolster the finances of
King Henry VIII (ever a prodigious spender) resulted in the royal
coffers retaining but a fraction of the spoils. These were acquired
by the rising ranks of the middle classes who were by now well
represented in the lower assembly of Parliament and, in the course
of six reigns, the monarchy became an impotent front for the
landed gentry.

Spoils for the nouveaux riches

Still the plundered names of the country landowners evoke their
monastic ties, as in Woburn Abbey and Beaulieu, and date from
the times in which the new generation of squires bought their
respectability, with titles in the upper Chamber or a seat in the
House of Commons, to reflect their aggrandisement and who,
through Stuart and Hanoverian reigns, consolidated their wealth
into this century until the First War began the eclipse of the 'old'
order.

The prosperity established by monastic influence in the Thames valley underwent material change, naturally, when the Tudor magnates pillaged and demolished the monastic buildings, in order to embellish or rebuild their residential properties in the neighbouring countryside. Scarcely a great old house exists which is not adorned with the stonework taken from a monastic quarry.

Buildings of substance and marvel were built as ornaments of beauty, proudly displayed by Englishmen who had gained an unshakable confidence in the vision of their homeland. The estuary fortresses at Tilbury and Gravesend and the defensive portcullis of the Tower, downstream, highlighted the protection afforded by the waterways of the Thames.

There is one man in particular who adapted the River Thames to his own character and left an indelible mark, both on the course of the river and English history: William the Conqueror. The key to an appreciation of the two most famous fortresses in the British Isles – the Tower of London and Windsor Castle – and the key to much of historical significance in English history, lies within these two strongholds, on which subsequent major events were staged in the centuries that followed the great Norman's presence.

WILLIAM THE CONQUEROR'S THAMES

William took hold of the main artery of the island kingdom's communications by choosing both sites carefully, upstream and down. If the Norman garrison in the White Tower kept watch over London, so did his encampment at Windsor, chosen by the military strategist as being within a day's march from the Capital, should an insurrection by the citizenry beleaguer his forces and require a rapid deployment of reinforcements. What history was to prove time and again was spotted by William the Conqueror, namely that control of these strategic sites ensured victory over rival contestants for the mantle of the Kingship. For the main overland routes that connected southern and central England crossed through the Thames valley:

> Watling Street joined Dover to Chester and intersected the Thames at the 'horse-ferry' betwixt Lambeth and Westminstrer. The East Anglian route along Icknield Way was an ancient barbarian track and cut through the Thames valley at Dorchester and at Wallingford, while Ermine Street crossed the river at Cricklade, connecting the Berkshire hills to the fertile highground of Hampshire communities.

The fourth main route was the Fosse Way which crossed the
headwaters of the Thames where the metal mines of Cornwall
became linked to the Pennines.

By choosing strategic positions for the defence of their strongholds, the Conqueror and his barons either built or resurrected a
chain of bastions that stretched throughout the kingdom and so
cemented the Normans' domination of the island races. Windsor
Castle is *the* outstanding example, as King John's troops were to
prove in holding the fortress for the Crown against the combined
forces of the Barons and even the King of France. This castle so
nearly enabled King John to retain his kingdom in the campaign
that followed the truce at Runnymede, not forgetting that most of
the south of England had fallen to his enemies.

Within four years of landing at Hastings, meanwhile, William
had constructed the Round Keep on the terrain above the
'winding shore' at the bend in the river [Wind-sor]. With forests to
the south and surrounded by water, on three sides, he chose the
steep cliff which overlooks the water meadows of Ea-ton [Eton]
on the far bank. There he held court with his Norman barons and
consolidated his grip over the quarrelsome kingdom he had won.

Some twenty miles downstream, the impregnable White Tower
was built in 1067, on the eastern perimeter of the City of London.
On a natural mound above the shingle of the river's pathway, it
was built to intimidate the populace and was whitewashed, to be
seen from afar in the sunsets over the London marshes. Visits to
both these magnificent places put history in perspective and are
therefore logical excursions to make at the start of a visit to
London. For this reason alone, an account of Windsor (and
Runnymede) is included in the excursions to follow.

Liquid history upstream

In all, the range of choice provided on the banks of the Thames is
not to be missed by anyone who would rather exchange the bustle
of London's crowded thoroughfares for the tranquil panorama of
the enviable river settings. Nowhere may the bold edifices of past
grandeur be seen to better advantage than in the regal splendours
of England's royal heritage on the Thames. This book covers
many accessible places on the river, upstream of Westminster,
which may appeal, for example, to the traveller intent on visiting
Hampton Court and wishing to explore further afield. While
Henry VIII's palace affords a prime reason to venture upriver,

Richmond, beside Kew, should not be missed – once a renowned royal residence in its own right – and still combining the glories of nature with London's landscape 'where countryside meets town'.

Our Royal Heritage

Before seeing such places, there will be those who demand a visit to the greatest shrine of all: Westminster Abbey. As the lone survivor of the monastic purge, it became the main repository of England's royal heritage since its foundation by Edward the Confessor in 1065. This glorious sanctuary, which also housed England's mediaeval Parliament for three hundred years (in the Chapter House until the 16thC), stands out in the list of principal sights that repay its visitors handsomely. For there, at Westminster, under the shadow of the nation's famous 'time-piece', where the *Great Highway* provides our rendezvous with upstream Thames, our journey into history properly begins.

River services are most frequent during the summer months (April – October). Winter schedules can vary greatly, where such exist. Passengers intending to embark on rivercraft should remember to ascertain return timetables.

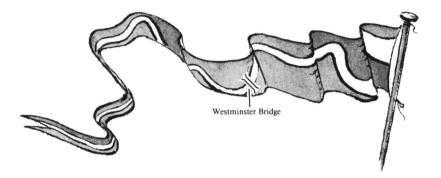

Westminster Bridge

─────────── UPSTREAM FROM WESTMINSTER ───────────

From CHARING CROSS PIER   To: Cadogan Pier
                                 Chelsea Harbour Pier

Water transport: Riverbus service

Frequency: Every 15 minutes between
                                0700 and 2300 hours (weekdays)
                                1000 and 1800 hours (weekends)

Journey times: Approximately 10 minutes or less between
                             piers

Further information: Thames Line (Operator) T.941–5454

From WESTMINSTER PIER   To: Kew [one way: 1½ hours]
                                 Richmond [one way: 2½ hours]
                                 Hampton Court [one way: 3½ hours]

Water transport: River steamer, usually licensed bar

Frequency: Every hour, or on the half hour during peak
                             demand, between 1015 and 1600 hours

Journey times:
                             } See Appendix and pages 70 & 71
Further information:

GENERAL NOTES FOR BOATPERSONS

The Tideway is the name given to the tidal stretch of the River Thames and normally refers to water passing between London Bridge and Teddington Lock. The Assistant Harbour Master welcomes navigational enquiries: [01] 481–0720.

The Tideway's 'Highway Code':

One of many important rules of the Highway Code is the 'give way' rule – upstream traffic always gives way to any craft travelling downstream which if observed will ensure safe passage. The rule has its origin in the days when unstemmed tides ebbed back to London Bridge at uncontrollable speed, in part caused by the famous Bridge itself acting as a bottleneck through which the raging torrents swept all in its path. (The custom of 'shooting the bridge' was an ill-advised pastime that is later referred to).

Like some practitioners of the **other** Highway Code, boatpersons take considerable pains to show courtesy to other 'Highway' users when altering course and changing direction. This is not done by hand signals or eletronic flashers, but is announced by the time-honoured blast of a hooter. These sound signals give an added dimension to the many unexpected noises that permeate the river Highway.

One short blast:	Vessel going to starboard	going right, of bow
Two short blasts:	Vessel going to port	going left, of bow
Three short blasts:	Vessel going astern	going backwards
Four short blasts:	Vessel unable to manoeuvre	going nowhere
Four short blasts, followed by one blast:	Vessel turning round, to starboard	going about turn, clockwise
followed by two blasts:	Vessel turning round, to port	going about turn, anticlockwise
A continuous blast:	Vessel in danger, distress signal	going under?

In the most serious instance, the 'Lutine's' bell may have to be rung – once, to report a total shipwreck – where it may be heard downstream, in the proximity of Lime Street, City of London. The bell was salvaged from the wreck of the warship which sank on 9th October, 1799, with loss of every soul (bar one, who died after being rescued), off the Dutch coast. The Lloyd's underwriters faced a dreadful financial loss, hence the bell is hung at their world headquarters, and, their chairman sits – when not praying against calamity on the High Seas – in his 'official' chair carved out of the Lutine's rudder.

Should you hear the bell tolling *twice*, be not alarmed unduly: a ship is merely overdue. If yours, there is little you can do, except thoroughly enjoy the extended moment on the river Thames.

THE GREAT CHAM of literature, as Smollett dubbed Dr. Johnson, enjoyed himself on the River. Of that there is little doubt –

> It is well known that there was formerly a rude custom for those . . . upon the Thames to accost each other as they passed in the most abusive language they could invent; generally . . . with as much satirical humour as they were capable of producing.

> Johnson was once eminently successful in this species of contest. A fellow having attacked him with some coarse raillery, Johnson answered him thuse:

> "Sir, your wife, under pretence of keeping a bawdy house, is a receiver of stolen goods."
> Boswell.

That remark is scurrilously obscure.

Of the meaning of the best known lines of Johnson, there is not the slightest doubt even if Boswell elicited them by suggesting:

> a doubt, that if I were to reside in London, the exquisite zest with which I relished it in occasional visits might go off, and I might grow tired of it..

> **"Why, Sir, you find no man, at all intellectual, who is willing to leave London. No, Sir, when a man is tired of London he is tired of life; for there is in London all that life can afford".**
> *Dr. Samuel Johnson: remark attributed by*
James Boswell, Life of Johnson, [29 Sep. 1777).

A word about the weather. As Dr. Johnson drily observed –

> When two Englishmen meet, their first talk is of the weather.
>
> *(The Idler, No. 11).*

Today's visitors to these shores will, of necessity, soon pick up the habit.

Travellers to London in the last century underwent a twenty-four hour indoctrination in the weather –

> To sleep in London, however, is an art which a foreigner must acquire by time and habit. Here was the night watchman, whose business it is, not merely to guard the streets and take charge of the public security, but to inform the good people of London every half hour of the state of the weather.
>
> For the first three hours I was told it was a moonlit night, then it became cloudy, and at half past three o'clock was a raining morning- so that I was well acquainted with every variation of the atmosphere, as if I had been looking from the window all night long.
>
> A strange custom this, to pay men for telling them what the weather is every hour during the night, till they get accustomed to the noise, so that they sleep on and cannot hear what is said.
>
> *Letters from England, by Don Manuel Alvarez*
> *Espriella (Robert Southey)[1807].*

While in London, or anywhere in England, one of life's more affordable luxuries must be the umbrella, as protection against the unpredictable elements.

The umbrella was introduced into England (1756) by Jonas Hanway, philanthropist and a contemporary of Dr. Johnson. They lived near one another, at Red Lion Square (Holborn) and Gough Square, respectively. Of the two, Johnson was probably less pessimistic about the weather, hence the use of tinted spectacles in the 'televised' illustration.

Of Hanway, Dr. Johnson had this to say (in keeping with his renown for something to be said about everything):

> Jonas acquired some reputation by travelling abroad, but lost it all by travelling at home.
>
> *(Boswell, ibid, p.126 [1770].)*

The great lexicographer was alluding to Hanway's authorship of *Travels to Persia* which was followed by his less than well-received volume, *An Eight Days' Journey from London to Portsmouth.*

Those venturing out and about on the water should take warm clothing as, on the river, lower temperatures and breezes are encountered. A spare pair of comfortable shoes will prove a god-send.

Venturing on the River

FOR THE MOST REWARDING INSIGHT into London, past and present, an excursion on the river Thames is still unbeatable value.

Of all the wide array of places on offer to the traveller who ventures on the *Great Highway*, those upstream are the most picturesque. For journeying to Kew, Richmond or Hampton Court – where the Thames's riverside glories are most closely grouped and displayed – the traveller has a choice of routes to follow.

Commencing the journey at the central location of Westminster Pier carries an obvious drawback that it can take between 3 and 4½ hours to reach Hampton Court: to save time, travel part of the course by rail, and take a boat-cruise on the best stretch upriver. If the latter decision is reached, a suggestion might be to take a train to Kingston, where steamers ply upstream to Hampton Court, taking 30 minutes, and down the other way to neighbouring Richmond and Kew, taking one hour to Richmond Pier: likewise, a train or tube to Richmond provides relatively quick access to those delightful destinations.

Readers are referred to the sections accompanying the river maps and pages which provide general information and time-tables. In all cases up-to-date information should be checked by telephoning enquiries to the relevant operator of services.

Taking to the water

For a preferred outing by water, it is worth taking extra clothing, as the temperature tends to drop by a degree or two from the breeze coming off the water. Providentially, most of the river-craft are licensed to serve alcoholic refreshment, for those who prefer to keep warm by other means.

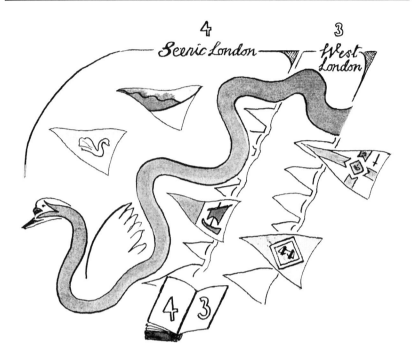

By river bus or steamer

Much of Central London is now accessible by fast new riverbus, a welcome service introduced by Thames Line, linking Upstream and Downstream in little over thirty minutes:

> Chelsea, (*Chelsea Harbour Pier, Cadogan Pier*), and
> Westminster (*Charing Cross Pier*),
> South Bank (*Festival Pier*),
> the City (*Swan Lane Pier*),
> Southwark (*London Bridge City Pier*),
> Rotherhithe (*Cherry Gardens Pier*),
> the Isle of Dogs (*West India Pier*),
> and even London's City Airport, at a pier to be
> decided near *Gallion's Reach*.

Many sightseers may therefore prefer to explore the famous haunts of Central London by riverbus rather than by overland or underground. Joining the new – if regular – commuters they can share a river view of London on Thames. Time will tell how fully this service will be appreciated.

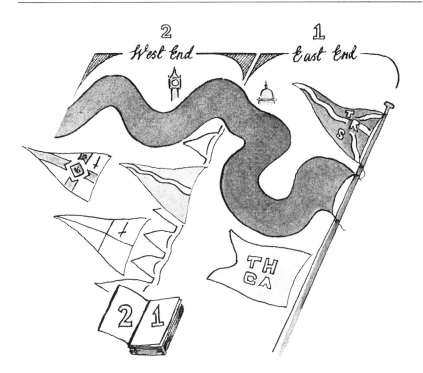

GENERAL INFORMATION

The chapters that follow are divided into a sequence of locations 'to aid the visitor's digestion' of the riverscape beauty and historical associations offered on the banks of the Thames. Places to visit, together with opening times, are listed in the Appendix.

How to use the maps

The river Thames flows through London to its estuary mouth at the Nore. At the front and back of the book are to be found the following sections of the river:

Inside front cover { Map 1   East End;
                      Map 2   West End;

Inside back cover { Map 3   West London;
                     Map 4   Scenic London.

These maps should be read in conjunction with the informaton listed in the Appendix of local places to visit and with the specific riversides narrated in the text. The next chapter commences a river journey upstream from Westminster.

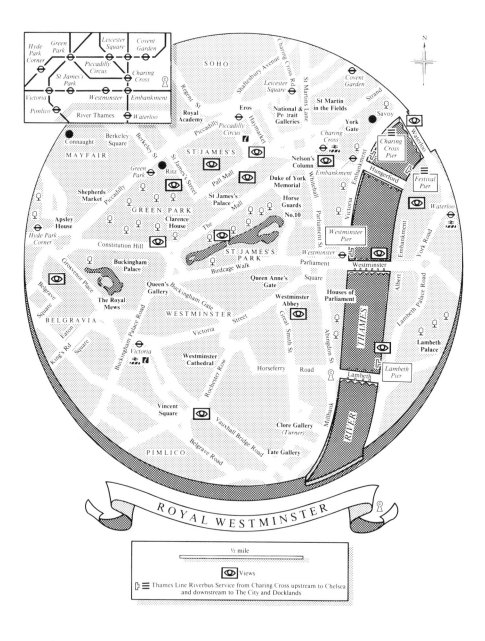

Upstream from Westminster Bridge

FOR MANY TRAVELLERS, the *well known* Westminster Pier will be the starting point for excursions on the Thames. A summary of the points of interest on and around the Westminster skyline is provided in the accompanying sections and an account of the path of the Thames above Westminster Bridge is recited until the outskirts of the city are reached: thereafter individual excursions are sketched of chosen locations from Kew to Windsor [upriver]. The book concludes with an opening account of the Downstream section of the river from Westminster.

Westminster Bridge

The stone bridge – only the fourth to have been built over the Thames, when erected in 1750 – was well enough in place by 1805 for William Wordsworth to extol an autumnal view in his celebrated poem. However, the structure was replaced (Thomas Page, 1862) after its piers gave way, caused by flow of water that was unleashed after the distinguished neighbour (London Bridge) gave way (1831), (when the nursery rhyme about *its falling down* had its effect). Despite a mighty increase in the velocity of overland traffic, the present structure has happily withstood the test of time.

Seven iron arches rest on giant granite plinths, allowing a maximum headroom clearance of 17 ft. 8 in. at mean highwater springs. At Westminster the centre span depth is about 4 ft. at mean low water springs, the shallowest draught of all London's bridges. Aspiring mariners may rest assured that should their vessel run aground and spring a leak, it is nigh impossible to drown.

At the bridge end of the pier is the imposing sculpture of *Queen Boadicea* (or Boudicca) (by T. Thorneycroft, 1902) who in AD 61 avenged her husband's death and revolted against the Romans with blood-curdling savagery, as suggested by the knives in the chariot wheels. (She is the only Queen in the British Isles to lie buried under a railway station, with the chauvinistic name of King's Cross).

The Palace of Westminster

The familiar sight of the Palace of Westminster, its reflected beauty rippling in the water, commands the view up river. The Houses of Parliament were built in 1860 (Sir Charles Barry, and Pugin) in Tudor gothic style and replaced the mediaeval palace which burnt down in 1834. Westminster Hall built in 1099, where monarchs lie in state, still survives. The Duke of Wellington had a hand in the choice of its proximity to the river. Following his brush with rioters whom he thwarted at the time of the Reform Bill (1832), he took the view that the legislative assembly should be as close to the river as possible, to facilitate an escape should revolution ever sweep the realm!

The Victoria and Albert Embankments

Victoria Embankment, on the Westminster bank, buttresses the entirety of Central London which bulges into Pimlico on the bend of the river. From Westminster to the Monument, in the City, this elegant structure conceals the main sewers and protects the District Line underground. On the 'South Bank' (eastwards) is the Albert Embankment. Both were designed by Sir Joseph Bazalgette and constructed in the 1860's. This corridor of granite walls, eight feet thick and more than a mile in length on either side, channels the Thames, free-flowing at high tide.

Westminster Bridge looks more carefree at low-tide, when the seven arches appear to make light of their load, an illusion created by the waterline lapping the sturdy granite pillars embedded in the Thames.

Lambeth Walk

On the South Bank, the gaunt outline of Old County Hall (left) and (right) St. Thomas's Hospital (named after the doubting disciple [John XX, 25] stand prominently across the water. Patients with this unrivalled view are said to take their time to recuperate, a most unwelcome – but pardonable – drain on the resources of the National Health Service. Paying patients get as good a view, but have to think twice before overstaying. The welcome greenery behind the grime of London bricks and mortar

points to the walled garden of His Grace, the Archbishop of
Canterbury, residing in the splendid and historic isolation
of Lambeth Palace. Shrouded in secrecy beside the pretty
silhouette of St. Mary's and with its own famed garden – tended
by the Tradescant Trust – both places are worth a visit, the former
on written application to the eminent cleric, or one of his
minions. There, on the corner of Lambeth Bridge and Pier, may
be had a very fine view from the celebrated Lambeth Walk,
near the Stairs where King Canute allegedly 'stemmed the tide' in
1030 A.D.

— *Passing below* —
LAMBETH BRIDGE

Lambeth Bridge, by G. Topham Forrest (1932), replaced a
suspension bridge, (1862) and extends on five steel arches supported
on granite piers, 776 ft. in length and 60 ft. in width. Westminster
Bridge by comparison is 1160 ft. long and 85 ft. wide. The bridge
is painted in the attractive livery of red and brown. This crossing

place was the site of the old 'horse ferry' which is commemorated in the name of the road leading from Westminster. It was also where James II carelessly dropped the Great Seal of England into the river while making good his exit from the kingdom on the night of December 11th, 1688. Should a mud lark by chance stumble on it, the Keeper of the Privy Purse would doubtless consider salving the royal conscience with the equivalent where-withal of a King's ransom. The dull corporate skyblocks and bulky municipal buildings encroach on the river where it bends, dominated by the Millbank Tower, 387 ft. high, (owned by, and known as, the Vickers building). Now the symmetrical classicism of the Tate Gallery comes into view, on the right.

The Tate Gallery

88

Rendered in high baroque (Sidney Smith, 1897), the façade possesses a worthy air, airily suggestive of the remarkable collection of paintings housed within. There should be a pier outside, where riverboats could moor while their passengers enjoy the artists' views of the river Thames, upstream and down, as an appetiser for the feast in store for them on their river excursion.

And the Clore Gallery of Turners

The Tate, as the *National Gallery at Millbank* is commonly known, was presented to the nation by the sugar baron, Sir Henry Tate, along with his collection of 65 paintings of the modern genre. This generous endowment formed the nucleus of the outstanding collection of works now on view which has been built into the major British gallery of modern art. As if Tate's gesture was not enough, the art-dealer Sir Joseph Duveen (as he then was) presented a gilded wing, together with some of the rare canvases which he had amassed with his fortune, in the early part of this century. As Lord Duveen he went on to even grander things when, as the reader may recall, he co-founded the National Gallery of Art in Washington, establishing a permanent home for the European paintings that he had procured for his rich and famous clients. To fill it he relied on the ingenious solution of encouraging them to leave their wonderful works of art to that gallery, thereby gaining posthumous fame and a reprieve for their heirs from the taxman's depredations.

Best of British

The Tate, which has received its own fair share of generous donations, enjoys the best collection of *British* art. Particularly magnificent is the collection of Turners, England's master in oils and water-colours. The artist himself left his masterpieces to the nation – folios exceeding 19,000 works of art – and now housed in the splendour of the Clore Gallery, an elegant new extension, the gift (1987) of another family of benefactors on whom fortune smiled, and who have enabled an appreciative public to return the compliment.

Back on the boat the more mundane views appear on a stretch of the left bank of the river at Nine Elms Reach, Vauxhall.

— *Passing under* —
VAUXHALL
BRIDGE

Vauxhall Bridge, by Sir Maurice Fitzmaurice and W.E. Riley (1906), replaced John Rennie's great iron structure of 1806, and features distinctive sculptures adorning the sides (Alfred Drury and F.W. Pomeroy, the latter noted for his figurine, Justice, atop the Old Bailey, downstream). For those who care to know, the dimensions of the bridge are 759 ft. in length by 80 ft. in width.

The Temple of Power

The massive hulk of Battersea Power Station looms out of the gloomy industrial wasteland of the south bank. Designed by Sir Giles Gilbert Scott, of that extraordinary family, in 1936 the huge structure (335 ft. in height, including the chimney stack) is now planned to be converted into an entertainment complex, whatever that might be, now that the uncompromising old giant has given up smoking, which is just as well since London's suppliers of fresh fruit and vegetables moved next door, (from Covent Garden) in 1974. For those who wish to be punctual at the opening of the Entertainments Centre in 1990, they should arrive well in time for the ceremony at 2.30 p.m. on May 21st.

Opposite, on the Pimlico bank, converted warehouses provide smart Londoners with tables on the river, at either the *Villa dei Cesari*, – perhaps he did have one on the Thames – or, moored beside it in the floating restaurant of *the Elephant on the River*. (Perhaps Caesar also had one accompany him up the Thames?). Behind the dull flatness of commercial hoardings, the bulk of Dolphin Square, a fashionable apartment block, holds sway amidst the rejuvenated terraces of what was once a London suburb. Pimlico was where a Miss Mary Davies lived, at Ebury Farm, before she met Sir Thomas Grosvenor who married her

(1676) and thereby added to his small fortune, not only an heiress, but all the fields at the back of Buckingham Palace –

> A marshy spot, where not one patch of green,
> No stunted shrub, nor sickly flower is seen.
> *[according to Mrs. Gascoigne, prior to 1825].*

King George III had foreseen the potential that existed in the district adjoining the new royal residence. His then Prime Minister (Grenville) would not provide the princely sum of £20,000 to buy the land and thus Grosvenor Place, and the fields behind, were developed into a fashionable district by the ubiquitous Lord Grosvenor. The boggy site was filled in by Messrs. Cubitt and Smith with soil excavated from downstream at St. Katherine's Dock in 1825. The district is Belgravia which owes its name to the Leicestershire village (Belgrave) that belonged to the Dukes of Westminster (as the Grosvenors have become).

— Passing under —
GROSVENOR BRIDGE

Grosvenor Bridge (1967) replaced the first railway bridge across the Thames which had carried passengers to Victoria Station, a few hundred yards north, for the first time in 1860.

The River Thames sweeps between historic Chelsea and Battersea with their many literary and historical associations.

Places to visit within walking distance of Cadogan Pier, Chelsea, – see Appendix for details – include:

North of the River –

Chelsea Embankment: Crosby Hall – Chelsea Old Church – Chelsea Physic Garden – Carlyle's House;

Royal Hospital Road: National Army Museum – Chelsea Royal Hospital – Ranelagh Gardens;

King's Road: Shopping and Squares [Paultons, Carlyle, Markham, Sloane];

Further afield, by London Transport: Natural History Museum – Geological Museum – Victoria and Albert Museum – Royal Albert Hall – Knightsbridge stores [Harrods, Harvey Nichols] – Kensington Palace – Kensington Gardens;

South of the River –

Battersea Park [Sub-Tropical Gardens, Lake, The Parade] – St. Mary's Church – Old Battersea House [William De Morgan Collection] – Battersea Power Station [Leisure Complex]

Chelsea Reaches

Chelsea Bridge, by G. Topham Forrest and E.P. Wheeler (1934) replaced an earlier structure of 1858 (by Thomas Page). A distinguished construction with handsome ironwork, it marks where the *Chelsea Reach* of the river flowed at its widest point, west of London Bridge (until the construction of the Chelsea Embankment, Bazalgette, 1874).

Wren's Royal Hospital

The riverscene at last becomes more attractive, with the fine vision of Wren's Royal Hospital (1689). The home of Chelsea's In-Pensioners – army veterans – was built as a result of the supposed influence of Nell Gwynne on King Charles II. The hospital's lovely garden is now the renowned venue of the 'Royal' Chelsea Flower Show, which marks the official opening of springtime in England (towards the end of May). It always rains on the opening day, a Monday, as any taxi-driver will confirm. The site was long a fashionable place of amusement known as Ranelagh Gardens (formed out of the 18thC estate of the first Earl, thus named) which rivalled Vauxhall Gardens on the opposite bank.

> Every night constantly I go to Ranelagh; which has totally beat Vauxhall. Nobody goes anywhere else – everybody goes there. My Lord Chesterfield is so fond of it, that he says he has ordered all his letters to be directed thither.
>
> *Walpole to Conway [June 29th, 1744].*

Such was the rivalry between the two haunts that decoys were planted in either gardens to attract the ear – and eye – of passers-by with blandishments of the other place over the water. Both were places to see or be seen in –

> amphitheatres with little boxes into which everybody that loves eating, drinking, staring, or crowding is admitted for twelve pence . . . the fireworks . . . the gardens of pleasure . . .
>
> *Walpole to Mann [May 26th, 1742].*

And even places in which to get lost –

> The ladies that have an inclination to be private take delight in the close walks . . . where both sexes meet, and mutually serve one another as guides to lose their way, and the windings and turnings in the little Wildernesses are so intricate, that the most experienced mothers have often lost *themselves* in looking for their daughters.
>
> *Tom Brown's Amusements p.54 [1700].*

At Chelsea and Battersea the fine vision of parklands spreads out on either side, and the distinctive riverside terraces make a special feature at Cheyne Walk, Chelsea Embankment.

On the south bank Battersea Park occupies former mudflats which were overlaid with soil excavated from the Royal Victoria Docks in East End's Canning Town. It was opened by Queen Victoria in 1858 'for the pleasure of Her Majesty's subjects during recreational pursuits'. Whether the Peace Pagoda, introduced, somewhat incongruously into the treeline in 1985, adds to the serenity of the setting is for the passer-by to decide. From the Parade, where the Japanese Shrine sits in dappled shade, a superb view of the *Royal Hospital* can be had. The scarlet figures which distinguish the landscape are the In-Pensioners in their tunics and tricornes (three-cornered hats).

For the Japanese-minded

Japanese photographers may care to note, while here, the best view of Wren's Hospital.

Japanese visitors to the shrine should not miss, while on the South Bank, the Soseki Museum in Clapham, where Soseki Natsume, the distinguished novelist, lived whilst in London.

Likewise, a visit to the Victoria and Albert Museum will reveal the works of Utagawa Yoshitora, artist and printmaker, a pupil of Itagawa Kuniyoshi, who popularised the 'floating-world' prints when Tokyo was 'opened' to the outside world in the 1850s.

俺のことには かまうな: 自分の事は自分でしろ. (?)*

* Old Japanese saying: "Mind your own business".

Herewith his eyewitness account –

London, the capital city of England, lies on the river Thames. There are a great many buildings, and the whole population is prosperous . . . the number of students normally at university is never less than several tens of thousands.

The women are extremely lustful and the men are both shrewd and cunning. To fulfil their ambitions they build large ships with which to sail the oceans of the world. They trade in all manner of goods and make enormous profits for themselves.

From – A Compendium of Famous Places in Barbarian Countries:
[published by Yamadaya Shojiri, 1862].

'Barbarian' Englishmen and their women still maintain their traditions, tirelessly, to this day.

Westwards on Chelsea Embankment, the famous Physic Garden, presented to the Society of Apothecaries in 1722 by Sir Hans Sloane, still opens to the public. Visitors may see for themselves where was grown the first cotton-seed to be sent to America in 1732, with such profound consequences for the Deep South. Beyond Cadogan Pier – one stop by Thames Line riverbus for those of their passengers who wish to exchange the sights of

Westminster for those of Chelsea – is Cheyne Walk, with a host
of literary and artistic associations, bisected by the endearing
structure of Albert Bridge.

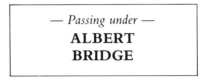

— *Passing under* —
ALBERT
BRIDGE

This delightful iron suspension bridge, in caramel and whipped
cream livery, was designed by R.M. Ordish in 1873, and intended
as a foot bridge. Fortunately, it has not totally given way to the
traffic. Bazalgette, (again), modified the cantilever designs with
this, resulting suspension design. Pairs of minarets gather the steel
cable which is attached, in ornamental loops, to each shore.

OLD CHELSEA

On the north bank, Cheyne Walk continues where the bridge intersects, leading from Oakley Street, which occupies the site of the *Manor House,* erected by Henry VIII (*1536*) and associated with three of his wives –

> – Henry had married Jane Seymour, his 3rd wife, secretly in Chelsea the previous year;
> – His 4th wife, Anne of Cleves died there (1556); she was the longest living of his 'two' widows;
> – Catherine Parr, his 6th wife (who also survived *him*) continued to reside there with her 4th husband (Sir Thomas Seymour).

Along the Chelsea Embankment, many of fame resided, where Blue Plaques are in their element –

Cheyne Walk

No. 4, George Eliot, novelist, (died here, 1880, after a residence lasting 19 days – see Wimbledon –);

No. 16, Queen's House (tenuously associated with Catherine of Braganza), home of Dante Gabriel Rossetti, pre-Raphaelite painter, (from 1862 almost till his death, 1882);

Embankment memorials: Rossetti fountain (by Ford Madox Brown); The Boy David, a sculpture by E. Bainbridge Copnall; in the gardens opposite Cheyne Row, seated bronze figure of Carlyle (by Sir Edgar Boehm, 1882);

If the *Kings Head and Eight Bells,* a 400 year-old Thames-side Pub, is packed, a pleasant alternative is to be found in Phene Street at the *Phene Arms.*

Cheyne Row

No. 24 (formerly no. 5), the Sage of Chelsea, Thomas Carlyle lived from 1834 until his death in 1881 (Carlyle House was opened to the Public in 1897, where his memorabilia are not allowed to gather dust); for 47 years Carlyle played host to his great contemporaries who, between them, probably discussed every topic under the sun, e.g. –

Tennyson: In my old age I should like to get away from all this tumult and turmoil of civilisation and live on the top of a tropical mountain! I should at least like to see the splendours of the Brazilian forests before I die . . . – If I were a young man I would like to head a colony out somewhere or other . . .

Carlyle: O, ay, so would I, to India or somewhere; but the scraggiest bit of heath in Scotland is more to me than all the forest of Brazil; I am just twinkling away, and I wish I had had my Dimittis long ago . . .
                                                      [Memoirs and Reflections]

No. 22 (Upper Cheyne Row), where Leigh Hunt lived (1833–1844);

Further on in Cheyne Walk are *Carlyle Mansions* where **Henry James, O.M.,** lived from 1912 until his death (1916);

Continuing Westwards, in *Cheyne Walk* –
No. 74, James Abbott McNeill Whistler, artist, died (1903);

BLUE PLAQUES

Out of monuments, names, wordes, proverbs, traditions, private
recordes, and evidences, fragments of stories, passages of bookes, *and the
like*, we doe save and recover somewhat from the deluge of time.

Lord Bacon. Advance of Learning. [1620].

I ask anybody who is in the habit of taking long walks in London or in
other cities, whether it is not an immense relief to come on some tablet
which suggests a new train of thought, which recalls to the mind the
career of some distinguished person, and which takes off the intolerable
pressure of the monotony of endless streets.

*5th Earl of Rosebery. Prime Minister 1894–5
1st Chairman, the London County Council [1901].*

Distinctive blue plaques are an agreeable feature of the Capital city and
were initiated by the Royal Society of Arts in 1866, later adopted by the
London County Council at the time when Lord Rosebery transferred his
talents across Westminster Bridge. Posthumous 'street fame' honours the
residential association of a noted individual, such as (in the words of the
committee) –

> he or she shall have had such an exceptional and outstanding
> personality that the name is known to the well-informed passer-by.

In the majority of cases the passer-by is flattered by the committee's
oblique compliment, although in some instances the onlooker is flattered
even more –

> (– *who* was 'Ouida', Maria Louisa de la Ramée d.1908, of Ravenscourt
> Square in Hammersmith, upstream? –)
> Whereas; everyone knows who the 'Father' of Lawn Tennis was –
> because the plaque at 33, St. George's Square, Pimlico, gives his
> name – Major Walter Clopton Wingfield (1833–1912).

The by-ways of Chelsea abound with blue plaques, especially on the
Embankment, where time may be pleasurably spent savouring the 'late
and great', and even the 'not-so-great', while also recovering somewhat
from the roar of London's traffic, if not from the deluge of time.

Nos. 97–100, Lindsey House, the sole surviving 17thC mansion in Chelsea, resided in by the 3rd Earl; Sir Marc Isambard Brunel and Isambard Kingdom Brunel, his son, engineering genii, (1811–1826);

No. 104, Hilaire Belloc, (1900–1905); Walter Greaves, Turner's boatman, protegé and artist, lived (1855–1897);

No. 109, Philip Wilson Steer, artist, lived and died (1942);

No. 119, Turner lived from 1846 until his death, (1851).

Chelsea Old Church

The historic Chelsea Old Church, dates back to the 12thC. It was but substantially rebuilt in the 17thC. Restored in 1964 after War damage, it contains, among many numerous associations, the 16thC *More* Chapel, which the famous scholar built for his private use in 1528 and which escaped later destruction. A statue of Sir Thomas More stands outside (L. Cubitt Bevis, 1969) and honours his period of residence in Chelsea, as also does the monument within, (right of Chancel, designed by More in 1532 intending to rest here with his second wife. Beneath, a long Latin epitaph especially composed for his first wife). Note the obliteration of the word 'hæreticisque' which evidenced his fatal theological dispute with Henry VIII.

Crosby Hall

Across Roper's Garden (named after Sir Thomas's son-in-law) stands Crosby Hall. One of the City of London's finest residences to survive the Great Fire, it was originally built in Bishopsgate, downstream. Prior to Sir Thomas's tenure – he lived there in 1523 – Crosby Hall boasted royal associations. One such was Richard III, maligned by Tudor propagandist William Shakespeare who drew the splenic character in his play from Thomas More's less than accurate and salutary account. The Hall was moved stone by stone and timber by timber to its present site, in 1910, perhaps giving rise to the practice which culminated in the wholesale removal of London Bridge to Arizona in 1973.

In Chelsea, Sir Thomas lived at Beaufort House, commemorated in the name of the street leading from King's Road to Battersea Bridge. Crosby Hall, his old City home, is open to the Public: now lovingly occupied by members of the British Federation of University Women, of whose emancipation the loving Sir Thomas himself would particularly have approved. What Sir John Crosby, the builder, a robust 15thC wool merchant, would have made of all this one can only wonder.

Also buried in Chelsea Old Church is a remarkable woman of a rather different hue to martyred More, but of the same vintage. Jane Dudley, Duchess of Northumberland, was mother-in-law of Lady Jane Grey (the 'nine day Queen'), beheaded in 1554, and wife of John Dudley, Earl of Warwick and Duke of Northumberland, whom she saw beheaded on Tower Green together with their son Lord Guildford Dudley on Tower Hill. Yet another son died *in* the Tower. However, the Duchess lived to see the restoration of the family's name before she died in 1555. Her son Robert, it will be recalled, rose to being Elizabeth I's favourite on whom was bestowed the title of the Earldom of Leicester. (His seat, Kenilworth Castle, was where Shakespeare may have acquired an early knowledge of Court pageantry). Her daughters-in-law included Robert's wife, Lettice Knollys, through whom the Duchess acquired a stepson, Robert, Devereux, Earl of Essex, the courtier who overplayed his hand at the Virgin Queen's Court. Of her ten other children, Ambrose was reinstated to the Earldom of Warwick, and her eldest daughter became mother to Sir Philip Sidney. (Any questions so far?)

Chelsea China and Battersea Enamel

The famous pottery 'Chelseaware' (established in 1725, by Nicholas Sprimont, but removed by William Duesbury of Derby – hence the 'Chelsea Derby' – in 1784) was manufactured in the vicinity of Lawrence Street, out of view of the river. Across the river, too, fine potteries thrived. There was Doulton's Faïence and Terra-cotta Manufactory at Vauxhall (founded 1815) and opposite, at Battersea, the snuff-box factory of Sir Stephen Janssen, c.1750–56, which produced the exquisite pieces known as 'Battersea enamels'.

The Secret Walkway beneath the Thames

Further west on the Embankment, where Cheyne Walk terminates, stand the proud gates of Cremorne House at Cremorne Pier. There, a tunnel under the Thames connected Chelsea worshippers who preferred to attend services at St. Mary's, on the Battersea shore. In regular use until the advent of the last War, when the authorities – with single minded tunnel vision – sealed up its entrances. The 18thC tunnel was subscribed for by members of St. Mary's congregation who, tiring of the extortionate demands of the ferry boatmen, clubbed together for the tunnel being dug. Were the twain of Chelsea and Battersea to meet again, the subterranean passage might provide a rendezvous.

Battersea Power

The Temple of Power, as the defunct Power Station on the South Bank was christened by agnostics, is considered an outstanding example of industrial architecture. Its hulk and bulk would be missed by Londoners far and wide. For the observer, the height of each fluted chimney is 30 ft. short of the tip of St. Paul's dome lantern [365 ft.] but the very fact of its mighty construction has ensured its survival: there was no demolitionist in the kingdom who dared undertake its safe removal. It is now due to open as a spectacular entertainments centre, when the converted 'temple' can pander to the prayers of mammon.

Battersea Park

Between Chelsea and the Albert suspension Bridges lies the attractive expanse of Battersea Park, set in 198 acres with a beautiful four acre sub-tropical Garden beside the *Serpentine* Park Lake, a favourite promenade of South Londoners and with a fine view of Chelsea Hospital. It was in the Fields that the Duke of Wellington fought his celebrated duel with the Marquis of Winchelsea [March 29, 1829]. The spot is probably the marshland out of which the lake and park were landscaped with surplus material from the Docklands.

Preposterous royal antics

Who can forget that King Charles II enjoyed bathing at Battersea Reach? Nell Gwynne didn't; nor did that Clumsy Knave, Captain Blood, who hid in the rushes (1670) before attempting – and muffing – an assassination. Blood was also pardoned for a separate attempt to steal the Crown Jewels (1671), being caught red-handed. It is generally thought that these 'preposterous antics' were designed to help Charles enrich himself. Perhaps the earlier attempt on the King's life was a ploy to distance their complicity? Every student of history will gladly recall that the life of the Merry Monarch ended peacefully (unlike his father's). No blood stains on Charlie junior!

Battersea Dogs' Home

Those who lead a dog's life are often to be found in the vicinity of the Battersea Dogs' Home, a boarding kennels for stray and faithful hounds (including King Charles spaniels) who have yet to discover the meaning of being 'man's best friend'. Ornithologists also flock to Battersea, considered one of the best London locations for serious bird-watching, being on the direct flight path of many species of migrating and other feathered friends. The black swan and bean goose are regular callers to the lake.

— Passing under —
BATTERSEA BRIDGE

An imposing iron structure, by Bazalgette (1890), which replaced the spanning wooden structure of Henry Holland's (1772), much noted by artists, from Turner, Girtin, et al. to Whistler with his well-known painting in the Tate.

Here the river curls southwards at Battersea Reach and leaves the elegance of Chelsea behind. The stark landscapes of Wandsworth and Fulham come into view around a further bend. On the Battersea bank stands the attractive parish church of St. Mary's, with its vestry window facing due west. It was here that Turner sat, over many years, in his quest of setting the sun on his canvases, which he stored a ferry ride away.

Chelsea's harbourside luxury

Opposite now rises the luxurious Chelsea Harbour Marina, – only two stops by river bus from Charing Cross Pier – with the golden marker buoy rising and descending atop the main tower, denoting the Thames's tidemark; the group of buildings a redeeming feature of an otherwise gaunt commercial wasteland. The dominant shadows of Lots Road Power Stations – which supplied London's first underground with electricity, 1904- and the ugly chimneys of its counterpart, the one at Fulham, still blight the landscape.

Battersea village

The name of Battersea, ('Peter's Eye' or Island) lingers in its ancient association with the patrimony of St. Peter's Abbey at Westminster:

Derivation: 'Patric-esy' (Domesday Book, 1086)
'Batrice-sei' (Pope Adrian IV – the one and only English Pope, Nicholas Breakspear, 1157)

(Pronounced: Batter/sih).

The riverside village of Battersea clusters below Battersea Bridge linking it with Chelsea. Upon the dissolution of the monasteries, ownership of the manor reverted from the Abbot of Westminster (who had much enjoyed its famed asparagus beds) back to the Crown; and was acquired in 1627 by the venerable family of St. John, (pronounced 'sinjun': the surname of the Viscounts Bolingbroke). In 1763, the Lordship of the manor passed to Earl Spencer, whose family more recently provided a princess for the heir to the throne whose title is borne in the Prince of Wales' Drive, which commemorates a previous holder, later King Edward VII.

HRH The Princess of Wales

The connection between Battersea and Princess Diana's ancestors was a real one: they shared in its development from a small-time settlement adjoining the Thames marshes into a fashionable residential neighbourhood. It is again enjoying popularity, as an overspill for the Sloane Ranger brigade who, ejected from expensive Chelsea, are known locally as –

Sloane Dangers.

One Spencer ancestor was responsible for obtaining from his peers in Parliament sanction for the bridge in 1766. Another assisted in the general development of residential accommodation and provided the Park for recreational use. Today, the association

is maintained in Althorp (pronounced 'All-throp', the family seat) Primary School, and in the names of streets and in the local housing estates. The village character is hard to find – largely bull-dozed into the ground – but a stroll along the riverside to the Parish Church and in the vicinity of the High Street repays the wanderer.

ST MARY'S CHURCH

The natural bedrock on which the Parish Church stands was surrounded by marshes that stretched over to Lambeth and provided a rare point of access to a river crossing. From the earliest times, Battersea vied with Westminster as one of two important landing stages in this part of the Thames. The historian, Maitland, claims both Emperors Claudius and Julius Caesar pursued the harried Britons at strategic Battersea Reach. Long before the church was built the river at Battersea had sacred connotations. The great Celtic Battersea Shield (now in the British Museum) was probably cast into the water here as an offering to the river god.

St. Mary's occupies one of the earliest consecrated sites on the southern bank of the Thames. It was conveyed by the Conqueror

to the Abbot of Westminster in 1067. It was indicative of its then importance that Henry Yevele, master-builder of the famous nave at Westminster, was dispatched upstream to oversee its fabric. Traces of his handiwork survive in the East Window.

Overlooking the great westward sweep of the river towards Putney, St. Mary's steeple commands a vantage point which did not escape the eagle eye of Turner. He spent as much time here interpreting 'his' Thamescapes and the glories of the sunsets due west from his favourite seat in the bow-windowed Vestry alcove, as he spent in Cheyne Walk.

Restructured in 1777, St Mary's façade of classical lines in dark red brick is faintly grand without being fussy. Its forthright whitewashed portico faces the riverbank and, between its columns, 'Turner's' vestry alcove gracefully inclines towards the river.

A helpful friend

The interior of this 18thC church is standard fare but with some fascinating adornments. To gain access may require a little leg-work; the doors are locked in the face of vandals. The keys may be procured from the Vicarage, a few hundred yards down the High Street at Vicarage Crescent. Alternatively, you may write, in advance of a pilgrimage, to:

The Hon. Verger, (Fred Hammond) 83, Tyneham Road, Battersea, SW11 5XG

Fred will show you his church with a disarming courtesy and vividly explain to you the treasures within. For those who do not encounter the memorable Battersea born-and-bred verger there follows a description of the Interior – a mere soupçon of Fred's intriguing revelations.

Many of the Virgin Mary's bountiful graces may be seen in *Her* place of worship at Old Battersea. The cavernous interior is full of grace, the chunks of decorative relief suitably restrained so as not to impose on the beholder. The wide flat ceiling broadens the feeling of space. The tripartite wooden gallery deftly marks its contours, inviting you up to its wooden cloister. Before ascending to the north gallery to pay homage to Roubiliac's outstanding work of art (the Bolingbroke Memorial, 1751), various items prove an excellent distraction.

– THE EAST WINDOW –

The outline pointed arch is the handiwork of Yevele in 1279; repaired in the 16thC when Sir Thomas, Anne Boleyn's (pronounced Bullen) father, donated it in honour of his great-granddaughter, also an Anne, who married Sir John St. John of Battersea. The heraldic glass [1630] contains the sequence of the St John family's descent and a forceful reminder of its Tudor connection, with the portraits of Margaret Beaufort (mother of Henry VII), Henry VIII and Elizabeth I. Observe the inset pomegranate between the Tudor rose-petals, thought to signify gentle birth – the possessor of 'pomain' scent banished the unpleasant human stench of fellow-citizens. In fact, the St. John family, as proud Plantagenets, while not relishing the Tudor parvenus, were still prepared to brag, in glass, of their royal relationship.

The flowing colours of the glass-ware were expertly repaired after inflictions of war damage, and are intrinsically valuable, being *hand-painted* not stained.

On either side a pair of decorous stained-glass cameos captivate the eye with the lustre of natural light, faintly glowing upon the themes of the Sacrificial Lamb and the Dove of Peace [James Pearson, 1796: blitzed 1944, miraculously restored] – the latter so lifelike as to appear as an open window on the sky.

– THE PULPIT –

Like a giant tulip sprung to life in some deserted rockery, the pulpit was designed to withstand and inspire the oratory of those who mounted its delicate cast-iron stairs. Beneath, on the Litany Desk, carefully opened at Fred's favourite page, lies the folio prayer book, which was a gift from the Austen family, two of whom – the poetess and the rash Lord Winchelsea (who challenged the Iron Duke to the duel in the Park) – attended worship here.

In the Sanctuary, you can find Turner's favourite chair on which he sat when studying the cloud effects and sunsets that greeted him from the oriel vestry (centre aisle, west end).

The Hayward Quartet, four stained-glass murals set in pairs at either end of the church aisles, are a proud addition to Fred's collection and depict scenes from the lives of four local worthies. The designs and manufacture were commissioned of John Hayward in 1976 and are high on Fred's list of priorities. Clockwise from north aisle:-

left   1. **JOSEPH Mallord William TURNER, R.A.**, allegorical studies; the window was donated by the Morgan Crucible Company; (ask Fred about the significance of the Plumbago Capensis plant featured.).

2. **WILLIAM BLAKE,** 'poet and visionary', commemorating his wedding in 1782 to a local girl, Catherine Butcher, spinster of Battersea, and afterwards –
   To see a world in a grain of sand
   And heaven in a Wild Flower
   Hold Infinity in the palm of your hand
   And Eternity in an hour.

Blake is much better known for *Jerusalem*:

HYMN NUMBER ONE

And did those feet in ancient time
Walk upon England's mountains green?
And was the holy lamb of God
On England's pleasant pastures seen?

And did the Countenance Divine   Bring me my bow of burning gold!
Shine forth upon our clouded hills?   Bring me my arrows of desire!
And was Jerusalem builded here   Bring me my spear! O clouds unfold!
Among those dark Satanic mills?   Bring me my chariots of fire!

I will not cease from Mental Fight,
Nor shall my Sword sleep in my hand,
Till we have built Jerusalem,
In England's green and pleasant Land.

(*Milton:* preface.)

---

right
(south aisle) 3. BENEDICT ARNOLD (1740–1801), General in George Washington's victorious army and somewhat poorly appraised in English history: shunned by the British and Americans alike and somewhat shabbily treated. By all accounts, he was the 18thC equivalent of a latter-day commando, and brave with it, to the last. Realising his war wounds would hasten his day of reckoning (he is buried in the crypt), he refused amputation of a leg, preferring –
   'Being born with two legs of the Good Lord,
   To die the same way.'

4. **WILLIAM CURTIS,** botanist, author of 'Flor Londiniensis', progenitor of the Royal Horticultural Society, founder member of the Linnean Society and Demonstrator of Botany at the Society of Apothecaries, Chelsea; Died 1799.

Ascend to:
North gallery –

(The Roubiliac monument): **HENRY ST. JOHN, Viscount Bolingbroke,** lauded by Pope, Swift and Smollett, but in the political climate of the time reviled by Walpole and Dr. Johnson as 'a scoundrel and a coward!'. Impeachment 1715 led to his attainder entailing forfeiture. But his estates were restored in 1723, whereafter he retired from public life. His epitaph alludes somewhat coyly to his troubles –
"Here lies Henry St. John, in the reign of Queen Anne, Secretary of War, Secretary of State, and Viscount Bolingbroke; in the days of George I and George II something more and better . . ."
Observe – the skill of Roubiliac on the tri-coloured marble statuary. His second wife was the niece of Mme. de Maintenon, mistress of Louis XIV.

SIR OLIVER ST. JOHN, Viscount Grandison, effigies executed by Nicholas Stone, mastermason, 1631;

SIR JOHN FLEET, Grocer, Lord Mayor of London 1693; fine carvings by Grinling Gibbons;

South gallery –

JOHN CAMDEN d. 1780 & daughter d. 1791; Observe – rare example of Coade's famous artificial stone statuary, executed 1792.

SIR EDWARD WYNTER, d. 1685, the fullsome Epitaph makes entertaining reading; the proud descendant of Admiral Wynter (of Armada fame) and of the less fortunate Thomas Wynter (blamed in the Gunpowder Plot); who included in his heroic exploits –
Alone, unarm'd, a tyger he opprest,
And crush'd to death ye monster of a beast;
Thrice twenty mounted Moors he overthrew
Singly on foot, some wounded, some he slew,
Dispers'd ye rest.
– What more could Samson doe?

Fred may at some point lead you into the crypt. Be not alarmed if he suddenly begins to tap-dance on the stone floor: Fred is about to share a secret! Which is the hollow flagstone and what *is* its secret?

┌─────────── *THE SECRET WALKWAY TO CHELSEA?* ───────────┐

Publisher's Note: This information is witheld, in the so-called 'public interest': The Publishers are advised that this harmless piece of information may be regarded as classified knowledge within the meaning of an Official Secret. The Publishers therefore recommend readers to other sources. (In other words, 'Ask Fred – or, the First Lord of the Admiralty'.).

— *Passing under* —
BATTERSEA
RAILWAY BRIDGE

Opened in 1863 to carry the West London Extension Railway (WLER) intended to connect the south to the north of England, it was a favourite target for Hitler's bombers, trying to bring about the 'North-South' Divide which eluded them. The existence of such a divide is now proclaimed by some left wingers not far removed from this bridge.

Here, 3½ miles upstream of Westminster Bridge, the gaunt industrial landscape takes over, with rare exception until the Chiswick Reach bend in the river, beyond Hammersmith.

HOW TO AVOID BEING BORED

Rather than face *a long period* of passing a monotonous wasteland on this part of the boat trip, one is better advised to choose the less taxing alternative journeys by overland route, in order to spend the same amount of time enjoying the loveliness of the Thames Upstream. For the popular destination of Hampton Court – still over sixteen miles away by water! – or the equally desirable locations of Kew or Richmond, a train from Waterloo to Kingston, or to Richmond (via the District line underground) is recommended, where plenty of local rivertrips in pleasant surroundings are on offer in these higher reaches.

— *Passing under* —
WANDSWORTH
BRIDGE

The stone edifice (E.P. Wheeler, 1938) replaced an iron lattice bridge of 1873, and stands amidst the wharves and warehouses crowding on the bend, and, before the green oases (of, on the left, Wandsworth Park, and opposite, Hurlingham Park) relieve the forlorn demeanour of the Thames. Hurlingham House is a rare survivor of the riverside mansions that gave rise to the river being dubbed 'the aristocratic Highway' and is now the exclusive Clubhouse of members expert in polo, croquet and self-comforts, to name but a few of their pursuits. Here was inaugurated the first

Westchester Challenge Cup (1886), the game having been taken to the States by the energetic Editor-in-chief of the New York Herald, James Gordon Bennett, (of 'go find Livingstone *alive*' fame).

'*The dismal image . . .*'

Few European cities have a finer river than the Thames, but none certainly has expended more ingenuity in producing an ugly riverfront. For miles and miles you see nothing but the sooty backs of warehouses, or perhaps they are sooty fronts: in buildings so very expressionless it is impossible to distinguish. They stand massed together on the banks of the wide, turbid stream, which is fortunately of too opaque a quality to reflect the dismal image. A damp-looking, dirty blackness is the universal tone.
. . . The whole picture, glazed over with the glutinous London mist, becomes a masterly composition. But it is very impressive in spite of its want of lightness and brightness, and though it is ugly, it is not insignificant. Like so many aspects of English civilisation that are untouched by elegance or grace, it has the merit of expressing something very serious. Viewed in this intellectual light, the polluted river . . . the atmospheric impurities . . . become richly suggestive . . .

Henry James. Portraits of Places, 1883.

Although the soot is largely gone since when '*London at Midsummer*' was published, much of the scenery seems little changed from Henry James's day. It is conceivable that the rejuvenation of the river – so laudably hatched in the London

Docklands scheme – will percolate upriver. This may remind the neighbouring authorities, in time, that they are custodians of the finest of assets: the neglected highway.

Beyond the exclusive club house of Hurlingham, where crisp cucumber sandwiches are daintily nibbled behind its porticoed columns, lies the New Kings Road. Until 1830, this was the sovereign's private road from Chelsea to the royal palaces at Kew, Richmond and Hampton Court. The road peters out at Putney Bridge (where monarchs chose to continue their journeys by water).

— *Passing under* —
FULHAM RAILWAY BRIDGE

Identified by its trellis girders (designed by William Jacob, 1889,) and –

— PUTNEY BRIDGE —

A sturdy design by Bazalgette, (1884) which replaced the wooden toll bridge of 1729, it was long a source of profit to the Bishops of London. A stone's throw away, on the right bank, lies their London seat, Fulham Palace. The inner courtyard, with pretty clocktower, is worth a visit by any venturer to Fulham, perhaps to watch the 'Varsity Boat Race (from the Putney Towpath, opposite), which commences at University Stone.

'Varsity Boat Race

The boat-race between Oxford and Cambridge University Boat Clubs is the chief aquatic event of the year, usually rowed on the second Saturday before Easter. The dark and the light blues – have competed on the Tideway and – but for a few mishaps – completed the present course since 1845. The event was first held in 1829. The distance between Putney and Mortlake is 4 miles and 400 yards. The race was the idea of two Harrovians who were friends at Trinity, Cambridge, one being Charles Wordsworth, nephew of the poet. It is almost surprising that the course was not set from Westminster Bridge, but there were, of course, no boat houses there.

A 'village in the bog'

The derivation of place names such as Putney and Fulham is a
matter of linguistic record: Putney, from the Norman holdings of
the Poultney family, and Fulham from 'Foule Ham' meaning
'village in the bog'. But local loyalties, pretensions or even
vanities give credence to absurdly picturesque histories of the
names in question. In these two rival parishes it is said that two
blacksmith giants, living on either shore, threw a large hammer
from side to side, calling out (so it is alleged) –
> 'Put, nigh!'
and calling back –
> 'Full, home!'
. . . As the Iron Duke said when addressed as plain 'Mr. Smith' –
'If you believe that, you'll believe anything.'

Putney High Street leads up the hill (where Algernon Swinburne
the Victorian poet, lived at the *Pines*, passing his pre-Raphaelite
days 'between the lintels of literature and life') to Putney Heath
and Wimbledon Common, being lovely open spaces. Swinburne
himself was fond of a walk and was remembered for his 'elastic
stride' as when, truly, a man of letters –

> *walking the Wimbledon postman off his legs.*
> J. Douglas: *Chambers's Cyclopaedia Vol. III [1922].*

Friends and relations

At Putney Park (now a social club, supposedly vying with
Hurlingham) Beatrix Potter spent childhood moments with her
young cousin Caroline while a batch of elderly relations lived up the
hill, towards Roehampton. They narrated to Beatrix some of the
animal stories, viz. *The Tailor of Gloucester* which she immortalised.
Of hedgehogs, *Mrs Tiggy-Winkle* may have frequented Putney Park.
Interested persons may wish to visit the garden wall of 2, The
Boltons (near Earl's Court underground) where *Mrs. Tiggy-Winkle* is
actually buried.

Cromwell's church

Hardby, the Putney parish church of St. Mary is almost squeezed
out of its ancient perimeter on the riverbank with an early 15thC
tower and long associated with the family of Cromwell. Thomas
Cromwell rose to power under Cardinal Wolsey (the butcher's
son) from his own lowly station as son of a Putney blacksmith. He
was the instrument of King Henry VIII in the extermination of
the monastic orders and their properties in 1537. The family were

able to move from Putney on the 'acquisition' of two of these foundations at Huntingdon. Thomas's grandson, Oliver Cromwell deposed and had executed Charles the Martyr. He became the Lord Protector during the Commonwealth and radically changed the political scenery of England as mercilessly as Thomas did the physical landscape. Had he accepted the crown as offered to him by Parliament his descendants might well have been ruling to this day. Instead, his son Richard, the last Protector that England has wished to see, lived in exile in Paris (and died unloved in 1701). North of the bridge stands Fulham parish church (All Saints) where several Bishops of London lie buried. Here also lies Theodore Hook, the 19thC prankster, born with a perverse sense of humour.

> The social hostess, Mrs. Tottenham, of Brewer Street, Soho, was the butt of one of his pranks, when, to avenge his not being included on her guest-list, he arranged for thousands of invitations to be issued to an evening at her home, to which half of London Society turned up. The resulting chaos and affront led his friends to insist he leave town. One, the Prince Regent, found him a sinecure in 1812 in the post of Treasurer of Mauritius. A 'grave deficiency' being discovered in the 'public chest', Hook scooted off to St. Helena where he encountered by chance one whom he had done down.

> *You again, Hook; I trust you're not staying here only because of your health? When are you returning home to face the music?*

> *No! Alas, no! I am told there's a deficiency in the chest. Medical orders, you know.*

Hook's memorial window was placed there by anonymous subscribers in 1893.

Behind the church lies Fulham Palace, approached from Bishop's Avenue. The Tudor Quadrangle is among the most picturesque to survive in London, built by Bishop Fitzjames (1522), wherein the impressive Great Hall is situate, used by Bishop Bonner for examining heretics. Between the Palace and the river lie some 28 acres of mature parkland, once encircled by a moat and now partitioned off by the thoughtless local council. A pleasanter walk along the river is had on the opposite bank, along the towpath to Barnes and Hammersmith Mall.

Beyond Putney lies Barnes where the river curves northwards, nigh on 180°, at Barn Elms Reach. The distinctive terracotta-coloured brick warehouse furniture depository of Harrods, the Knightsbridge store, may be seen, with its shapely cupolas, rising above the reservoirs. Overlooking Barn Elms Reach are the drab pre-war wharves that comprised a once thriving light industrial area, now being restored, piecemeal, in a worthy attempt to emulate the schemes of redevelopment in Downstream Docklands. Docklands West, as this almost impenetrable Hammersmith riversite may become, does boast an excellent place of refreshment: the *River Café*. Situated at Thames Wharf, in a complex renovated by Richard Rogers, (the architect noted for the Pompidou Centre in Paris, and the new, eye-catching Lloyds Building in London), it is run by Ruth Rogers, his wife a first-rate cook. The Café is open from 8.30 a.m. and serves North Italian food, setting the pace for some other restaurants in London. At high tide, standing clients, who are tall, can sometimes get a glimpse of the River.

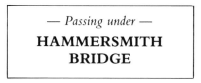

— *Passing under* —
HAMMERSMITH BRIDGE

– *Six miles upstream of Westminster* –

Bazalgette's Hammersmith Bridge dates to 1887 when it replaced a suspension bridge (1827). From the north bank of the river at Hammersmith Mall, a popular riverwalk for pedestrians, the bridge cuts a striking silhouette.

A feature of the river terraces are the many pubs which mostly share, with the handsome residences alongside, interesting historical associations: the 17thC *Ship Inn*, complete with verandah (for a select few), and the *Dove Inn*, particularly so. James Thomson, author of Rule Britannia, supposedly finished a once celebrated poem 'Winter' in the latter hostelry. This was perhaps as well since, returning to Kew by boat, he caught a chill and died. His is a salutary lesson to anyone who neglects to take warm clothing on water excursions, where, as you have been warned, the temperature often drops appreciably. The walk from Hammersmith Bridge to Chiswick is of great interest, combining Upper and Lower Malls – the latter especially attractive, again with distinctive pubs, the *Rutland* and the *Blue Anchor*, set amidst 18thC cottages and riverside properties.

The Malls are segregated by the Creek, now dammed, where the 'High Bridge' joined a row of old cottages.

No. 14, At Sussex Cottage, WILLIAM MORRIS set up his first 'Kelmscott' Press (1890), hence the name given to –

No. 26, where he lived until his death (1896); Morris, craftsman, designer and philosopher, liked to imagine the waters which run below his windows had passed the meadows upstream of his grey-gabled country home, Kelmscott, near the source of the Thames.

Two stanchions mark the site of the occasional residence of Catherine of Braganza (1687–92) by Rivercourt Road and Furnivall Gardens (named after the social reformer, a 19thC doctor), where a swathe of green cuts a welcome pathway to the river. Of many renowned residents, the distinguished Thames historian, Sir Alan Herbert, lived at –

No. 12, Hammersmith Terrace. A ship named after this engaging writer, independent member of Parliament and wartime River fireman is moored at St Katherine's Dock (Near the Tower of London).

On the south bank is the ultimate home (1969) of the former City of London school, St. Paul's, now occupying the spacious meadows at Barnes. Founded by Dean Colet in 1509 with a benefaction from the Mercer's Company, it removed to Hammersmith in 1884. The original number of boys was 153 (representing the exact fistful of fish miraculously caught by St. Peter).

St. Paul's 'old boys' include –

John Milton, the poet; **Duke of Marlborough**, the soldier;
Edmund Halley, of 'comet' fame; **Samuel Pepys**, diaryist;
John Strype, historian; **Judge Jeffreys** – who astonished his father
when, as a schoolboy, he first saw the Lord Mayor passing to a feast
and opined he would one day be an honoured guest – as Lord
Chancellor! –, and, of course, **Viscount Montgomery of Alamein**,
the great modern soldier.

— Passing under —

BARNES
RAILWAY BRIDGE

An elegant iron structure (1849, by Locke) nine miles upstream of
Westminster, which connected the Richmond railway line to the
London network north of the river, marks the divide where
London officially ends, and the Middlesex (North bank) and
Surrey (South bank) commence. The finishing post for the
winning stroke of the University boat race crew is shortly past
the *Ship Inn*, opposite Duke's Meadow.

Here the scenery begins to change, imperceptibly at first, where
the river seems wider by the absence of less dominant buildings
and with the effect of more abundant meadow and treescape.

Barnes

Barnes Village, with its duck-pond beside the Green, and
wayside Pubs, lies just behind the elegant row of 18thC riverside
residences, known as Barnes Terrace, which come into view.

At **Millbourne House**, lived **HENRY FIELDING** (1750), and **SHERIDAN**
the actor, sometime later;

At **No. 10**, lived **GUSTAV HOLST** (1908–1913), composer of The Planets
Suite.   54

At Barn Elms was the local manor owned by Sir Francis
Walsingham. It stood near the river and was famous for its
obvious associations with Elizabethiana – she gave it to him.
Nearby lived Jacob Tonson, antiquarian and secretary of the
Kit-Cat Club formed in the early 18thC. Members met here,
including Congreve, Vanbrugh, Walpole et al., whose portraits
formed a famous gallery of 42 three-quarter length works, by
Sir Godfrey Kneller. They now hang in the National Portrait

Gallery. The Club took its name from a type of mutton-pie sold by Mr. Christopher ('Kit') Cat, tavern keeper at old Temple Bar, in the City, where they first assembled.

The terrace of the elegant 16thC *Ship Inn,* affords a prime view of the finishing post for the winning stroke of the University boat race crew. The beer flows down Thames Bank from the nearby Mortlake brewers, Watney, whose brew is as famous as the brewery is unsightly. It stands on the former Mortlake manor, whose present titular lord is Earl Spencer. Whether the manor's seigneurial rights include a quaff from Watney's best red barrel is presumably a personal matter of taste.

By the parish church of St. Mary's leads a passageway to the Thames where the famous Mortlake Tapestries – to be seen hanging at Ham House and Hampton Court upstream – were worked by diligent Flemish Weavers in the 17thC.

— *Passing under* —

CHISWICK BRIDGE

With the longest concrete arch on the river (spanning 150 ft.), it was built in 1933 (Sir Herbert Baker) to support the arterial roadroute of London. At Duke's Meadows on the Middlesex (right) bank, the Boat Race ends and Mortlake Reach commences. The bridge was christened by Edward, Prince of Wales in 1933.

Chiswick House once afforded his lordship, the 3rd Earl of Burlington, a Thames riverfrontage. Behind the Meadows, out of sight, stands Burlington's 'ornamental villa', Chiswick House, a redeeming feature of the district which has swallowed much of his lordship's river frontage as well as much other land in ribbon development. Burlington's villa, and another little jewel, Hogarth's House, are worthy of a detour on foot.

CHISWICK HOUSE

The classical style (1725) of this Palladian mansion was one of the first 18thC examples to revive the purer school of architectural harmony out of the Baroque period which it replaced. The architect Palladio's style caught on in England, due in no small measure to Lord Burlington, who had studied the Italian master on his Grand Tour. It was this style that Nash successfully popularised in the Regency period when, by using stucco upon brick, he emulated the expensive stone-cut façades of the super-rich, for the terraced residences of the merely well-to-do.

The interior of the house (William Kent, Burlington's *protegé*) is imposing, though lacking sufficient atmosphere to be an agreeable experience. At least the house and parklands survived the threat of demolition (1929) and the interior decor is of a high standard, viz –

Domed octagonal Salon (Kent),
Diane and Endymion (Sebastiano Ricci):

In Greek mythology, Endymion was given eternal life and youth by Zeus on Mount Latmus; the moon goddess Selene came nightly and embraced him. This resulted in her giving him fifty daughters – which says something for his stamina, and her devotion; all lovingly painted by the Italian artist.

Burlington was a leading patron of the Arts, fittingly remembered in London to-day where Burlington House, Piccadilly,
houses the headquarters of the Royal Academy of Arts, and a host
of learned societies, including the Royal Society. The reader may
recall that it was Burlington whose Palladian designs for building
the Mansion House, in the City of London, were rejected, as a
result of a Common Councilman enquiring, in committee –

> Who was Palladio? Was he a Freeman, and was he not a Roman
> Catholic?   *[18thC.]*

– perhaps he mistook him for the great Architect of the Universe?

Only a short walk from the banks of the Thames (traffic
allowing) is:

HOGARTH'S HOUSE

The gifted painter William Hogarth R.A. lived in Chiswick, in a
little house he built himself, to get away from London (where he
lived off Leicester Square). This house, which he described –

my little country box by the Thames [1749]

– was lived in by England's first great portraitist in oils from 1750
until his death (1764). The *Queen Anne-styled* doll-house is well
worth a visit, and is filled with this artist's works, including his
famed etchings, viz –
>A Harlot's Progress [1732]
>Marriage a la Mode [1745]
>An Election [1755/8]

Visitors will absorb the lovely personality of 'Hogie' (to his
friends), a man of utter distinction who played a role of great
benefaction in the 18thC.

> For example, he masterminded the funding of the Foundling
> Hospital in Bloomsbury, for his friend Captain Thomas Coram, the
> grand old mariner, as well being instrumental in the early activities
> of the founding of the Royal Academy.

> *Note* – Those who visit the Thomas Coram Foundation in
> Bloomsbury may wish to gaze at Hogarth's full-length portrait of
> the sea captain, possibly as fine a study of character as any to be
> achieved in brushstroke.

Soon, at the next river turn, beyond Kew Railway Bridge, the first inklings of prettier surroundings are sensed.

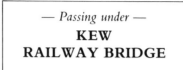

— *Passing under* —
KEW
RAILWAY BRIDGE

Opened in 1869 to connect the South-Western Railway extension the iron bridge spans – with somewhat delicate latticework – the bend of the river below Brentford. It was designed by W.R. Galbraith. By this time, the intrepid boat tripper has notched up the 15th mile from Westminster Bridge. After one and a half hours – or two, more likely – the traveller will be thirsty for the finer views, now afforded upstream.

The monotonous shores of Vauxhall, Pimlico, Battersea, Wandsworth, Fulham and Hammersmith are soon forgotten as the riverbank changes to the scenic views of Kew and Syon Park, at Syon Reach.

Time to relish the picturesque townscapes of Richmond and Twickenham, nestling beneath stately Richmond Hill and time to enjoy the lovely progression from Kingston, past Teddington Lock, that leads to Hampton Court, around the lip of landscaped Tudor parkland. Many a boat traveller, now taken with local views, may feel that an *overland* departure from Central London, (via Waterloo or Victoria) to Kew, Richmond or Kingston is a time-saving option to be preferred on a future occasion.

London on Thames was *just so* seen by Rudyard Kipling [1865–1936] in the following verse, entitled **THE RIVER'S TALE (PREHISTORIC):**

TWENTY bridges from Tower to Kew—
(Twenty bridges or twenty-two)—
Wanted to know what the River knew,
For they were young and the Thames was old.
And this is the tale that the River told:—

"I walk my beat before London Town,
Five hours up and seven down.
Up I go till I end my run
At Tide-end-town, which is Teddington.
Down I come with the mud in my hands
And plaster it over the Maplin Sands.
But I'd have you know that these waters of mine
Were once a branch of the River Rhine,
When hundreds of miles to the East I went
And England was joined to the Continent.

I remember the bat-winged lizard-birds,
The Age of Ice and the mammoth herds,
And the giant tigers that stalked them down
Through Regent's Park into Camden town.

And I remember like yesterday
The earliest Cockney who came my way,
When he pushed through the forest that lined the Strand
With paint on his face and a club in his hand.

He was death to feather and fin and fur.
He trapped my beavers at Westminster.
He netted my salmon, he hunted my deer,
He killed my heron off Lambeth Pier.
He fought his neighbour with axes and swords.
Flint or bronze, at my upper fords,
While down at Greenwich, for slaves and tin,
The tall Phoenician ships stole in,
And North Sea war-boats, painted and gay,
Flashed like dragon-flies, Erith way;
And Norseman and Negro and Gaul and Greek
Drank with the Britons in Barking Creek.

And life was gay, and the world was new,
And I was a mile across at Kew!
But the Roman came with a heavy hand,
And bridged and roaded and ruled the land,
And the Roman left and the Danes blew in—
And that's where your history-books begin!"

KEW

HOST TO THE MOST RENOWNED GARDEN in the world, Kew Parish is centred on the old Village Green, a stone's throw from the Thames, beside the gateway to 300 acres of choice horticultural exotica. The Royal Botanic Gardens were established in 1759 by Augusta, Princess of Wales. It was to her son, George III, it will be recalled, that the brewer Whitbread of Clerkenwell, City of London, boasted –

> That he had butts enough, he knew,
> Placed side by side, to reach along to Kew;
> On which the king with wonder swiftly cried:
> 'What, if they reach to Kew, then, side by side,
> What would they do, what, what, placed end to end?'
> To whom, with knotted, calculating brow,
> The man of beer most solemnly did vow,
> Almost to Windsor that they would extend . . .
>
> *John Wolcot: (extract) A Satirical Poem [1787]*

Kew became an eminently fashionable neighbourhood after Frederick, Prince of Wales (Augusta's husband) took a lease of the Kew estate in the 1730s. From 1802, Kew Palace was the regular residence of George III, Queen Charlotte and some of their 15 children, before the king withdrew to Windsor (1805).

Kew Green

Royal associations abound in the rows of imposing Georgian dwellings overlooking the tree-lined Village Green, where cricket has been played for upwards of 200 years. In summertime the picturesque setting provides a perfect back drop to games of cricket, whose fielders almost encircle the brick church of St. Anne (consecrated 1714) beneath its distinctive octagonal cupola. In the churchyard are to be found the tombstones of the Royal Academician painters –

JOHAN ZOFFANY (between the apse and the wall closest to the A307 Road), who died in 1810 at Strand-on-the-Green (over Kew Bridge) at the ripe old age of 87, and his contemporary –

THOMAS GAINSBOROUGH, Britain's finest portraitist? (southside path, the one monument with railings), d. 1788;

FRANCIS BAUER, botanical artist to George III,
and JEREMIAH MEYER, miniaturist painter to Queen Charlotte.

St. Anne's lightly classical exterior is matched within. The *Royal Gallery* [1805], is associated with George III who regarded

this 'his' church, as did the Duke of Cambridge, his 7th and youngest son, (the one who was reputedly prone to interrupt long sermons with entreaties for good harvest or the weather). The coat-of-arms depicted are those of their forbear Queen Anne, another patron.

In the *South Aisle* are memorials erected to Meyer (who designed the realm's coinage for George III), and Archbishop Laud (who lived on the Green at King's Cottage and regularly participated in worship). This church continues to be well-patronised. In 1951, St. Anne's Easter Thanksgiving was shared by millions of listeners to the B.B.C. in a first ever live television broadcast from a church.

An Engaging moment

Ties with royalty have since continued for many years, although Buckingham Palace had been purchased and was to become the principal residence of George III's heirs. There was even a royal knot tied in the nave by Queen Mary's father, the Duke of Teck when he proposed, during Sunday matins, to Princess Mary of Cambridge – a union which proved a love-match: (Queen Mary married George V. This much-loved couple were the present Queen's grand-parents). Perhaps the lines, entitled *On Early Love*, to express the youthful dawn of sacred feelings shared, were whispered –

> Ah, I remember well (and how can I
> But ever more remember well) when first
> Our flame began, when scarce we knew what was
> The flame we felt; when as we sate and sighed
> And looked upon each other, and conceiv'd
> Not what we ayled, yet something we did ayle,
> And yet were well and yet we were not well.
> And what was our disease, we could not tell.
> Then would we kisse, then sigh, then looke: and thus
> In that first Garden of our simplenesse
> We spent our child-hood. But when years began
> To reape the fruit of knowledge: ah, how then
> Would she with grave looks, with sweet, stern brow,
> Check my presumption and my forwardness.
>
> Yet still would give me flowers, still would me show
> What she would have me, yet not have me know.
>
> > *from – Hymen's Triumph!*
> > *Samuel Daniel [1562–1619] (lauded by Coleridge)*

Outside the porch, sweethearts are much in evidence in the shade of summer, under the colonnades of lime: clustered on the grass verges outside the Pubs that continue to rival Whitbread's heirs at Kew Green. Although Kew is an ideal place for a picnic, there are also some good eating places, *Pissaro's Wine Bar*, for example. There is a lovely walk beyond the terraces at Ferry Walk, beside the river. So too, across the dainty span of Kew Bridge (opened by Edward VII, in 1903), to quaintly-named Strand-on-the-Green.

Strand-on-the-Green

Strand-on-the-Green lies beside the river and contains a further batch of delightful 18thC houses, many converted from fisher-men's cottages, and denoted by anti-flooding protective step walls to their front doors. In addition to Zoffany, among other distinguished locals, the poet Dylan Thomas resided at *Ship House Cottage*. The *City Barge* (No. 27) claims a 15thC charter and is named after the proximate mooring of the Lord Mayor's bygone water chariot, whereas the *Bull's Head* (No. 15) is only 350 years old, but with exactly the sort of exposed, tarred beams you would expect as proof of age. Both pubs are best approached from Kew Bridge, (in under twenty minutes, if walking).

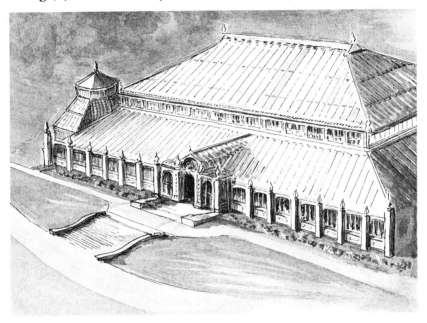

KEW GARDENS

Kew Gardens, as the Royal Botanic is known, fully justify their world ranking. The devotion to their upkeep is repaid by the delight of visitors. The Gardens are at their best in April (spring daffodils and flowering cherries) or early summer (azalea and rhododendron) when you can put a piece of sunshine in your pocket. The Gardens are known to cater to the most arcane tastes of the specialist, and the valuable Souvenir Guide caters to such a person, as well as to those who may be less demanding. At Kew a million visitors a year swarm through the turnstiles, still one of the cheapest passes – 50 pence – to one of the most delightful surroundings, anywhere, in the world. Three hundred acres of magnificent gardens, which vary in leaf as widely as an artist's spectra of colours, run amok of the pathways, avenues and tracks which wander, sometimes on purpose and sometimes amiss, by the unusual buildings, temples and follies dotted about the leafy terrain. Kew is the perfect place to take a picnic, as the ducks had discovered – until their keeper realised they would die from obesity, unless the more thoughtless members of the public refrained from feeding them.

There are no litterbugs here as the by-laws are strictly enforced by plain-clothes park attendants.

Kew's 'Treasures' include –

> *Princess of Wales Conservatory* – where a fabulous collection (1500) of herbaceous plants find shelter under high-tech conditions, ranging from the oppressive humidity of the Tropics to the dry intensity of the Desert; controlled by buttons, built into the innovative designs of the new building (1987), Wilson and Simmons;

> *Palm House* [by the lake] the lofty Victorian glasshouse (Decimus Burton. 1848 – predating the Crystal Palace of 1851 – and still standing),

> *Temperate House* (Burton's second experiment in weather-control, 1862), for all the other plants that did not fit in the first greenhouse; someone once mistakenly left a monkey there believing that it was where the bananas grew. It was in the other glasshouse that they grew. Instead the monkey searched high and low for one of those trees from Brazil – where by repute the nuts come from.

> *The Pagoda* – Sir William Chambers designed the striking land-mark (163 ft. high) in 1762 for the Dowager Princess of Wales, who founded the botanic garden two years previously. On her death (1772), George III purchased her residence, Kew House (since demolished) where he lived in utmost simplicity.

> *Kew Palace*, or the Dutch House, (1631), which was an annexe to Kew House, was acquired by George III, and Queen Charlotte died there in 1818.

> In the southwest part of the gardens is the thatched *Queen's Cottage* which George III built as a tearoom, a couple of years before the Boston Tea Party, in 1773, soured his taste for some things foreign.

Despite the tragedy of destruction inflicted by the storms in the autumn of 1987, when so many of the grand old trees were 'cast to the winds', the gardens at Kew retain an incomparable vista of nature's landscape at its best; and in each of the seasons, Kew is

imbued with nature's specialties. Some say that Spring is their favourite moment, when England's parklands assume a cloth of gold, and where, at Kew, the daffodils herald the passing of another winter. A delightful account of the unfolding of nature comes from one of the finest writers in English prose –

> When we were in the woods below Gowbarrow Park, we saw a few daffodils close by the waterside. As we went along there were more and yet more; and at last, under the boughs of the trees, we saw there were a long belt of them along the shore. I never saw daffodils so beautiful. They grew among the mossy stones about them. Some rested their heads on the stones, as on a pillow; the rest tossed, and reeled, and danced, and seemed as if they verily laughed with the wind, they looked so gay and glancing.
>
> *Dorothy Wordsworth, [1807].*

The sister of William, the poet, – 'she gave me eyes, she gave me ears' he once said – Dorothy was writing of a beauty-spot near Ullswater, in the Lake District (just 299 miles, north of Kew), but her interpretation of nature lends itself to this garden on the river, which she visited, whilst travelling through London with her brother.

For the reader who wishes to compare her exquisite handiwork
to her illustrious brother's, the following verses may be of
interest –

> I wandered lonely as a cloud
> That floats on high o'er vales and hills,
> When all at once I saw a crowd,
> A host of golden daffodils;
> Beside the lake, beneath the trees,
> Fluttering and *dancing* in the breeze . . .
>
> For oft when on my couch I lie
> In vacant or in pensive mood,
> They flash upon the inward eye
> Which is the bliss of solitude;
> And then my heart with pleasure fills . . .
> And *dances* with the daffodils.
>
> *William Wordsworth, Poems [1807]*

Syon Reach

From Kew Gardens the stately home of Syon House, in the setting
of Syon Park, may be viewed across the Thames. Visitors enthuse
over the contents of this Percy seat, remodelled in the 18thC by
Robert Adam, and considered his miracle work. Said Basil Taylor
of the result –

> *'You're almost in the middle of a jewel-box'*

The Park, landscaped by Capability Brown at about the same
time, contains the first national gardening centre; but those
travelling by Shank's pony may prefer to feel they 'saw' Syon
from the relative convenience of Kew Gardens opposite. What
may disappoint those who do cross the river is the 20thC
desecration of the northbank: the environmental cancers of
Brentford and Hounslow conceal, none too well, abysmal
community planning and squalid public sector housing, in a
commercial sprawl that treats the river as its sewer. The former,
and once delightful, *old* village of Isleworth was not spared the
post-war ruination. Even the dutiful parish church, once protected on its flanks both by water and by the imprint of the duchy
and set in a fabulous position on the riverbend, has been wrecked.

Isleworth Parish Church

<u>All Saints</u> – The nave of the 14thC church, was gutted in 1943: not,
as presumed by enemy action but by the arson of two gutter-
snipes, who also desecrated four other churches in the vicinity.

The brick appendage, grafted in 1970 to the surviving church tower, graphically illustrates the insensitivity of modern architects to their environment. The importance of the church site was, and is, its aspect to the river: but the 'window-strips' (designed perhaps to inhibit plump pigeons from perching on the sills) blindly shut out this view. The Micawberish optimism of the church pamphlet in its penultimate paragraph has a message for 'friendly strangers' with whom you *may* wish to be identified –

> there is so much more that could, and indeed should, have been written about this intriguing church, but the limitations of space within the covers of this little history has necessitated many omissions . . . and it is hoped you will come back again and again.

(or not, as the case may be.)

The replica of the ornamental sundial, erected in 1707 by the wife of a governor of Jamaica, offers visitors from the international time zones in Isleworth, Jamaica, Jerusalem and Moscow an opportunity to check the accuracy of their watches, and contains a thoughtful reminder

> *WATCH AND PRAY*
> *TIME PASSETH AWAY LIKE A SHADOW.*

Nearby is the *London Apprentice*, a pub bandied in many leisure manuals as 'still a favourite place to get away to'. It was precisely so, once upon a time, when workers apprenticed to the famous guilds in the City rowed upstream on festival days to this neck of the river. Brave the stained and beer-sodden floorcovering and smeared glass (1988), and inspect the handiwork of Italian craftsmen (employed on the Adam decorations to Syon House) which is still preserved in the carved ceiling of the upstairs restaurant.

The Percy Seat

The park provides an ideal setting for an occasional mansion, as well as a lion. Now confined to the roof-top compound, the king of the jungle is the crest of the Percy family, whose southern residence Syon House is. The armorial feature, with its conspicuous and vertical tail, was floated up the Thames by barge from Charing Cross Pier, where the beast previously commanded attention astride Northumberland House, in Northumberland Avenue. There, the awkward question arose as to which way that part of the animal with the tail should point. After an argument

between the resident Duke and his Kingly neighbour, the statue was finally and defiantly rotated on its axis so that the hind-quarters faced the direction of the royal residence!

At Isleworth Stairs

The convent, founded by Henry V (1415) and dissolved by Henry VIII, was used to incarcerate his disgraced Queen Katherine Howard, in 1541, after her downfall, for infidelity. From Isleworth Stairs, the royal barge delivered her to the Tower. Before the decade was out, Henry himself lay at Syon House when his coffin rested en route to his burial at Windsor. Chroniclers allude to the ghastly condition of his huge putrefying body being attacked by the ravenous rodents of Syon's cellars: a sight to be relished by the ghosts of Anne [Boleyn] and Katherine [Howard].

Then, Protector Somerset acquired the deeds and married off his son to the sister of Lady Jane Grey (the 'nine day queen' who became another victim of imprisonment at Syon, till she, too, followed Katherine's fate further down the Thames). Towards the end of the century in 1594, the Percy family took the lease of the estate, the freehold of which was granted in 1604 to the 9th earl. On this site of the old nunnery the 1st Duke of Northumberland built his riverside mansion in 1766, still lived in by the family of his Grace, the 10th Duke.

Syon House

In showy contrast to the gloomy exterior – the castellations relieve the boredom – the *interior* boasts the best of Adam's handiwork: the Great Hall, considered outstanding by experts of neo-classicism and the ornate Ante-Room, to mention a couple of his lordship's caverns. The Duchess's tiaras are not anywhere immediately apparent, but almost everything-else-worth-anything is highly visible. There is a good guide book for visitors.

The 'Northumbrian' landscape, the joint creation of a Percy and one Brown ('Capability'), distinguishes the fifty acres that stretch from the riverbank and contain the idyllic setting of the lake. The private grounds, closed to public access, afford a dream come true: those seeking one, may prefer to spend their time upstream, such as in neighbouring Twickenham or Ham, or opposite, at dainty Kew . . .

Another Adam jewel

An interesting comparison to Syon is the seat of the noble Earls of Jersey at Osterley Park, (also by Adam), situated at the beginning of the M4 (Heathrow) motorway which bisects the grounds. The long distance motorist should have little difficulty finding it, unlike pedestrian users of London's travel network (Osterley, Piccadilly tube). Those who do will not be disappointed.

Osterley House

Osterley House was built (1576) for Sir Thomas Gresham, founder of the Royal Exchange, and one of Queen Elizabeth 1st's most prominent Englishman. In the 18thC the Child family (of bankers) acquired the estate – one of the largest in London – and invited Sir William Chambers, (who was followed by Robert Adam) to remodel the interior. Their lavish handiwork may be enjoyed to this day since the family, whose titles include the Earldom of Jersey, retired to *their* Channel island, leaving this property to the nation, in 1923.

UPSTREAM SERVICES FROM RICHMOND-UPON-THAMES
[Underground to Richmond (District Line) or British Rail from Waterloo]

To: Kingston	[one way: 1 hour]
Water transport:	Riverbus steamer, usually licensed bar
Frequency:	**From Richmond Pier**
	[01] 892–0741
	From St. Helena Pier
	Turks Launches – [01] 546–2434
	Departure times: 1200, 1430, & 1700
To: Hampton Court	[one way: 1½ hours]
Water transport:	River steamer, usually licensed bar
Frequency:	From Richmond Pier
	[01] 892–0741
	From St. Helena Pier
	Turks Launches – [01] 546–2434
	Departure times: 1200 & 1430 [May – September]

RAILWAY TRAVEL
By British Rail from Waterloo [Tel. (01) 928–5100 Passenger information]

TO RICHMOND: (river destination)
Outward journeytime takes approximately twenty minutes, faster in peak periods.
MON–FRI: very regular frequency of services
SAT–SUN: regular services (every half-hour).

TO KINGSTON: (river destination)
Outward journey takes approximately thirty minutes.
MON–FRI: very regular frequency of services
SAT–SUN: fairly frequent services

TO KEW BRIDGE: (Gardens)
Outward journey takes approximately twenty minutes
MON–FRI: frequent services (every thirty minutes)
SAT–SUN: fairly frequent services

Visitors may marvel at the rococo decor: Walpole described the Drawing room as –

worthy of *Eve* before the Fall.

What he thought of *Adam's* State Bedchamber (domed-poster replete with bedhead decorations of exuberant naked loined youths riding dolphins), he chose not to commit to paper.

UPSTREAM SERVICES FROM KINGSTON-UPON-THAMES

To: Hampton Court   [one way: 30 minutes]

Water transport: River steamer, usually licensed bar

Frequency: *Departure times: 1030, 1115, 1200, 1315, 1345, 1430, 1500, 1545, 1615, 1700 [May – September]*

Enquiries: Turks Launches – [01] 546–2434

UPSTREAM SERVICES FROM HAMPTON COURT

To: Runnymede

Enquiries: French Bros. [0753] 851900

DOWNSTREAM SERVICES FROM HAMPTON COURT

To: Kingston Pier   [30 minutes]

Frequency: From Turks Landing Stage
Departure times: 1115, 1200, 1230, 1315, 1345, 1430, 1500, 1545, 1615, 1700 & 1730

To: Richmond Pier   [1¾ hours]

Same times of departure, as above.

Note: All journey times are approximate.

LONDON UNDERGROUND

By London Underground [Tel. 222–1234 Passenger information) 'Tube' trains run from approximately 0700–2300, seven days a week.

TO RICHMOND – District line (13 stops from Victoria): allow forty-five minutes to one hour

TO KEW – District line (12 stops from Victoria): allow thirty-five to forty-five minutes

General Note:
    Return journeys approximate in frequency and journey-time to above information, contrarywise.

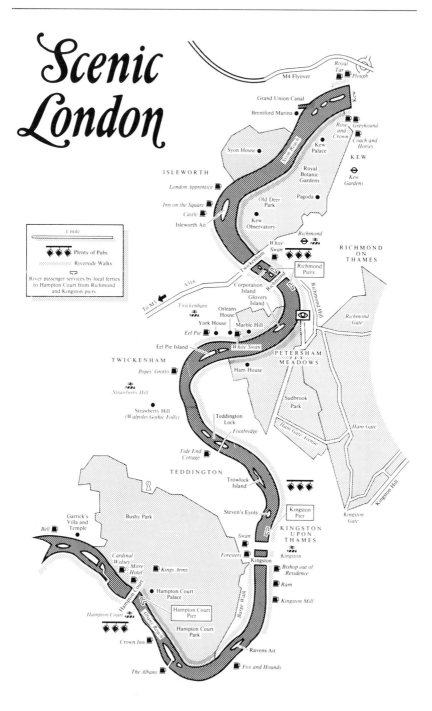

Scenic London

M4 Flyover

Royal
Tar
Plough
Kew

Grand Union Canal

Brentford Marina

Rose
and
Crown

Greyhound

Coach and
Horses

Syon House

Kew
Palace

KEW

ISLEWORTH

London Apprentice

Royal
Botanic
Gardens

Kew
Gardens

Inn on the Square

Old Deer
Park

Pagoda

Castle

Isleworth Ait

Kew
Observatory

Richmond

White
Swan

RICHMOND
ON
THAMES

Richmond
Piers

1 mile

Plenty of Pubs

Riverside Walks

River passenger services by local ferries
to Hampton Court from Richmond
and Kingston piers

A316

To M3

Twickenham

Corporation
Island
Glovers
Island

Orleans
House

York House

Marble Hill

Richmond
Gate

Eel Pie

Eel Pie Island

White Swan

PETERSHAM
MEADOWS

TWICKENHAM

Popes' Grotto

Ham House

Strawberry Hill

Strawberry Hill
(Walpoles Gothic Folly)

Teddington
Lock

Footbridge

Sudbrook
Park

Ham Gate

Tide End
Cottage

TEDDINGTON

Trowlock
Island

Garrick's
Villa and
Temple

Bell

Bushy Park

Steven's Eyots

Kingston
Pier

Kingston
Gate

KINGSTON
UPON
THAMES

Cardinal
Wolsey
Mitre
Hotel

Kings Arms

Swan

Foresters

Kingston

Kingston

Bishop out of
Residence

Hampton Court
Palace

Ram

Hampton Court
Pier

Hampton Court
Park

Kingston Mill

Crown Inn

Ravens Ait

The Albany

Fox and Hounds

RICHMOND-UPON-THAMES

At Richmond and Twickenham

A visit to Richmond-upon-Thames may be combined with excursions to the adjoining neighbourhoods of Kew, Petersham, or on the opposite bank, Twickenham, depending entirely on the time available to the sightseer. A way of saving travelling time from Central London is to alternate between a river route and overland by train. A suggestion might be to take the tube to Richmond (14 stops from Victoria) and then incorporate a river excursion amongst the prettiest river scenery to hand.

A logical solution to seeing Upstream Thames without spending a day on the water (from Westminster Pier and back) is to go by train or Tube to Richmond and catch the steamer. As the best riverscapes are between neighbouring Kew and Kingston, opposite the unfolding banks of Isleworth, Twickenham, Teddington and Hampton Court, this method is ideal for visiting Hampton Court and its interesting neighbours.

Richmond-upon-Thames

Richmond Town centre is compact and whether an arrival is by river, rail or car, the leafy Green adjoins the main shopping street and, like the Hill, is next door to the beauty of the river. Richmond Park sits on the top of the hill, a beckoning expanse of countryside for the hearty walker. The view from the Terrace should not be missed and, for those who have the time, a window table in the dining-room of the Petersham Hotel may afford a memorable occasion (but *definitely not* within the reach of everyone's pocket).

At the bottom of the famous hill, Richmond Bridge shows off its charm – designed by Kenton Couse, 1777 – and from its arches a commanding view, upriver and down. The bridge leads to Twickenham with its own lovely riverbank, and – at a pinch,

traffic congestion as it is on the Richmond bank – a place to
remember for parking.

The view from Richmond Bridge

The view from the bridge is one long sweep of tranquillity. On
the southern flank, the deep trough of the river meanders, girdling
the Hill. Spreading back towards Kew, the line of trees and
shapely buildings slope down to the waterline, where vessels rest
in the lee of Corporation Island. Beyond the harmony of linear
scale shown by the new Riverside development, the outline of
Twickenham Bridge (Maxwell Ayrton, 1933) protrudes across the
river. By Old Deer Park, the twin bridges of Richmond Footbridge
and Weir – a most striking construction which contains the first
sluices upstream of Westminster – and even the Railway Bridge
are congruous to the stylish locality.

In the early morning, or sometimes at dusk, swans glide about
the rivermists and part the surface of the water with ripples
trailing in their wake. Then, the reflected branches of the trees
unthread and weave about in slow motion. The air is that much
stiller and it is time to sit and take one's ease.

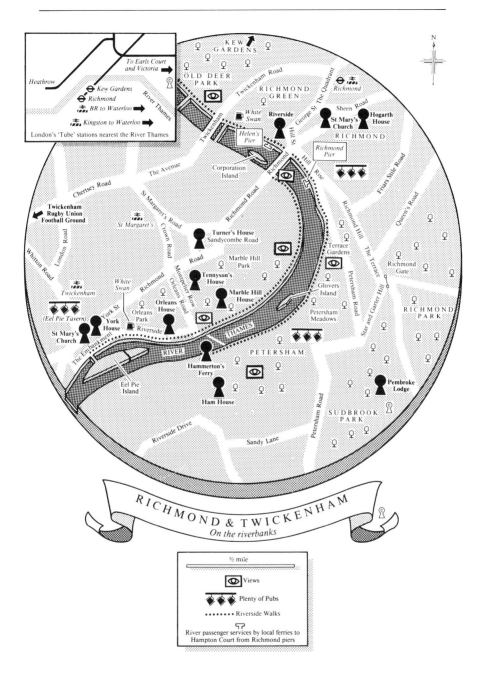

London's 'Tube' stations nearest the River Thames

Heathrow

To Earls Court and Victoria

Kew Gardens
Richmond
BR to Waterloo
Kingston to Waterloo

KEW GARDENS
OLD DEER PARK
Twickenham Road
RICHMOND GREEN
Richmond
Sheen Road
White Swan
Riverside
St Mary's Church
Hogarth House
Helen's Pier
RICHMOND
Richmond Pier
Corporation Island
The Avenue
Chertsey Road
Twickenham Rugby Union Football Ground
St Margaret's Road
St Margaret's
Turner's House
Sandycombe Road
Marble Hill Park
Terrace Gardens
The Terrace
Richmond Gate
Tennyson's House
White Swan
Twickenham
Marble Hill House
Glovers Island
RICHMOND PARK
Orleans House
Orleans Park
Petersham Meadows
(Eel Pie Tavern)
York St
York House
Riverside
St Mary's Church
The Embankment
RIVER THAMES
Hammerton's Ferry
PETERSHAM
Petersham Road
Eel Pie Island
Pembroke Lodge
Ham House
SUDBROOK PARK
Riverside Drive
Sandy Lane

RICHMOND & TWICKENHAM
On the riverbanks

½ mile

Views
Plenty of Pubs
Riverside Walks
River passenger services by local ferries to Hampton Court from Richmond piers

Beside the bridge, near where the ferries come and go, stands the finest, recent riverside development on the Thames completed 1988: (Haslemere Estates, architect Quinlan Terry). If not so considered, there are many residents who would like to learn where else to look. Developers of the Canary Wharf, in East London, perhaps should be reminded of what may be accomplished, as opposed to being merely built? Richmond Riverside, as the complex is christened, houses the Richmond Tourist Information Centre and the long-awaited independent Museum of Richmond, among many fortunate tenants of the pleasing neoclassical buildings. The Museum promises to their visitors an interesting and well-run (for their money, just 80 pence) display of local history, second to none along the length of the river. The Curator, Kate Thaxton, and the Museum's president, John Cloake, deserve inaugural congratulations for their good works.

Explorers "on the town" who determine to leave no stone unturned – such are the many historical associations built upon Richmond's riverbank – may like to include a visit to the burial place of Edmund Kean, the Shakespearian actor, in the parish church, and the house, nearby, where Virginia Woolf lived, between her Bloomsbury sojourns as it were, in Paradise Road. If Paradise, reported missing by Milton in 1663, but valiantly regained eight years later, were ever to re-emerge in London, it might be in the haven of Richmond-upon-Thames.

Van Gogh's Earring

Vincent Van Gogh lived at Holme Court in Twickenham Road, where he taught for a short spell in 1876, as a blue plaque records. When he came to London three years earlier at the tender age of twenty, he lodged at Mrs. Loyer's Lambeth boarding house where he fell under the lasting spell of the landlady's daughter, Eugenie, who heartlessly rejected his proposal of marriage and became engaged to a better looking lodger. He would walk his lovesick round to South London and back, sporting one of Miss Loyer's earrings as a sign of unrequited love. Disillusioned, he banished the final reminder of his besotted heroine, and it is said that the earring was abandoned to the Thames, off Richmond Bridge. As is well-known, the ear that was pierced parted company with its owner after an argument with Gauguin some eight years later, so that art historians are chary of ascribing to a small chunk of metal its full intrinsic value. But with the price of Miss Loyer's favourite bouquet, Sunflowers, fetching what it does, a modest investment

This view of the Thames at Richmond was painted by P.A. Rysbraeck c.1730. His work may be admired at Orleans House, which was acquired with N A-C F help. 'STEM THE TIDE – join the N A-C F now and stop more works of art from flowing away!'

246

in a waterproof metal-detector to search the foreshore and river bed, could provide the means of an inflation-proof retirement.

Richmond Green

Historic Richmond Green is a beautiful centrepiece in the midst of one of England's prettiest riverside townscapes. Queen Elizabeth I most certainly thought so – where else did she choose to die, other than in surroundings she preferred.

The site of Richmond Palace was between the old Gatehouse and the river, and bordered by Old Palace Lane. While the Palace no longer stands, a cluster of the old buildings' fabric survives on the far edge of the Green, where Old Palace Lane leads down to the riverbank. There, the *White Swan* Pub hides away, an ever popular retreat for residents and others who stumble across its welcoming hearth.

Leading off the Green are many cobbled lanes and alleyways offering a full range of antiques and curios – Duke Street, Paved Court, Brewers Lane, connecting with George Street and a variety of other Pubs and eating establishments. Readers who find time to browse in the old bookshops (there are plenty here and on Hill Rise, beyond the Bridge, leading to Richmond Hill) may like

to share the experience accorded to William Cobbett – when he
was eleven years old –

> As young William went looking for work in Kew Gardens, in 1773, he
> passed a bookshop in the town and, with his last threepence, bought
> Swift's Tale of a Tub [1704].
> Thereupon he read the work and pronounced himself 'seized' with –

> *the birth of intellect.*

> *William Cobbett: Reflections*

The subject of books is deeply personal – of course –

> Some books are to be tasted, others to be swallowed, and some few
> to be chewed and digested.

> *Francis Bacon: Essays, 'Of Studies [1610]*

The Palace

Beyond the Tudor Gateway, emblazoned with the coat-of-arms
of Henry VII stands Old Palace Yard, immediately behind The
Green. It was this Henry who rebuilt the earlier palace (gutted by
fire in 1497) of his grandfather Henry V, who had also endowed
the largest Carthusian monastery in England – Shene – with
riverside land adjoining, now Old Deer Park. His grandson
changed the name of the palace from Shene to Richmond, after
the Yorkshire title [an Earldom] held by his Tudor family.
Earlier, it was the site of a royal residence from the time of
Plantagenet kings – Edward III died here, as did Richard II's first
Consort, Anne of Bohemia, a victim of the Plague in 1394. In a
public act of grief, Richard demolished Shene Palace built by his
grandfather with such care. This therapy must have been successful for he married Isabella of Valois the following year.

Relics of the old buildings exist beyond The Wardrobe (hardly
large enough for the 'dress-sense' of Elizabeth I, but indispensable
to all such creatures), in the fabric of Trumpeter's House. Nearby
Maids of Honour Row related to those in Waiting on a later
Queen, Caroline, when Princess Royal, who lived in Richmond
Park at Ormonde Lodge with her husband, the future George II,
and their family of eight. Beyond, the river tow-path passes under
Richmond Railway Bridge and Twickenham Bridge, past the Old
Deer Park and Kew Gardens which flank the river walk to Kew
Green – affording some 2½ miles of splendid views.

St. Mary Magdalen

Off Red Lion Street, by its churchyard, stands St. Mary's. The parish Church deserves a look-in, where the monuments include one to Simon Bardolph [d. 1654], and one to Robert Cotton [d. 1591] a rather grandly labelled domestic servant in his day – gentleman of the Removing Wardrobe of Beds to Queen Mary, then Groom of her Privy Chamber, and Yeoman of the Wardrobe to Queen Elizabeth. Other interesting memorials are to Edmund Kean, the Shakespearian actor (by the west door), and James Thomson, who died, poetically speaking, at the tender age of forty-eight. Had he not written 'Rule Britannia', the birth of Britain could have passed unnoticed and the island kingdom just remained (if not sunk) in the oblivion of the 'azure main'. The masque of *Alfred* (in which 'Rule Britannia' features) was first performed in 1740. Born and bred in Scotland, Thomson came up to London town some fifty years before Dr. Johnson could rudely point his kith and kin in the same direction of "the high road to London".

Thomson lived convivially at his house in Kew Foot Road where he enlarged his 'rural domain' by paling two fields so that his many friends, invited to visit, might admire both his enclosure, and also, where –

> the walk runs round the hedge, where you may figure me walking any time of the day, and sometimes at night.

Regrettably, as previously noted, the poor poet died after catching both a boat from Hammersmith and a fatal chill.

Virginia Woolf in Paradise Road

In 1915, the newly-weds Leonard and Virginia Woolf took lodgings in Richmond, seeking a home 'outside Bloomsbury'. They found what they were looking for near the church, in Paradise Road (a block or two south of the railway station which helped to keep *The Bloomsbury Group* alive by contact), and they moved in to their new residence, called Hogarth House, where they founded the Hogarth Press. This sideline was to become their principal source of income and her published work, *Monday or Tuesday and Kew Gardens*, was written here during weekends. These presses later imprinted the work of other authors, e.g. T.S. Eliot, to the profit of all. Virginia soon yearned to return to her literary and social paradise in Bloomsbury, which they both did in the following decade. There her health gave out, alas.

Close by, the varied assembly of old houses, Georgian villas and picturesque dwellings, in the Vineyard, and Lancaster Park, make for a pleasing detour towards Richmond Hill and the Terrace, with the lovely view.

— THE VIEW FROM RICHMOND HILL —

There will be some who agree with Mary Russell Mitford –

> The principal charm of this smiling landscape is the river, the beautiful river, for the hill seems to me overrated. The celebrated prospect is, to my eye, too woody, too leafy, too green. There is a monotony of vegetation, a heaviness. The view was finer as I first saw it in February, when the bare branches admitted frequent glimpses of houses and villages.
> *[A visit to Richmond, 1832]*

In her day, at least, it was possible to ameliorate the view with a spanking dinner at the hostelry beloved of Charles Dickens and noted by Benjamin R. Haydon, as one of the three summits of human happiness (the first, a purity of soul that comes from 'doing your duty', the second, 'success in great schemes'), the third, a 'lovely girl who loves you in the dining room of the Star and Garter' on Richmond Hill –

> sitting after dinner on your knee, with her heavenly bosom palpitating against your own, her arm round your neck playing with your hair, enough of consciousness to keep her cheeks blushing, her eyes lustrous, & her lip shining, and her form twining & bending, while you are sufficiently heated to be passionately alive to the ecstasy without having lost your senses from its excess – claret on the table and the delicious scene of Nature in Richmond Park beneath your open window, moaty, sunny, out of which rise the wandering voice of the cuckoo, moaning its distant echo, and the singing of the birds in the Groves, while the sun, who throws a silent splendour over all, sinks into the lower vaults & the whole sky is beginning to assume the tinged lustre of an afternoon.
>
> *[Diary, 2 June 1816]*

The *Star and Garter* is now the *Petersham Hotel* – where the view is still available but the raunchy maids of Richmond who gained Dickens's vaulting praise have not been revamped in the £1 million facelift of an hotel that so far lacks any 'stars' and has carefully dissociated itself from any 'garters'.

A superior eye for the view

Sir Joshua Reynolds must have enjoyed the view from his home, Wick House (designed by Sir William Chambers, 1772) in Nightingale Lane, above the *Petersham Hotel*. The Terrace now affords one of the finest views to be had in London.

The largest royal park in England

Richmond Park is the largest royal park in England, exceeding 2,500 acres and the haunt of the herds of fallow and red deer, unique to London. The stags are at their prime in the season of late autumn, when nature inflames their coats flush-red – as also their temperament – be warned.

Young and old deers

Although the Old Deer Park of Shene never brushed with the higher ground of the Park, Charles I extended and enclosed the royal hunting ground by annexing what he dared of common land between, and presumably resented to this day by a handful of the

old, lowly, families of Richmond and Shene. The older oaks were planted in his reign and are over 400 years old. Some royal lodges remain – White Lodge, built for George I who would undoubtedly have acquired a novel command of the English language from the lips of huntsmen in full cry, had he chosen to live there, which he never did. Perhaps his tutors felt that an occasional lapse into profanities might soften a teutonic ear, with the ripeness rather than the subtlety of a 'foreign' language. The lodge was built in 1727 and reflects the style of upstream Chiswick House.

More royal ties

The Duke of Windsor (Edward VIII) was born at White Lodge and his brother (George VI) began married life there with H.R.H. Queen Elizabeth, The Queen Mother. To-day it is the home of the Royal Ballet School(open to visitors in the month of August).

Another Old Lodge

The Isabella Plantation and Woodland Gardens are renowned for their 'blooming display' of azalea and rhododendron, best seen in May. Nearby is the site of Old Lodge, (demolished) built for Sir Robert Walpole as a retreat from Downing Street, and across the Park stands Thatched Lodge, the residence of one of England's most popular Princesses, Alexandra, whose anniversary of her

Silver Wedding to the Hon. Angus Ogilvy was recently (1988) celebrated by her happy family.

A Virginian Reminder

For American citizens, the sentiments attached to Richmond's placename afford many historic ties. Some link the view from Richmond Hill with that of the James River that William Byrd thought similar, when he gave the Virginian city its name in 1737; others point to the coincidence that the founding colony and its chief town should bear the name of the Virgin Queen and her palace. Literary buffs prefer to jog their memories up Richmond Hill where they hope to be served exhilarating cups of municipal tea at Pembroke Lodge. There to re-enact, perhaps, the moment in 1859 when the authoress of *Uncle Tom's Cabin*, Harriet Beecher Stowe, called on Lord John Russell (to take tea, as arranged by Lord Byron's widow whom she was visiting), and who noted of the household –

> *so New England-like.*

Whether the decor, or service, of the cafeteria will provoke the same thought for today's visitor out of New (or Old) England, rests on the shoulders of the owners, the Commissioners of the Crown Estate, who can't wait to stop serving their dreadful tea and sell the place off.

The ubiquitous preserve of Henry VIII

Near Pembroke Lodge is the Mound, where the royal hunting party could view the chase and where, by a far-fatched tradition, Henry VIII awaited confirmation of Anne Boleyn's execution, by searching the eastern sky (western from Greenwich) for the rocket that was fired at her send-off. In fact, the temporary widower was in Wiltshire on that day, May 19th (1536), but legends do abound.

'The Poet of Nature'

At the Pembroke Lodge entrance may be found the memorial Lines on James Thomson, 'the Poet of Nature', which begin –

> Ye who from London's smoke and turmoil fly,
> To seek a purer air and brighter sky.
> Think of the Bard who dwelt in yonder dell,
> Who sang so sweetly what he loved so well.

Think as ye gaze on these luxuriant bowers,
Here, THOMSON loved the sunshine and the flowers . . .
John Heneage Jesse [d. 1874]. Memorial plaque in Richmond Park.

**Dr Thomas Augustine Arne, the musical composer of the
stirring tune ("Rule Britannia") lived downstream in Chelsea (at
215 King's Road, later lived in by Ellen Terry, Actress), for those
who wish to know.**

**Today the view, set on the promontory above the river pattern
in the valley, commands a sweeping panorama towards the setting
sun, Windsor Castle, and all the way downstream to St. Paul's
(whose dome can be seen) in the City, beyond.**

RULE BRITANNIA
– A Favourite Anthem –

When Britain first, at Heaven's command
Arose from out the azure main,
This was the charter of the land,
And guardian angels sang this strain:
Rule Britannia, rule the waves!
Britons never will be slaves!

2. The nations not so blest as thee
   Must in their turns to tyrants fall,
   Whilst thou shalt flourish great and
   free
   The dread and envy of them all.
   Rule, Britannia, etc.

4. Thee haughty tyrants ne'er shall
   tame;
   All their attempts to bend thee
   down
   Will but arouse thy generous flame,
   But work their woe and thy
   renown.
   Rule, Britannia, etc.

3. Still more majestic shalt thou rise
   More dreadful from each foreign
   stroke
   As the loud blast that tears the skies,
   Serves but to root thy native oak.
   Rule, Britannia, etc.

5. To thee belongs the rural reign;
   Thy cities shall with commerce
   shine;
   All thine shall be the subject main,
   And every shore it circles thine.
   Rule, Britannia, etc.

The Muses, still with freedom found,
Shall to thy happy coast repair;
Blest isle, with matchless beauty crowned,
And manly hearts to guard the fair!
Rule, Britannia, Britannia rule the waves!
Britons never will be slaves!

TWICKENHAM

– (*Twik-n'm*): *a tweak or a twick – a place to observe [Anglo-Saxon corruption]*
– *Ham: a village.*

Richmond Bridge connects the Twickenham bank where, again, the unending town may finally be said 'to meet' country. Lovely walks lead around the riverbend to Twickenham, long associated with literary and artistic residents, Horace Walpole and Turner, in particular.

Despite the urban encroachment of humanity, Father Thames has kept watch over the beauty spots, which are maintained by one or other of Her Majesty's municipal bodies. Given time and an imaginative resolve, Father Thames will yet approve of the changing compromise. Whether a quorum of Fielding, Pope, Walpole and Tennyson, notwithstanding Turner, could share the beliefs of the past with those of the present will be a matter for the historical agendas of the next century.

Marble Hill House, the compact Palladian mansion composed in the handsome parklands on the slopes of the river, is a familiar gem to the day-tripper, in an unfolding passage of highpoints, *en route* to Hampton Court. How many would abandon ship (the ferry never stops) were they to be given the chance of wading ashore and exploring the royal and literary connections that cast their spirits still, in the lanes that thread about Twickenham?

Turner's hideaway

Designed by Turner in 1810, Sandycombe Lodge shows up the practical nature of the extraordinary man, for its unpretentious dwelling to which he could retreat from the social clamour of the art world which he so disliked and at the same time, pursue his painting. It is remarkable that success never turned his head, especially at the young age of thirty-four, when he bought this strip of land with the fruits of his acclaimed labour. The trappings of wealth counted for little in comparison with his single-minded purpose, to become, as was later acknowledged, the greatest artist that England has produced.

Turner's prescience enabled his countrymen to inherit the gift of so many of his works, presented along with his monetary

largesse, for all to enjoy in perpetuity. This is now a reality in the
Clore Gallery at Millbank, downstream.

Turner at Millbank

Thanks to the generosity of Vivien Duffield, of the family of the
late Sir Charles Clore, who salved the conscience of the nation by
providing the funds for this lovely Turner shrine, any number of
his works of art may be soaked up in the fastest place in London in
which to lose an hour. Many local scenes are hung – the big ones,
the glories, the quick ones, the snaps and the sketches. All with
that gift supreme – a vision of colour; the splash of carpets woven
through the skies; the tactile wetness of the seas; the flake of his
oils rendering land minerals of rust; foliage in breathfuls of the
breeze that squeezes from each frame. Light, studied, analysed and
captured on canvas by this, true first (and perhaps best) of the
Impressionists and arguably the finest abstract painter. Which, one
wonders, were completed at his Twickenham hideaway?

Twickenham developed from a small Saxon community and in
the 18th/19thC became known for *the* supply of fresh produce to
London market. Turner's father, a barber of Covent Garden, used
this to advantage when he came to live here. A gallant commuter
in his old age –

> *Why, lookee here, I have found a way at last of coming up cheap*
> *from Twickenham*

he wrote to a friend, explaining his journey up to town, where he
still kept shop for his son, in the Queen Anne Street gallery, West
End:

> *– and found out the inn where the market-gardners baited their*
> *horses I made friends with one of 'em, and now, for a glass of gin a*
> *day, he brings me up in his cart on the top of the vegetables.*
> > Thornbury's *Life and Correspondence of J.M.W. Turner,*
> > 2nd ed. pp118/9 [1870].

As a barber in Maiden Lane for many years, he was no stranger
to the goods consigned to Covent Garden, though he can hardly
have imagined he would one day spend the hours of sunrise and
sunset, packed on top.

Turner kept a boat at Richmond –

> . . . from which he painted on a large canvas direct from Nature.
> Till you have seen these sketches, you know nothing of Turner's
> powers. 　　　　　　　　*from –* Trimmer's *account. [c. 1812].*

Turner on the riverbank

Turner was to put the time he spent on the River to optimum good use. Many of his *so-called* landscapes are little less than prime studies in skyscape to which he lent the props of scenic detail, much as a craftsman in precious metals may enhance the effects of a stone in its proper setting:

> **e.g.** Tree-tops and sky, c. 1807 [Room 103, Clore Gallery, Millbank).

It was also from the Thames that Turner imagined the classical grandeur of nature, in his *scapes* –

> *observe* – **Sunset on the River**, no. 2311 [c. 1807];
> **Landscape**, no. 5486 (the benchmark for Modern Art)
> **'Sunset'**, no. 4665;

23

> **'Moonlight a study at Millbank**, no. 459;
> Exhibited at Clore Gallery, Millbank.

> *compare* (for fun) – Turner's *Italian idylls* with Claude's canvasses.

If you squint your eyes at Richmond Hill – or from it if you're on it – you may even share the view that Turner forged into many a masterpiece which quite outstripped Claude of Lorraine (when at *his* best).

Visitors to London may choose a rewarding experience of combining a visit to the Clore Gallery and, possibly after a superb lunch in the adjoining Tate Restaurant, hot-footing it to Richmond, where a skiff awaits them. There, at leisure – especially after some good claret from the Tate's fine cellars – a discovery of Turner's colours in the sky may be enjoyed and modestly appreciated.

Opposite Sandycombe Road and adjacent to the main entrance of Marble Hill, stands the imposing Georgian terrace – Montpelier Row. At number 15, Tennyson, the poet, lived in town. Orleans Road leads to the Riverside, where Hammerton's unpredictable ferry service crosses to Ham House.

FATHER AND SON

Turner and his father lived at Sandycombe Lodge between 1814 and 1826. While "Son" spent much of his time in travel –

> Sandycombe sounds just now in my ears as an act of folly, when I reflect how little I have been able to be there this year, and less chance (perhaps) for the next in looking forward to a Continental excursion, and poor Daddy seems as much plagued with weeds as I am with disappointments.
>
> *[J.M.W.T., letter 1st August, 1815]*

"Old" Dad ensconced himself at Twickenham the whole year round, and, it seems was always working in the garden or catching cold when 'released from the chore of farming'.

As a boy, Turner spent much of his time away from Covent Garden (at his uncle's house in Brentford). He knew the Thames valley well, as his sketchbooks testify. The influence of the broad reaches of the Thames was lifelong; this effect on his vision of nature, as reflected in her waters, profound –

> Resplendent stream, thy bank relives its haste
> A simple stone yet marks where Thomson lies
> Along the hill and Putneys airy waste
> He looked and Nature sparkled in his eyes
>
> Place then amidst thy upland groves
> The Eolian Harp soft tuned to Nature's strains
> Melifluous cheering Thamesis as he roves
> Rich with the tribute of the verdant plains.
>
> *[Poem by J.M.W.T. commemorating Thomson's own verse entitled*
>   *Aeolian Harp, a copy of which he hung in his own gallery).*

Marble Hill House

Built as a summer pavilion for one of George II's mistresses, Henrietta Howard, Countess of Suffolk, in the early 18thC, the Palladian mansion stands in grounds spacious enough for the sort of entertainment expected, not only by royal command, but by her own lavish circle intent on the social season. The house is furnished in the style of contemporary 18thC taste, here and there a little sparse, perhaps, but it all makes for an undemanding walkabout, in well-proportioned rooms, with lovely views beyond. The lack of tell-tale signs which are absent from the royal mistress's bedroom irritate the curious, particularly when there are two to choose from. The other one was Mrs. Fitzherbert who became a royal bride, but no queen. In 1785, she was secretly married to the Prince Regent, later George IV, but they left Marble Hill for his grander Pavilion beside the sea.

The grounds contain a mature park, which Alexander Pope, the Countess's close neighbour at Cross Deep, lost no time in laying-out to his design, and which bears his imprint. The largest black walnut in the British Isles is still there – easily identified by its trunk – if not, by its marker tag. The river walk from Richmond Bridge passes the park, in its course to the village, where convivial local pubs have earned Twickenham the Londoners' affection. Richmond Hill is seen to the fore, by the bend where Horse *Reach* lies.

French Connections

This aspect of opulent river footage once housed more ornamental villas per square mile than almost anywhere else: Francis Bacon's Twickenham Park; Mount Lebanon adjoining Orleans House; and Horace Walpole's at Strawberry Hill, and the French aristocracy in refugee encampment at York House. The Octagon, adjoining the gallery of Orleans House, is the only portion of the Thames terminus for the twice-exiled king of France, Louis Phillippe, Duc d'Orleans. Happily for those who go, are the open-air concert recitals staged at Marble Hill.

YORK HOUSE

A bend in the roadway, to make way for the brick-walled raised garden of York House terrace, temporarily severs the company of Father Thames. The road rejoins the river, passing under a raised garden bridge which connects the house to its terrace by an inconspicuous entrance. The garden frontage is well hidden by the natural elevation of the terrace and the well clipped hedges. Beyond lie well-stocked borders and pond, trim packages for the eye, until the fountain spurts from nowhere and the wonder of nudity and bosomry, draped about the boulders of the rockery, all of a sudden presage a scene change.

Sir Ratan Tara, the wretched 19thC tycoon, bought the property but suffered from melancholia and thus planted his lovelies, purposely oversized, so that he and his guests could view the nymphs at play, from the distance of the house. Thus he hoped to raise his spirits from the depression caused by his disease. James II received York House as a wedding present from his father-in-law, Lord Clarendon. Both of his daughters, Anne and Mary, later Queens of England, were born here in the 17thC.

York House would make a fitting residence – (should the Mayor and Aldermen agree) – for any couple with royal connections, just as it also did for the Comte de Paris and his bride, in the last century. More especially it might suit a Duke and Duchess with a name that fits, otherwise unable, like so many young couples starting out these days, to find an ideal home that they can afford so close to town. Those who do occupy the 'desirable' residence, in future, should set about saving poor Ratan Tara's stone-faced damsels, persecuted by the vandals, and looking very under the weather.

Strawberry Hill

In 1747, Sir Horace Walpole set the style of 'gothic' back in fashion when he purchased Strawberry Hill and began his extraordinary reconstruction of the property. It became an architectural land-mark in his clever revival of a discarded style. In the same year, he wrote to a friend –

> You perceive by my date that I am got into a new camp, and have left my tub at Windsor. It is a little plaything house that I got out of . . . (Mrs. Chevenix, a toy woman), and is the prettiest bauble you ever saw . . .

His father, Sir Robert (first Prime Minister in England) had died two years previously, leaving his fourth son with ample means and both the time and an imaginative disposition to create his 'Gothic Castle' out of the 'toy-woman's cottage'. The fanciful name was about the only item in the title-deed not to be altered. Walpole's residence glories in the interiors and combines, with the airy castellations of the façade, an exuberance and novelty rarely seen elsewhere. This house was much copied in Victorian 'community architecture' by the very rich in England. It also influenced domestic architecture in the United States, where innumerable brown stone mansions in affluent suburbs derived their style from the vogue that Strawberry Hill created. The Gallery, the Hall, the fan-vaulted ceiling copied from the Henry VII chapel at Westminster, no less – the vestibules, the grand rooms and the small – are a delight to encounter. No visitor, finding an opportunity to visit Strawberry Hill, should fail to do so, there to share with its original creator the notion that –

> every true Goth must perceive that (the interiors) are more works of fancy than imitation.

Some would describe it all as pure fancy-dress in stone moulding – a creation that caused Walpole to restrict visitors by allocating tickets, such were the crowds that flocked to see it. The 'Admissions' Secretary to the Principal of St. Mary's College (the fortunate occupants) restricts the flow today to a 'select' trickle: small wonder, she is an elusive lady to make contact with, unless by registered post, be warned (1986–7).

POPE'S GROTTO

> Not with more glories, in the ethereal plain,
> The sun first rises o'er the purpled main,
> Than issuing forth, the rival of his beams,
> Launched on the bosom of the silver Thames . . .
>
> [from 'The Rape of the Lock']

Alexander Pope the 'wasp' of Twickenham, had completed much of the *Iliad* by the year of Walpole's birth (1717), writing up to fifty verses a day, despite the poet scholar's aversion to all Greek, but Homer. Pope was then twenty-nine and well on his own way to fame. He regarded himself with enormous self-esteem, as rivals discovered if they crossed him. He also enjoyed the ear of the Prince of Wales, which may have added to his self-confidence (and to his sense of his own importance). Pope lived with his mother at Cross Deep and in his famous grotto played host to the foremost literary names – Gay, Arbuthnot, Congreve, Fielding (a 'Twickenhammer', of nearby Holly Road), Swift and also Voltaire in the period of his exile. Pope even boasted, to the envy of the lesser poets, his early acquaintance with Dryden –

> All fly to Twit'nam, and in humble straint
> Apply to me, to keep them made or vain . . .

There are who to my person pay their court:
I could like Horace, and though lean, am short.
[from 'The Prologues to the Satires']

As a man – sophisticated, able and clever – Pope's appeal, though dated
to the modern ear, must principally lie in his zest for life; – no more so
than when he is parrying one of his lady-friends, Lady Mary Wortley
Montagu – (an exceptional woman and way ahead of her time). She
introduced the Turkish practice of inoculation against smallpox into
England, among other advanced ideas she held, some of which inflamed
Pope. So did Lady Mary's 'English rose' complexion – she was an early
practitioner in the art of skin care – among her other refinements that
moved Pope –

> I am fourscore miles from London, a short journey compared to that I so
> often thought at least of undertaking, rather than die without seeing you
> again. Though the place I am in is such as I would not quit for the town, if I
> did not value you more than any, nay everybody else there; and you will
> convince how little the town has engaged my affections in your absence
> from it . . .

– LOCKING IN TO LADY ARABELLA . . . –

Shortly after this missive, there was to be a parting of the ways.
Meanwhile, Pope was soon busy elsewhere, this time adding spice to the
same fragility of human passion that inspired much of his prose and
poetry. He had turned his attentions on Arabella Fermor, a leading
beauty, and the theft of her lock of hair by her lover, Lord Petre –

> This nymph, to the destruction of mankind,
> Nourished two locks, which graceful hung behind,
> In equal curls, and well conspired to deck,
> With shining ringlets, the smooth ivory neck . . .
>
> The advent'rous baron the bright lock admired,
> He saw, he wished, and to the prize aspired . . .
> *The Rape of the Lock. [1714].*

Pope launched into detail, which he intended in jest – 'to laugh them
together again' – but, when the poem was published, had the opposite
effect. The butts of his pen suffered instantaneous estrangement, *as well as*
his own. To discover which of the two locks was stolen makes for a good
read, a work endemic of the 'wasp of Twickenham', lauded by Professor
George Saintsbury, no less –

> For though Ben Jonson was a greater, and Dryden a very much
> greater, critic than Pope, neither had so fully co-ordinated his
> gifts . . .
>
> Though still to polish it a little, he has already rearranged the
> Drydenian couplet, (so as to deprive it of much of its stateliness . . .

and irresistible momentum), to substitute for these a much greater polish, a constant glitter instead of the intermittent glaze . . . and a sort of castanet accompaniment of rhyme which, till wearies the ear utterly of it, is singularly attractive.

On one occasion in his life, Pope slipped up literally, when he fell in the Thames: his French friend and admirer wrote –

Sir, I hear this moment of your sad adventure. The water you fell in, was not Hippocrene's water, otherwise it would have respected you. Indeed I am concerned beyond expression for the danger you have been in, and more for your wounds.

Is it possible that those fingers which have written the rape of the lock and the Criticism, which have dressed Homer so becomingly in an English coat, should have been so barbarously treated? . . . I hope ser you are now perfectly recovered.

rely your accident concerns me as much as all the disasters of a master ought to affect his scholar. Etc, etc,

Your most humble servant

Voltaire [Autumn, 1726]

Dear Voltaire, France's greatest anglophile, was able to visit Pope in his Grotto at Twickenham, during his period of safe haven in London [1726–1728], while exiled from the 'unjust' kingdom.

The famous Grotto may be visited on Saturday mornings only, as it also was by the leading wits of the day. But they took care not to overstay, a privilege not accorded the present traveller.

When Pope died, (30th May 1744), his deformed frame completely worn out by his incessant study and 'constant excitement', he left his property to his gorgeous girlfriend from Mapledurham to whom he had remained devoted for thirty years ever since he first set eyes on her, 'fair-haired' Martha Blount. In fact scandal cast doubt on whether her character was quite as fair as *her* locks, if not her fidelity to Pope; in an age of scandal that was soon forgotten.

Some other Petersham residents

OF PETERSHAM WATER MEADOWS, and riverbanks, or the freshening English shower, there is none so delightful a companion as Dr. Izaac Walton –

to soothe, instructe, and delighte the reader (1665).

– But turn out of the way a little, good scholar, towards yonder high hedge: we'll sit whilst this shower falls so gently

upon the teeming earth, and gives a sweeter smell to the lovely
flowers that adorn the verdant meadows . . .

Anglers abound on the Surrey bank outstaring their invisible
prey, skylarks dart and dive in playful combat overhead; the busy
world hidden behind distant Richmond Hill. River craft glide
below the treeline, their engines humming and chugging and a
lash of oars occasionally breaking forth in ripples that splash in the
breeze. Between field views this way and that, woodlands wander
and cluster by yesteryear's mansions, carefully planted in
ornamental lawns.

The meadows at Ham and Petersham provide for lovely
riverside walks, unburdened by urban encroachment, and seem
unruffled by the passage of centuries that have by-passed this
stretch of the Thames. There is plenty to interest every taste: from
the magnificent Jacobean residence of Sir Thomas Vavasour's
Ham House to Teddington and Twickenham a ferry ride away, on
the Middlesex side. Their countrified pubs and village lanes repay
an unhurried detour.

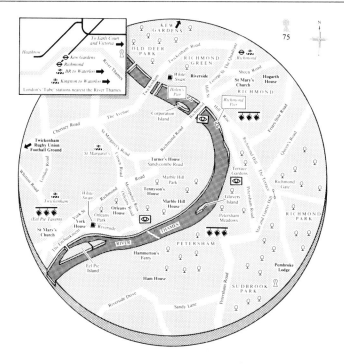

HAM HOUSE

By way of Hammerton's ferry – when it is running – or via Richmond, there is a genuine mansion to be found, almost in the state its illustrious 17thC owners bequeathed it. Ham House, perching ankle deep on the flat water meadow, often flooding the car park, is a delight, not only for its position but also for the contents which reflect the authentic tastes of the Duke and Duchess of Lauderdale. The Duke was a ruthless politician of Charles II's court, he –

'the coldest friend and most violent enemy that ever was known'

and married to a Countess in her own right (of Dysart), she –

'of a most ravenous covetnessness . . . violent in everything, a violent friend and a much more violent enemy'

as contemporary opinion states of the apparently well-matched couple. Their unliked portrait of 'Ye Graces' by Lely may be seen in the Hall Gallery amidst many of the Duchess's coveted acquisitions.

The house exudes 17thC authenticity; decoration, paintings, furniture and even the wall fabrics are mostly accounted for in the original inventories, and lend an atmosphere, rich but not overwhelming, often lacking in historic houses. The mansion is thought to have survived chiefly because the family spent their fabled wealth on a string of other properties following the famous Duke and Duchess's tenure of Ham, and never got round to converting this forgotten residence. To-day, largely due to the care and attention of the Victoria and Albert Museum, together with the National Trust, the house may be enjoyed to the full doubtless more so than by some of the Lauderdales' erstwhile friends.

The influential Lauderdales

England was once said to be 'ruled from Petersham' in the heyday (1666) of the *Cabal* (the word was made up the initials taken from the names of):

> Clifford,
> Ashley,
> Buckingham,
> Arlington, and
> Lauderdale,

the principal ministers of Charles II.

St. Peter's

St. Peter's was more than ever the Established Church for the influential set who encamped at Ham. The parish church retains its links with the past, the box-pews are a lovely feature, so too, the charming Gallery.

The present Queen Mother's parents, the late 14th Earl and Countess of Strathmore, were wed here (1881). The Hon. Elizabeth Bowes-Lyon followed on 4th August, 1900 (into the world, not to Ham), and herself married George VI, (who reigned, together with Queen Elizabeth his Consort, from 1936 to 1952). Londoners who survived the years of the Blitz rallied to the inspiration she provided 'in England's darkest hour'; and the Queen Mother's subjects continue to hold her in warm esteem, hence she is popularly called 'The Queen Mum'.

In the churchyard Captain George Vancouver lies buried [1798], having discovered himself to be a Columbus (the 2nd, but British) of the Canadian Pacific (British Columbia).

Village Character

This charming village remains largely unspoilt in this backwater of the Thames, as do most of the glorious residences in the vicinity. Neither – alas – have remained unscathed from the relentless flow of traffic through its heart.

Beyond, the river lane leads to the peace of the towpath and, back, to Ham House, or, on, to the Twickenham Bank, by ferry.

> 'Ahoy! and Oho, and it's who's for the ferry?'
> (The briar's in bud and the sun going down:)
>
> 'And I'll row ye so quick and I'll row ye so steady,
> And 'tis but *a penny* to Twickenham Town.'
> *Theophile Julius Henry Marzials [19thC]*

The visitor may opt to return to the Twickenham bank, if the ferryman will land. A ferry ride away is the (often submerged) roadway called Riverside, connecting Marble Hill with the village of Twickenham. Beside the landing stage, or what still does as one, the riverside garden of the *White Swan* makes merry with customers who have learnt to be choosy about pub food and

appreciate Mrs. Sutton's high standard of honest fare (1987), who put up with sudden showers in order that they may enjoy the lovely view and, the occasional sight of a footloose ferry passenger falling in the drink.

   A plain, but no ordinary pub is the *White Swan*. The upper-storey serving area and balcony is reached by the wooden stairs which, when the Thames floods its banks, encourages patrons to stay for the consumption of another 'one for the road' when the latter has disappeared from view. Just in case, an up-to-date timetable of the tides should be acquired by anyone intending to use the ground floor toilets.

There are similar pub signs in England, many adopted after the arrival of Henry VIII's fourth wife, Anne (of Cleves), whose Prussian background boasted an order of chivalry – the Order of the Swan; the badge being a silver swan surmounted by an image of the Virgin.

The local residents are probably content to believe their *local*'s pub sign is none other than a swan plucked at random out of the Thames. These graceful birds actually belong to the Sovereign, except for a rather large handful that, either by royal indulgence or ancient custom, are owned by one or other of two City Livery companies: the Dyers (one nick in the beak, denotes), or the Vintners (two nicks in the beak). Swan-Upping is a colourful ceremony in late July when cygnets are marked in this way – the Queen's swans are never marked – attended by the Keeper of the Queen's Swans. His presence therefore counts.

ST. MARY'S CHURCH

The handsome red brick church, sitting on higher ground fronting the Embankment, stands out with aplomb. The 14thC tower survived a disaster in 1713 when the body of the nave collapsed but James, the architect, replaced it with a gracious structure, picturebook Queen Anne style. On the exterior East wall – opposite the vicarage garden of Dial House, an unspoilt riverside property built for the Twining family from their tea-time takings – there is a poetic inlaid stone inscribed by Pope to his nurse, buried beneath the bumpy turf.

> Today *the House of Twining* is famous for its brands of tea, and has particularised the favourite blend of Charles, 2nd Earl Grey, resident of Ham Common on the other bank, before he became Prime Minister in succession to Wellington (and moved the Reform Bill).

Inside the church, the galleried aisles offer an empty clue to the affluence once associated with a house of prayer. Pope is naturally here, under the stone slab marked 'P' –

> *To one who would not be buried in Westminster*
> *(Warburton's tribute)*

– the brass plate, the gift of three American scholars, records the fact. Conversely, the monument of Sir Godfrey Kneller, court portraitist (who lived at Whitton House, Twickenham) – which stands in Westminster Abbey – was intended for this Church, where a special place is yet reserved, in the hope of his return.

> He said . . . By God, I will not be buried in Westminster. I asked him why not. He answered 'they do bury fools there.'
> *Sir Godfrey Kneller, remarks on his death-bed, November 1723,*
> *[quoted by Alexander Pope: letter to Lord Stafford, 6 July, 1725]*

The *Rysbrack* monument to Admiral Sir Chaloner Ogle is as showy as any to be found, and it may be presumed that this worthy gentleman, or his family at least, intended him to repose down river.

More Village Character

The church mould leads to Church Street, originally the old High Street, and mercifully preserved except for the crater, which is used as a car park opposite a deservedly popular *Eel Pie* Pub – comfortable and clean. The wide selection of food is good value – consumption of eels is not obligatory – and the bewildering array of ales, each with the specifics of gravity, most helpfully pointed out, are kept in prime condition according to discerning real ale drinkers. Those pressed for time, at any stage *before* 'closing time' may be glad to know that Twickenham Station (BR to Waterloo) is close by.

A stroll about the riverbank in this neighbourhood is a delight. It is all so peaceful, and easy to imagine the voices and the people of the past, who enjoyed precisely the same scene, and who have – by some subtle alchemy – imbued it with their unmodern, lingering elegance and charm.

Time Out

Here, where the reeds meet the fast-flowing current, and fishing rods loiter on the river, snatches of conversation may almost be caught in the air (as between one fisherman, *Piscator*, and a wayfarer, *Vivator*, – the characters of Vavasour's contemporary, the incomparable Izaac Walton) –

> . . . As I left this place, and entered into the next field, a second pleasure entertained me, 'twas a handsome milk-maid that had caste away all care, and sung like a nightingale; her voice was good, and the ditty fitted for it; 'twas that smooth song which was made by Kit Marlow, now at least fifty years ago; and the milk maid's mother

sung an answer to it, which was made by Sir Walter Raleigh in his yonger days.

– They were old fashioned poetry, but choicely good, I think much better than that now in fashion in this critical age. Look yonder, on my word, yonder they both be a milking again; I will give her the chub (perch), and perswade them to sing those two songs to us . . .

To the blandishments of *Piscator* who presents the milk maid's mother with his catch of the day, she replies –

O I know it now, I learn't the first part in my golden age, when i was about the age of my daughter; and the later part, which indeed fits

me best, but two or three years ago; you shall, God willing, hear them both . . .
   (The Compleat Angler, 2nd ed 1655) –

Izaac Walton, England's best known angler and first countryside commentator, feared that despite (or perhaps because of), his contemporary popular renown, he would not merit a burial and memorial in the Poet's Corner of Westminster Abbey (the Arlington cemetry of English *literati*). Presciently he scratched his initials on the memorial to Izaac Watt, a great contemporary who predeceased him, and whose accepting marble still bears witness to Walton's only memorial in that place of Literary Honour.

The language of the great artists – from poets and writers to the composers and the musicians – nearly always originates in the rhythms and chords of nature. In England and elsewhere in Northern Europe, where the profusion of bird-song breaks out each season, the sounds and notes of starlings, chaffinch, willow warblers and thrush – and the dozens of other varieties – may be listened to with the greatest of pleasure.

Take Beethoven for instance: in his Pastoral Symphony he places snatches of bird-song which may be detected by anyone who listens to the nightingale (flute) *in* Berkeley Square (?) or the quail (oboe) or cuckoo (clarinet) *in* the water-meadows of the Thames.

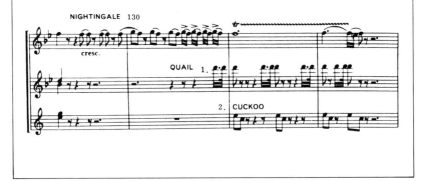

KINGSTON-UPON-THAMES

The quaint back-streets of Kingston, where they came down to the water's edge . . . the wooded towpath, the trim-kept villas on either side, Harris, in a red and orange blazer, grunting away at the sculls, the distant glimpse of the old grey palace of the Tudors . . .

– Jerome K. Jerome, Three Men in a Boat.

ROYAL KINGSTON-UPON-THAMES, the *other* one of London's two royal Boroughs (an honour shared by the Borough of Kensington and Chelsea) seems to have changed for the worse since *Harris* went 'messing about on the river'. Gone are the quaint backstreets and unhurried pace of the town: replaced by a snarling traffic system which divides the main thoroughfare, now spoilt with drab skyblocks and multi-storey car parks. Pockets of pedestrian cobbledom have survived, but hardly breech the void created.

'All change' for Hampton Court

For those who wish to combine the vaunted convenience of British Rail's train schedule from Waterloo, Kingston is a convenient point of river embarkation to Hampton Court (with perhaps an instant picnic, on the cruise, from the nearby shelves of the Royal Borough's branch of Messrs *Marks and Spencer*).

Kingston proudly guards the old Anglo-Saxon coronation stone which should be seen.

Cyninges-tun, or 'the place of kings by the water', grew out of the community that settled at one of the safest crossing-places upstream from Westminster. A thriving market town, it became the focal point of the surrounding hinterland. In 1628 a royal charter decreed that the rights of the 'Ancient Market' to supply market produce was extended to include a radius of twelve miles and this monopoly was preserved until the advent of frozen foodstuffs.

The cluster of Tudor frontages to survive in the Market Place bear evidence of the longtime prosperity of the local merchants. *Chiesman's* the department store, even has preserved a fine Jacobean staircase, for old-fashioned customers who distrust the workings of a lift.

Legal ties

Kingston acquired a legal respectability in this century when it was ordained the Assize town of the county of Surrey, in place of Guildford (equally respectable, in every other respect). This occurred when an irate judge, so it is said, found himself and his court constantly interrupted by the capers of music-hall artists who were rehearsing, noisily, in the Hall adjoining the Court-house in Guildford. He recommended to the Lord Chancellor that the town be forthwith relieved of its 'duties in maintaining the dignity of their lordships' office'. Lo, without further trial or ado, the court was removed! One particular Assize judge was Mr. Justice Darling. Once, in a case well known for the repartee that flowed between the very witty judge and erudite Counsel, the bench enquired –

Who, and what, is Mr. George Robey?

Robey was a famous and nationally celebrated music-hall artist (as the learned judge well knew). The question was put by way of seeking and taking 'judicial notice' – a rule prescribing the admissibility of facts being proved in court – of information that was otherwise excluded as hearsay evidence. Counsel's answer was a swift retort –

> *'M'l'd, Mr. George Robey is the Darling of the gods.**
>
> F.E. Smith (later Lord Chancellor Birkenhead) [1923]
> * A popular name for the music-hall gallery was 'the gods'.

The Coronation Stone

Directly outside the Guildhall is the old Coronation stone of the seven (asterisked) Anglo-Saxon kings of England, who were enthroned beside the river, in a ceremony conducted at the (restored) All Saints' Parish Church. William the Conqueror disputed the crown, left by the last of this pedigree, with the English King Harold II. In 1066 their confrontation led to the Battle of Hastings where William convincingly proved, by combat, his right to the crown of Edward the Confessor. The latter's grandfather, another Edward, was the last king – but one – crowned at Kingston; the first was the son of Alfred the Great –

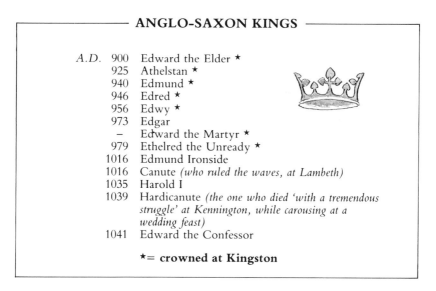

```
                    ANGLO-SAXON KINGS

        A.D.  900   Edward the Elder ★
              925   Athelstan ★
              940   Edmund ★
              946   Edred ★
              956   Edwy ★
              973   Edgar
                –   Edward the Martyr ★
              979   Ethelred the Unready ★
             1016   Edmund Ironside
             1016   Canute (who ruled the waves, at Lambeth)
             1035   Harold I
             1039   Hardicanute (the one who died 'with a tremendous
                    struggle' at Kennington, while carousing at a
                    wedding feast)
             1041   Edward the Confessor

                    ★= crowned at Kingston
```

'Hollywood' on view

A coin of each of the seven reigns is embedded in the base of the Greywether sandstone, the whole protected by the railings; so far to good effect. The medieval remains of the old bridge may be observed off Old Bridge Street which adjoins the existing bridge, erected in 1828. Other local points of interest include the Kingston Museum and Heritage Centre which boasts a unique collection of Hollywood's founder of authentic modern cinematography, Edward Muybridge, who bequeathed his work to the town of his birth (in 1930). Behind the town, on the London road, five conduit houses built by Cardinal Wolsey to supply Hampton Court with water may be seen. Nearby, the Lovekyn Chapel, founded in 1309, with Tudor fabric, continues to be used by the Grammar School and up the hill towards Richmond Park, members of another *old school*, American war veterans, may recall that General Eisenhower took up residence on Coombe Hill whilst in London.

In the Distance

In the distance, across the water, looms the parkland setting of Hampton Court, the most spectacular secular building in the kingdom.

The most fitting approach to this Tudor Show-piece is by water when, rounding the southern perimeter of Le Notre's landscaping which yields to the bending river above Kingston Bridge, the splendour of the palace takes hold. The candle-stacked chimneys overtake the slumbering tree-line, and, through the wrought-iron railings, standing on parade, the sculptured hedges, ornamental lawns, and fanciful facades beckon the eye of the beholder.

For those who have the time, an option might be to take a steamer from Richmond (1½ hours away, by river passage); alternatively, the shorter river-trip from Kingston Pier (30 minutes) still captures some of the prettiest moments to be had on a Thames outing.

HAMPTON COURT PALACE

The lands of the manor of Hampton were owned by the Knights of St. John, who were unable to drive a hard bargain with Wolsey when, in 1519 he decided to acquire their choice countryside, on which to build his second London residence. Within a decade, the son of an Ipswich butcher was to become the most powerful commoner in England, an exalted courtier, bearing on his breast the chain of office of the Chancellorship, and the pectoral cross of the Archbishopric of York, while on his head he wore the red hat of a Cardinal Prince and Papal Legate of the See of Rome. His plans for the splendour of Hampton Court were to reflect his self-esteem, which, in part, caused his downfall, just six years later. Not even the gift to the King of his Thamesside showpiece could stem his fall from grace, compounded by his failure in 1529 to secure a papal decree that would release Henry VIII from wedlock.

What Wolsey constructed, Henry embellished to an even more marked degree, building the magnificent Great Hall, the Chapel Royal, and creating the labyrinthine structure which was intended to project the Tudor name well beyond the boundaries of their recently acquired kingdom. His daughter Elizabeth inhabited the

Court (before settling at Richmond), making minor additions (her name in the year 1586 is preserved in brickwork encasing the bay window of the Tudor façade, as also in the Royal Stables). It was during the reign of William III and Mary that the layout of the State apartments and Baroque wings (designed by Wren), assumed today's pattern. *Dutch* William, it will be recalled, endured a lifelong revulsion for Louis XIV, his Dutch and English foe, and it was for Hampton Court that William III commissioned plans that, if they had been completed, would have outshone his detested rival's palace of Versailles.

– THE MOAT BRIDGE –

Visions of Tudor might and glory are assembled beyond the walkway. lined with the Queen's Beasts –

(Observe:)

White Greyhound of Richmond	**White Lion** of Mortimer
Yale of Beaufort	**Unicorn** of Scotland
Red Dragon of Wales	**Griffin** of Edward III
White Horse of Hanover	**Black Bull** of Clarence
Lion of England	**Falcon** of the Plantagenets

The heraldic beasts make an interesting background for a snapshot of the family group; (a twin set are displayed at Kew Gardens). The bridge leads over the moat immediately to the Great Gatehouse and the Tudor Base Court.

<u>Observe:</u> The oriel window, bearing the arms of Henry VIII, in the Gatehouse, built by Wolsey, 1521; the original stone weasels surmounting the battlements.

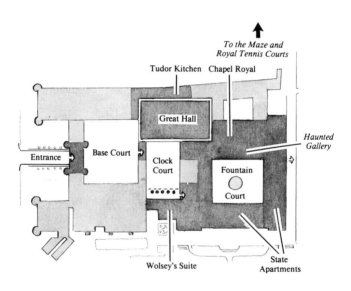

RIVER THAMES

– BASE COURT –

Facing the entrance is *Anne Boleyn's Gateway*, adjoining the west wall of the Great Hall, surmounted by the clock tower.

<u>Observe:</u> early example of Italian renaissance work, two roundels, by Giovanni dei Maiano, 1521, of Roman emperors; and, beneath the arch, the monograms 'H' & 'A' in the ceiling, possibly erroneously ascribed to Anne Boleyn, but it was not the custom to link the Consort's christian name. More likely, it was Wolsey's peace offering of Henry entwined with Aragon, before the edifice was appropriated in the name of the second wife.

– CLOCK COURT –

Opposite the great bay window of the Hall is Wren's 17thC colonnade, above which the royal apartments and private suites, now housing the Galleries, are located.

Observe: The Astronomical Clock, made in 1540 by the French clock-maker, Nicholas Oursian. The Dial [dimension of face, 7 ft. 10 in.] indicates, inter alia, the time of high water at London Bridge – a timetable which proved indispensable for estimating the arrival and departures of guests by river access.

Above the arch, Wolsey's arms; the 16thC terracotta cardinal's hat was expunged by Henry, but later restored.

Fountain Court was Wren's classical reconstruction of the earlier Cloister Green Court, enclosing the private State Apartments; dated 1694 and a pleasing contrast to the surrounding Tudor edifices.

– THE INTERIOR –

Each State Room is clearly marked with gold lettering above each door and display panels describe their contents to the visitor, who in fact tour the Interior in almost reverse order to that taken by yester-year's. Much of the Interior decor, including the 500 paintings and antique furniture, is original, with a preponderance of the collection dating back to Wren's refurbishment for William III, and to Queen Anne's tenure of the throne, on his death in 1702. From 1694, when Queen Mary departed, until her husband William overcame his sorrows (in 1699), work was interrupted; thus the Queen's Apartments are primarily those of Anne's doing. A portion of these apartments are now designated 'grace and favour' residences, for those suffering genteel poverty. The visitor may well be grateful that a tour of the interior does not include the whole palace – a daunting task, that one official estimated would cover a minimum period of three working days, or realistically a week, if more than a single minute was to be passed in each and every room (1,000).

– KING'S STAIRCASE –

The immensely elaborate stairwell, with a beautiful balustrade by Tijou, cascades between the grandiose sets of murals, by Verrio who died here in 1707, (still painting weird allegories to the political glories of his royal patrons).

Observe: The ornate ceiling. Verrio's reputed sexual appetite was the terror of the parlour maids and it was his practice to include an unflattering portrait of any damsel who had thwarted him, in whichever ceiling he was working on. At Hampton Court he must have had his way, as all the mythical ladies look appeasing.

– KING'S GUARDROOM –

Over 3,000 assorted hand weapons are on display around this enormous chamber, where the Yeomen of the Guard would have stood on duty.

– WOLSEY SUITE –

To the right, a panelled suite once occupied by the cardinal's personal retinue, being made up of a series of rooms housing some fine royal portraits.

<u>Observe:</u> undisturbed views of the Pond Garden.

Portrait of a Woman, in a floral dress beautifully painted by Marcus Gheeraerts (Flemish).

– STATE APARTMENTS –

The Apartments are divided, after a fashion, into the King's, Queen's and Prince of Wales' Suites. What may have made them bearable for royalty has largely been obliterated by the soulless hand of civil servants entrusted with the upkeep of the place. There are, however, important examples of the Italian schools of the 16th, 17th and 18th centuries, notably Tintoretto's *Esther and Ahasuerus*, Carracci's *Time and Truth*, Domenichino's *St. Agnes*, and the work of the Venetian painter, Sebastiano Ricci, who achieved high art with his portrayal of *the Continence of Scipio*. Indeed, the artist's notorious promiscuity lends pathos to the subject matter.

The Communication Gallery was probably the busiest – and most discreet – passageway in England at one time. Some of the many beauties seen at Court may still be seen – Lely's 'Windsor Beauties' – and may be compared with Kneller's 'Hampton Court Beauties'. Leading off the gallery was the King's State Bedchamber (for his use on formal occasions), entered through a number of interlocking rooms.

If the Queen did not wish to dally with the King, in any of his Presence Chambers, Audience Room, Drawing Room or Dressing Room, she could withdraw to her set of apartments which run the length of the East Front, with lovely views over the Park and Long Water.

– THE PRINCE OF WALES' SUITE –

Created Prince of Wales on the untimely death of his father, (Frederick Lewis), in 1751, George William Frederick (later George III), resided in this suite, after whom it is named. His suite contains a fine group of paintings, and not to be missed in the lobby, an earlier Prince of Wales, Henry Stuart, is charmingly portrayed with the Earl of Essex, dated 1610.

Beyond the Communication Gallery the oldest portion of the royal apartments are reached. Cardinal Wolsey's private closet is surprisingly small and may easily be missed. His motto may be observed in the ceiling –

Dominus Mihi Adjutor – The Lord is my helper

His Maker no doubt helped him 'Come unto Judgement.'

– QUEEN'S STAIRCASE –

Another superb balustrade by Tijou, and an allegorical subject '*Apollo and Diana*' (finely executed by Honthorst, in honour of Charles I and Queen Henrietta Maria) opens onto the Haunted Gallery, where some of Elizabeth I's tapestries are displayed. This quarter of the palace contains the oldest Tudor section. The Haunted Gallery also contains the ghost of Catherine Howard whose sleep walking outside the bounds of marital fidelity led to her execution for adultery in 1542. It was here, during her incarceration, that she escaped, seeking Henry's forgiveness as he sat in the (connecting) Royal Pew of the Chapel Royal. She was dragged screaming from his presence. Her ghost, which is still heard, walks the corridor at odd hours.

– CHAPEL ROYAL –

This Chapel was built for 'My Lord Cardinal' in 1520. The vaulted timber ceiling, encrusted with Pugin's constellation of stars is much to be admired. The Royal Pew commands a fine view from the upper 'stage', as remodelled by Wren. The woodwork by Grinling Gibbons, is noteworthy. Either side leads to the Holyday Closets, where Henry VIII prayed in turn for his queens to find God's mercy (if not his own).

– GREAT WATCHING CHAMBER –

Set behind Kitchen Court and overlooking the Great Hall is the Great Watching Chamber of Henry VIII where his predecessors' tapestries now hang, under the great panelling of the ceiling which was adorned in 1537 with Jane Seymour's arms, in honour of her giving birth to his son, (later Edward VI). The adjoining Horn Room, where food for the high table was prepared, leads to the Great Hall.

– GREAT HALL –

The Great Hall was built by Henry VIII in 1535 and forms his most important addition to Hampton Court. The hammerbeam roof, by Nedeham and one of the finest secular examples in existence, spans the dimensions of the Hall [106 ft. long, 40 ft. wide, and 60 ft]. high. Both Queens Anne Boleyn and Jane Seymour are commemorated in monograms and badges aloft.

Observe: The Flemish Tapestries, threaded with gold and silver, of great beauty, known as the *Abraham* set;

The Oak Screen, incorporating a minstrels' gallery, behind which the servants assembled.

– *TUDOR KITCHENS AND CELLAR* –

The Tudor Kitchens, including the King's Great Kitchen, are superb reconstructions of yesteryear, with their wide fireplaces and open hearths where, quite literally, an entire ox could be and was roasted, and are, reputedly, the best surviving examples in existence. The Wine Cellar and Beer Cellar vaults are extensive and provide an insight to the prodigious quantity of liquid refreshment made available at Henry's Court.

– *THE LOWER ORANGERY* –

A visit should be made to the Lower Orangery in the palace grounds. There, the finest works of art at Hampton Court – and amongst a handful of the best Italian examples of the Renaissance, in Europe to this day – may be inspected in Mantegna's *Triumph of Caesar*, a set of nine large tempera paintings.

Commissioned by the Duke of Mantua in 1485, in which city the artist flourished as court painter, the Gonzagas' collection of works of art had to be sold, when the family fell from power. The art-loving Charles I outbid the nobility of Europe (including Maria de Medici and Cardinal Richelieu) who scrambled to get their hands on the auctioned items. Charles I paid £10,500 in 1629, which has proved a shrewd bargain. In his lifetime many lampooned his acquisitions as a complete waste of the monarch's money, hence, when Raphael's *Cartoons* were purchased, the word acquired a sense of the derisory or bizarre.

– *THE WILDERNESS AND MAZE* –

On the north side of the Palace is the Wilderness, an intricate classical garden, designed for William III, of which a circular Maze was an integral part. The earlier purpose of a maze, in medieval times, was to refresh the spirit in an isolated environment. Whether a King of England really intended his subjects to lose themselves, as well as their anxieties is anybody's guess.

– '*A MIGHTY MAZE! BUT NOT WITHOUT A PLAN*' –

So ventured Alexander Pope when the Maze was constructed in the form laid out for Queen Anne (1714). Those who follow in his footsteps may may also recall the hopeless machinations of *Harris* – who led his friends, George Wingrave and Jerome K. Jerome, the author, plus a burgeoning assembly of 'lost' souls, around, and around, and around –

> They met some people soon after they had got inside, who said they had been there for three-quarters of an hour, and had had about enough of it. Harris told them they could follow him if they liked; he was just going in, and then should turn round and come out again.
> They picked up various other people who wanted to get it over, as they went along, until they had absorbed all the persons in the maze . . . and one

woman with a baby, who had been there all the morning, insisted on taking his arm, for fear of losing him.

Harris kept on turning to the right, but it seemed a long way, and his cousin said he supposed it was a very big maze.

'Oh, one of the largest in Europe,' said Harris.

'Yes, it must be,' replied the cousin, 'because we've walked a good two miles already.' . . .

Three Men in a Boat
(TO SAY NOTHING OF THE DOG)
Jerome K. Jerome (1st published, 1889).

The Lost Property Office does its best to cope with a brisk trade in abandoned parents, rather than their children who know perfectly well, as did *Harris* –

Follow the hedge on the right, after entering,
And follow the left hedge when planning to escape.

– THE ROYAL TENNIS COURT –

No visit to Hampton Court is complete without a peep at the 'Real' tennis courts – a fashionable game imported from France by the Tudors. The existing courts – where matches are currently played in tournaments that are even faster-moving than Wimbledon's – stand on the site of Henry VIII's original courts of 1529.

The River Aspect

On the south side of the palace are the Privy Gardens which stretch to the river bank. Here the exquisite screen and gateway by Tijou, complement the vista of the formal layout commissioned by William III, the Pond Garden (laid originally by Henry VIII) and the sunken Garden side by side with the Elizabethan Knot Garden, containing many scarce specimens suitable for aromatherapy.

The eastern aspect from the palace Broadwalk, leads to the Great Fountain and the mile-long Long Water stretching through Hampton Court Park, (here named the Home Park), towards the Kingston stretch of the river, at Hampton Wick. Beside the river,

the Barge Walk from Hampton Court Bridge (where the ferries berth) leads to Kingston Bridge. What for pedestrians is lost of the Park view, by the very long brick wall beyond the Pavilion, is made up by an assembly of river activities.

The Pavilion

Originally there were four 'summer' pavilions, where now exists the lovely sole residence in the parkland overlooking the Thames. Spare room in the palaces were appropriated to use as 'grace and favour' dwellings, and were (and are) in the personal gift of the sovereign. Many such apartments exist at Hampton Court, and, until the Pavilion was sold in 1987, it too was a prime example: Dickens' readers may recall in *Little Dorrit*, that the dowager mother of the failed gentleman, Henry Gowan, was granted 'grace and favour' at Hampton Court but showed her gratitude with spite! The great lexicographer, Dr. Johnson, was himself turned down in his request for 'rooms' in Hampton Court, which might have put an end to his enthusiasm for excursions upstream.

Most visitors to the palace precincts make their initial approach through the Trophy Gates, abutting the Outer Green beside the Bridge. On the far side is the Green which is worthy of a detour.

On Hampton Green

West of Hampton Court Bridge stands a cluster of riverside properties, including *Old Court House* – where Sir Christopher Wren died in 1723. Two along is *Faraday House* named after the great diviner of electricity, who lived there from 1858 until his death in 1867. Tucked snugly between the two, is *Paper House*, which probably served the purpose for one or other of its distinguished neighbours. There is no mistaking *The Royal Mews*, set back from the road, in subdued redbrick, inscribed with 'Elizabeth Regina 1570' – and still very much in use by the Horse Rangers Association (Patron: HRH Princess Michael of Kent). The stables (1538) enclose a courtyard that would probably look unchanged, even to *'Enery's* roving eye, and although the stable lasses seem far too occupied with their handsome charges to spend any of their time in dalliance, a treat awaits you should you offer to feed their wild oats for them.

A minor footslog in the direction of Hampton village leads to *Hampton House*, overlooking the River. It was purchased by David Garrick in 1754 who gave his villa the imposing facade (by Adam) and was mainly responsible for the village becoming fashionable. Garrick's ornamental temple, on the Thames bank, was dedicated to Shakespeare and contained the lifesize *Roubiliac* statue, now to be admired in the British Museum and from which the poet's image was copied onto the existing £20 Bank note.

Herewith an eyewitness account by the Scottish divine, Alexander Carlyle, 1758, when bidden to lunch and to practise a putt –

> GARRICK had ordered the wine to be carried to this temple . . . I said to (him), that while the servants were preparing the collation . . . I would surprise him with a stroke of golf, as I should drive a ball through his archway into the Thames . . . I had measured the distance with my eye in walking about the garden, and accordingly, at the second stroke, made the ball alight in the mouth of the gateway, and roll down the green slope into the river. This was so dexterous that he was quite surprised, and begged the club of me by which such a feat had been performed. We passed a very agreeable afternoon; and it is hard to say which were happier, the landlord and landlady or the guests.

Carlyle was very curious to meet Garrick's wife, the Viennese dancing girl, whom he had first observed on the packet-boat returning from Leyden, in 1746, disguised in boy's clothing, and whom Garrick married three years later. Had she dressed as a choirboy, a proposal might have come sooner than expected?

The Lion Gate

The northern entrance to the palace grounds is approached from Hampton Court Road which cuts past the green by Hampton Court Bridge, with the palace to the south, and with Bushey Park to the north.

Although the Lion Gate bears the Queen's arms, it is the *King's Arms*, a large pub overlooking the scenic Chestnut Avenue of Bushey Park, where people tend to stop and linger.

Bushey Park

Bushey Park incorporates 1,000 acres of parkland, and is a preferred nature reserve of Londoners, with its famous roaming deer. The imposing Diana Fountain – the moon goddess of the ancients, and famed for her fertility – is centred in the wide, round pond, a focal point of Wren's who planned a grander vista stretching as far as the eye could see. Instead, the woodlands have taken over, providing one of many serene walks to be snatched in Greater London.

It was here, at Bushey House, that William, Duke of Clarence lived 'blissfully' with the actress, Mrs. Jordan, for twenty years, until forced to forsake her for a suitable royal bride (Adelaide). His brother, George IV, had died (as did the next in line, Princess Charlotte) without leaving an heir. William IV, as he became, in 1830, spent the best years of his life as Ranger of Bushey Park. His residence is now part of the renowned National Physical Laboratory, well worth including in a visit to the Park.

Old Chestnuts

Londoners flock to enjoy the blossom of chestnut, in the mile-long Chestnut Avenue, on what they call 'Chestnut Sunday', in late May. It is lovely, too if it doesn't rain on that special day.

A Detour to Wimbledon

WIMBLEDON

Wimbledon (pronounced Wimbuld'n), meaning the village of Wymble on the hill (-'don'), in Anglo Saxon times was spelt Wimbledounying (967 A.D.). It stands back and over its river neighbours of Putney, Richmond and Kingston and is approximately 7½ miles southwest of central London.

WIMBLEDON VILLAGE sits almost smugly atop a promontory which shrugs off southern suburbia at its borders. The old village lies at the tip of Wimbledon Common threading northwards, over a thousand acres, to the Thames at Richmond and Putney. One of Caesar's encampments still exists on the perimeter of the Royal Wimbledon Golf Course. On the other side of the village, there is an endearing Parish Church, St. Mary's, with its Anglo-Saxon foundations. Below the escarpment, on which the steeple perches, lie the famous grass courts which have made the village name synonymous with the best in sporting worlds.

The busy world just passes by, and Wimbledon, sitting in its enviable location, retains a sleepy character, apparently remote from London's bustle. The pulse of the Capital barely filters through to this community; in the High Street villagers amble about their local business; their pedigree dogs accompany them, on theirs; people stop to talk with one another as if, with genuine time to spare, they mean to pass the time of day.

The local denizens seem to like the sound of their own bells, too, which ring in the peaceful hour from the belfry of St. Mary's – itself a landmark on the treelined hill above the tennis courts. Number Four (the clock bell that is, not the court) may often be heard by devout afficionados when the summer carries its peal beyond the lawns of the Wimbledon Tennis and Croquet Association. With its good local restaurants and hostelries, variety

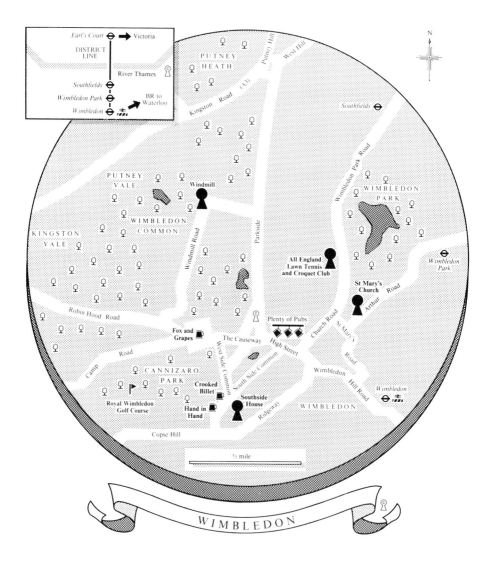

of places to see or visit, and lovely walks on its doorstep, Wimbledon village lies within easy access of Town, affording the visitor a difference from the usual outing.

The village High Street connects with the Common at a corner known as the Causeway, alongside the open space and pond, of South Side, (hence the name). Here and there a convoy of horseback riders emerge and mingle with the traffic, before passing out of sight from the thoroughfare. The street looks smaller than seems the London norm: lower buildings with older facades.

In spite of some encroachment by their neighbours, the oldest properties still proudly stand their ground (in what is left of it): of note, Eagle House, with its newly restored feature of the gabled motif, built for Robert Bell, founder of the East India Company. He fared rather better in commerce than another Wimbledon resident, Sir Theodore Janssen, who was ruined in the South Sea Bubble, 1720, and died a pauper. At least in his declining years Janssen must have been spared the attentions of the highwaymen, footpads and robbers who roamed the infamous Common. They liked to stop the coaches which ran their pistoll'd gauntlets between the staging posts of taverns, such as the local *Rose and Crown* and the *Dog and Fox*.

Smart service

In the stage-coach era, passengers had to contend with other, equally mundane hazards – as when unscrupulous landlords served up such piping-hot dishes that the hungry travellers could barely touch them during the short stop-over period allocated for a change of horses. Their meals were then returned to the cauldron and smartly served, piping-hot, to the next coach-load.

THE ALL ENGLAND LAWN TENNIS AND CROQUET CLUB

In June, 1877, the world's premier annual tennis championships were inaugurated by the committee of the exclusive tennis and croquet club. The tournament is now vested in the governing body of the Lawn Tennis Association (which spends some of its time, in the rest of the year, trying to teach British youth to gain the upper hand again).

Links with the past

The game's origin is obscure but was popularised by the French aristocracy after the crusading knights acquired the art of 'jeu de paume' – a game of the palm of the hand – in the course of their travels. By the 16thC the racket (and the net) had replaced the palm (and artificial mound), laying the basis for what is the modern game.

The ball seems originally to have been of a hard texture, cloth wrapped around animal hair, tightly stuffed, and a heavier object than its successor. When thrown, the server is thought to have called to his opponent –

– Tenez! - "Ready!" –

a corruption of old French (*tenes, tenyse*) from which the name of the game was derived. A servant kept the score by utilising the clockface in the courtyard, where the game was being played, and moving the hand forward a quarter, after each rally, hence the points are signified in the numerals 15, 30, and – until the 18thC when 40 was accepted – 45. Where the scores were even, "A deux" (*'Deuce'*, two more points) was called, and the race around the clock continued.

Royal links

In any event the game that Henry VIII introduced at Hampton Court was soon popularised and evolved into to-day's game; together with croquet, is the quintessence of the sporting round in every English country house. In England, tennis maintains its royal link through H.R.H. the Duke of Kent, the President of the Club.

The Duchess presents the prizes, both the trophies and – a recent custom – the cheques as well, in a finale to Wimbledon fortnight which is familiar to millions of television spectators. Many viewers like also to admire the elegant clothes which the Duchess "wears so well" and which were so neatly remarked on by her near (and dear) relation –

> One of those rare ladies who is the perfect coat-hanger – everything hangs exactly right.   *H.R.H. Princess Margaret [attrib., 1987].*

It was the great Tudor himself who cut such a dash –

> It is the prettiest sight in the world to see him play, his fair skin glowing through a shirt of the finest texture. . .
> *Venetian chronicler at Hampton Court [1519].*

State of the art

Both for performers, and spectators, the combined skills and flair displayed with prowess on the court raise the game, sometimes perhaps, to the status that the French Academy bestowed upon it in 1797 –

the only game that can rank in the list of arts and crafts.

One of today's master players has indeed likened his game with that of Art –

Some days, with brilliant strokes and a good sense of composition I can make a masterpiece; other days, less creative and inspired, I only produce insignificant studies. This comparison [to works of art] gives me a way to judge my own performance . . .

Tim Mayotte (1957–   ).

From the point of view of the select band of groundsmen at Wimbledon, they beg to differ on the finer point of equating the top 'seeds'. They may reckon they're not a patch on their own, – the special seed – that grows to such velvet perfection.

Lawn Tennis Museum

The history of the game, and the special part played by the Wimbledon Club, is fully explained in a display at the Wimbledon Lawn Tennis Museum. Directly overlooking the Centre Court – *(affording an uncluttered view of the hallowed turf)* – the Museum contains memories in store of the legendary players, who combined to set the standards of the golden age of tennis.

> Tickets to the Championship fortnight are in tight supply (as every member who reads the Personal columns of The Times appreciates) and are regulated by ballot of advance applications, each January. However, daily gate entry, which admits the bearer to any of the 18 'outside' courts [currently £5, or £3 after 1500 hours, being the cost of the ticket], allows admission by rota to Centre and Number 1 Courts, where 2,000 and 1,150 places exist, respectively, for 'standing room' only.
> The stewards also have a stock of 'returned' seat tickets which may be purchased, not from the touts, but from the Stewards' offices for a princely sum of £2. The chance to witness some of the best play happens in the first week, when the qualifying matches do not attract the capacity crowds, or those with an enthusiasm to see and be seen. Then, the atmosphere is quite as lively, moreover superbly entertaining, and, unlike the later matches, seldom ruined by the tensions that have overtaken supersports.
> Any spare seat represents the best value in town.

The state of dress

Would-be spectators at English sporting events may infinitely prefer the relaxed rules of dress adopted at tennis or cricket gatherings, to the hard and fast rigours of some of the season's fixtures –

> If you go with fashion you get middle-aged women showing thighs that should have been kept secret for years.
> *What* is the next stage? You start to have people stripping to the waist because they say it's hot. It [Henley] will begin to look like Lord's or Wimbledon; God forbid we should get down to their level.
> *Mr. Peter Coni. Q.C., Chairman of Henley Royal Regatta [1988].*

There is the nice story told of the Moss Brothers (whose name is synonymous with formal dress hire, beloved by the impoverished gentry), who were invited into the Royal Enclosure one year, at Ascot: when asked by a royal, how one or other Mr. Moss was enjoying himself, he replied –

> *Memorable, memorable, just stock-taking.*

Wimbledon Stadium

When England first went to the dogs, stadia such as the fine one at Wimbledon soon filled to capacity. In those far off days, some forty millions attended the sport of dog track racing, which has since dropped tenfold. However, the plush facilities offered at Wimbledon Stadium in Plough Lane, would seem to exclude it from those statistics. Meetings are frequent and frequently packed, in the bars, 'carvery' and terraced restaurant, where video-screens beam the prowess of the favourite to punters enjoying an evening meal. It is one of the few places that really indulge the restaurant-goer: waitresses are known to tip off the diner, who can only hope they are in the know.

Wimbledon Stadium built one of the first tracks (1928) and was the 'home stable' where *Mick the Miller* –

> the Red Rum of greyhound racing
> *(Michael Flaherty, racing clerk, [1988]).*

proved unbeatable. The heroic runner now rests in a glass case at the Natural History Museum, South Kensington where he remains *first* in the field of exhibits sought after by the public.

SOUTHSIDERS SEEM HELL BENT on spectator sports: Now it is the turn of Wimbledon Football Club, proud winners of the F.A. Cup at Wembley in 1988 – the first South London Club to win the premier trophy for over forty years (since Charlton Athletic F.C., in 1947) – and celebrating their centenary year in 1989.

Where will it end for all these wonderful persons? One place that the local vicar of the Parish of Wimbledon foresees is in his congregation, where all the sports-minded parties, in their singles and mixed doubles, as maybe, could overspill with praise. Allelujah.

ST MARY THE VIRGIN

> *Unto you oh men I call*
> *A gift to the church*

So reads the inscription on the *Striking* bell, dated 1867, and quite one of the youngest in St Mary's belfry. There is a peal proper of eight bells, the oldest dating back to 1313. The *Tolling* Bells continue the sweet resonance of their pitch, which have been

heard by local congregations since the century following Magna Carta.

If you meet the churchwarden, he will inform you of many things less startling than the Immaculate Conception: that the *Tenor* weighs 11 cwts (over 500 kilos), and the *Treble* an impressive 3 cwt. He is not making a personal remark about members of the choir but merely boasting of the physical attributes of his precious bells.

Worthy Wimbledon matrons attend to more pressing needs, as can be observed when entering by the west porch: a bulletin board prescribes the roster for flower arrangements, which, in any month except Lent, are a joy to behold. Clusters of seasonal flowers bloom from indiscriminate vases perching on ledges the length and width of the nave, a gesture which evokes the feeling of being in a cherished place.

The solid flint edifice of the external structure (restored by Sir George Gilbert Scott, 1843) disguises the radiance of the interior: a spacious Nave augmented by a wide tripartite Gallery, which once accommodated a prosperous middle-class Victorian congregation that could, by virtue of paying for the privilege of the balcony pews, look down their noses at the lower riff-raff.

The Warrior Chapel

Above the Chancel arch hangs an imperious carving of the Royal Arms, which contrasts starkly with whitewashed walls. The natural light diffuses well throughout, and illumines the faded naval Ensign that droops sadly from its mount. The forlorn memories of the Battle of Jutland (1916) linger in its folds which dip in homage to the war dead, to whom the Warrior Chapel (South Aisle) bears lasting witness. The flower of a generation of Wimbledon's youth is remembered; their names engraved on countless plaques, crowded upon each other in copper-plate inscriptions of English surnames, threading the brief years of their existence. Some, whose lives barely spanned their teens, are bearers of posthumous decorations.

An absent-minded husband

Sir Edward Cecil Knight Lord Cecil & Baron of Putney

Lord Treasurer Burghley

His First Wife Who in This Tombe is Named:

His Second Wife:

Viscount Wimbledon

of Wimbledon 3rd son of Thomas Earl of Exeter Grandchild of

The Cecil Mausoleum

An English family of great prominence, *dramatis personae* of Elizabethan fame, lies buried in the peaceful surroundings of its parish. The Cecils' association with Wimbledon began in 1550, when Sir William purchased the reversion of the Old Manor and begot the dynasty of courtiers – and confidants – of many Heads of State. This ancient family is entombed in a vast granite memorial commanding the centre stage of the Chapel.

In 1558 the first Lord Burghley joined the cause of Queen Elizabeth 1, who succeeded to the throne of *Bloody* Mary. So began the remarkable partnerships between the 'new' lords of Wimbledon and their sovereigns. They have strode the stage in public, successfully for over four hundred years. In private life the Cecils appeared to suffer the normal apprehensions of most fathers with high parental hopes and expectations: as when, in 1605, the grandson of Lord (Treasurer) Burghley was receiving an education in Paris – (the sights of which distracted many a youth then and since) –

'. . . The shame that I shall receive' wrote his father, the Earl of Exeter, 'to have so unruly a son grieveth me more than if I had lost him by honest death'

The venerable old gentleman did not live to see his grandson's redemption after his demise in 1598. Cecil junior not only consolidated the family estates around Wimbledon, acquiring part of the turf which has since bordered the famous enclave, but also sired a progeny of thirteen in a lasting marriage to Dorothy (née Lady Neville, of Belvoir Castle). Those who hanker to sow their wild oats and elect to do so across the Channel, may like to recall that no lasting shame was attached to Cecil's 'unruly' son.

By the inner wall of the Mausoleum, an old leper window, which allowed the worst afflicted to watch the elevation of the sacrament at a safe distance, has been excavated. There is more besides, of historical diversion to be found within the precincts and to wander round the churchyard is time well spent in a quiet backwater of an unhurried English scene.

Grand Houses

THE CECIL MANSION, Wimbledon House, was acquired by King Charles I for his consort, Queen Henrietta Maria, in 1639, and became her favourite country residence. It stood near the Old Rectory, adjoining the church, but was burnt down in 1785. By the turn of the 18thC, many grand mansions had been built, mostly overlooking the Common, and were followed by the Victorian era's fair share of leafy villas. Church Street leads back through the village, to West Side and South Side, where many of the older houses have survived.

Near the Common stands *Chester House*, built 1670, the home of the Reverend J. H. Tooke, whose election to the House of Commons in 1801 forced a change in the law, whereby clergy were made ineligible. The law still stands, but, would seem to be of little practical effect for such tiresome praters merely exchange the uncertainties of the hustings for the safety of the pulpit. The house was saved by one of the banking institutions, where training is now given to members of staff about to be let loose in the heraldic corners of the High Street, where an eagle 'displayed' beckons its prey.

Lady Ann Barnard, the novelist, lived across the village at Gothic Lodge on the corner of Woodhayes Road, beside the Common. A more recent literary association is to be found at 31, Wimbledon Park Road, in another lodge where resided a woman of equal or greater stature.

George Eliot at Holly Lodge

In 1859 Mary Ann Evans, and George Henry Lewes, the man she was to marry twenty years later, set up house together at Holly Lodge (". . . we expect, for many years to come"). It was here, as George Eliot, the foremost feminine novelist of her day (1814–1880), she completed *The Mill on the Floss*. Her "beloved husband" enjoyed the open air of the Common –

with glorious breezy walks, and wide horizons . . .

and 'the home entertainment' of their literary friends, Dickens invariably included. They did not welcome staying guests and perfected such an uncomfortable spare room that those who sampled a night swore never to repeat the experience!

Prying eyes

'When . . . I have a month or two of leisure, I should like to transfer our house . . . to someone who likes houses *full of eyes all around him* . . .'

Not even the garnish of holly and laurel saved them their privacy, and, in the autumn of 1860, some eighteen months after moving in, they moved out.

Understandably, Holly Lodge is not open to the public.

Wimbledon Common

Wimbledon is a dreary, high, bleak, windy suburb, on the edge of a threadbare heath.

So Virginia Woolf noted, in her Diary, on 30 January 1915. Living closeby at Richmond, she was entitled to her poor opinion, which she seemed generally to hold of any place beyond her beloved Bloomsbury. – "Bugs and all", if the reader recalls William Morris's opinion, when safely ensconced in Hammersmith Terrace:

I don't fancy going back among the bugs of Bloomsbury.
(Written to his wife).

There are many lovely walks across the breadth and depth of the Common, which, when taken with Putney Lower Common and Vale, provide a much-valued source of recreation for the outdoor pursuits of Londoners. The land, exceeding a thousand acres, was fortunately saved for posterity when, in 1871, local con-servationists succeeded in gaining the protection afforded by an Act of Parliament which was passed in the teeth of opposition by local speculators. A 'threadbare' garment, as they say, is better than no garment at all, as Virgina Woolf might have agreed.

Wimbledon Windmill

After the manorial rights were surrendered by the Spencer family in the last century, the Windmill also passed into conservationists' hands, who restored the structure. Possibly the last hollow-post flour mill in England, it was erected in 1817. The miller and his mill did more than provide the Lord of the manor with a staple diet: from his look-out post he doubled as the local patrolman. As well as spotting highwaymen, and bands of robbers, he was also privy to the spectacle of duellists, fighting for their honour. Those who salvaged it included Lord Cardigan (1840, versus Capt. Tuckett). There was even a duel between an erstwhile Prime Minister and a Foreign Secretary, 1809: but, diplomatically, honours were shared evenly between Canning and Lord Castlereagh without a sabre being rattled or a shot fired. A predecessor, William Pitt, lived through an encounter with George Tierney when they met on the Common in 1798. It is claimed that the last duel was fought on adjoining Putney Heath between the exiled Prince Louis Napoleon and Count Leon. The question of honour being practised in this manner was finally stopped through the civilising influence of

Prince Albert in the 1840s. *Habitués* of Wimbledon Common today include the peaceloving species known as the Wombles.

CANNIZARO HOUSE

To arrive at Cannizaro House is to make believe like Judy Garland and Fred Astaire. –

> We're a couple of Swells
> We stop at the best hotels,
> – But we prefer the country, far away from the city smells;
>
> We're a couple of Sports
> The pride of the tennis courts,
> In June, July and August we look cute when we're dressed in shorts!
>
> *Irving Berlin: Easter Parade*

Where better to daydream than in the refurbished hallway or on the landscaped terrace?

Set back from West Side Common the formidable frontage of the 18thC mansion stands out, salmon pink in sunshine but pale cocoa for most of the year. Beyond the gates of the driveway stretch centuries-old beeches at rest in this enviable parkland setting.

'Count Cannelloni'

An impoverished nobleman, one Francesco Platamore Cannizaro Count San Antonio, acquired the house from the Grosvenor family and stayed long enough for his Sicilian name to stick – but then left rather hurriedly, in 1836. The Contessa stayed put for another five years. In such agreeable surroundings, presumably she was left in as much peace as the grass-widow of Victorian music hall –

> O, O Antonio, he's gone away,
> Left me on my own-io,
> All on my own-io.
> I'd like to see him with his new sweetheart,
> Then off will go Antonio,
> In his iced-cream cart!

In 1987 a major British brewery, Scottish and Newcastle, opened its doors to what they believe will establish new standards of service for luxury accommodation in South London. Although Wimbledon is a far cry from New York, it is the kind of establishment that might have suited the cosmopolitan tastes of a Vanderbilt, or their friends, and swells.

Whilst the contents of the interior cannot match the previous collection of Greco-Roman antiquities, the decor will not disappoint the more fastidious eye.

The avid collector of antiquities was Lyde Brown, one time (18thC) Governor of the Bank of England, who filled the house with priceless works of art. Following his death in 1786, Catherine, Empress of Russia, snaffled the lot. They now form a showpiece display at the Hermitage. Those who venture to Leningrad may, with *glasnost* in the air, identify the relics from Wimbledon as –

early examples of Capitalist assets.

Cannizaro Park extends over 35 acres and offers Londoners, *for whom a public right of access exists*, one of the maturest landscapes within Greater London. Many of the rare trees and shrubs were introduced by Henry Dundas, 1st Viscount Melville, during his period of residence in London when serving in Pitt's ministry. It is known that the two politicians were friends and doubtless they enjoyed a woodland walk together – a welcome escape from the burdens of their office. Unfortunately, Pitt's visits were cut short when Melville was impeached in 1806. His erstwhile colleague survived but retired to Duneira cottage (around the corner) from where he could still enjoy the park's vista into a ripe old age. Meanwhile his old crony, Pitt, was doubtless laying out the next path of peace in other high places.

Visitors to the Park should take in the view from the lake and adopt a conservationist's approach by obeying the notice-board's injunction –

NO TADPOLING.

Uncommon mansions

Facing the Common, are many old residences on Southside among which is Lauriston House where lived William Wilberforce – the 18thC campaigner against slavery. Its interior is particularly distinguished with its staircase decorated by Angelica Kauffman. West Side, too, boasts elegant mansions where many of London's distinguished residents used to live: Lord Chancellor Lyndhurst at No. 6, with, as a close neighbour, Lord Chief Justice Mansfield, before he purchased Kenwood House in Hampstead, (now the Iveagh Bequest, and thanks to the Guinness family, open to the public).

Almost in the depths of the Common can be found the *Fox and Grapes*, where the Pub's proprietress, Mrs Holder, conducts her premises with a strict regard for the parsimonious hours of England's licensing laws that conflict with the true nature of her loyal clientele. *Julius Caesar's* Bar honours the Roman's period at Caesar's Camp, a nearby site avoided by golfers but within the golf course. For those of her patrons who are seeking a 'typically English Pub with a back garden', Mrs. Holder fields the enquiry with nonchalant simplicity:

> *"Of course there is, and much the biggest one, – my garden is the Common!"*   *[1987].*

The garden that offers equally fine vistas is to be found in Cannizaro Park, closeby, where *Count Cannelloni* lived on the Common.

Towards the Ridgway, on the 'Don' of Wimble, stand a pair of attractive pubs, both owned by the London brewer, Young and Co, who established themselves long ago in neighbouring Wandsworth –

> We have been round the bend since 1831 (proclaims their bill-board on one of the corners of their famous Ram brewery site).

Dispensing commendable ales of, not 'on', the house, they do offer, as it were, more than just an *Hand in Hand* with a *Crooked Billet*. Supposedly, Protector Cromwell's army were billeted on the shady slopes fronting the corner of the Common, hence the latter pub's name.

Opposite, where the bend in the road begins to dip, stands Southside House which surely justifies a diversion to Wimbledon.

SOUTHSIDE HOUSE

– 17thC Gentleman's residence with intriguing country house atmosphere:

Beneath the spread of bark and bough of grand old chestnuts, at the corner of South Side Common, a grimy brick wall beckons. Behind it is Southside House with its clock tower peeping through the treeline. The concealed tradesman's gate, on the corner of an alleyway makes do as an entrance to the mansion whose stately coachgates were closed and bolted longer ago than anyone can remember.

The pulley-bell is rusted and the long extinguished gas lamp is askew in the awning of old ironwork over the doorway. The date – 1716? – is incorporated as are two initials – BN – barely discernible, that lean in old age. Under the scrolls of identity, an electronic buzzer has been mounted in the wall. Serving the purpose of an old retainer, unseen, a tiny eye observes the caller and the electronic device unlocks the fastened lock; the door shrugs open.

The custom of the house is to enter not only by the back gate, but also by the back door, which immediately deprives those who have the urge to tug the large bell-chain by the front door, from hearing the grand gong shake throughout the house.

The cobbled courtyard thus entered, is enclosed by the old coach-house and stableblock wings. To the fore, on an island in the drive, stands a life-size bronze commemorating the family's son, Peter. Cast by Alasia, Princess Borghese, in 1980, his hands hold a contemplative poem (here recorded, to save the reader from falling into the pond while unravelling the lines, otherwise upside down) –

Rays of Star
Shedding on human pain
Drawing stumbling from afar
    That night
Groping fingers 'ward a wondrous light
In the myriad of the heavens, One you are
    This night . . .
Still, rays, your shedding rain!

It was written by Peter (John Viking Pennington Munthe), over Christmas in 1943.

Southside House's distinctive facade, built by Robert Pennington in 1687, antedates the taste that was to prevail after the arrival of the Prince of Orange on the English throne a couple of years later. Pennington, a royalist, sought safety in Holland during the *interregnum* (1649–1660), and thus became acquainted with, and admired, Dutch Baroque. The result is an elegant example of this style of architecture, rarely seen in London today.

Pennington set two statues – *Spring*, and *Plenty* – in waiting alcoves of the façade. One celebrates his daughter's birth, the other, his wife's gift of another child. He had lost his son in the Great Plague of London; hence his move to the 'clean aires' of Wimbledon, then thought a sufficient distance from the putrid contagion of the city. His earlier sojourn abroad was commemorated by his employing Dutch stonemasons to remodel the property who imported 'Dutche bricke' which has now mellowed into the warm colours that set off the quoin-work.

The pretty clock tower carries his monogram – P.M. – denoting his surname and his family's title, Muncaster, of which he was a younger son.

That Southside House was spared the finishing touches of three centuries' worth of owners is largely due to the successive string of ladies upon whom the estate devolved, who lacked the compulsion often shown by their male counterparts, to leave their imprint willy-nilly, on their family's principal possession. Hence, largely untouched and untinkered with by the many occupants since, Robert Pennington's residence remains the best 17thC example on view in London.

The interior of the house may be visited between the months of October and May when afternoon tours, starting on the hour, are conducted by the Curator. In the winter months the evenings draw in early, and the light fades. The portraits and other memorabilia on display lack modern lighting effects, so it is advisable to arrive in the early part of the afternoon. Whilst it is often the case that *other* peoples' family portraits are a 'bore' (Southside is top heavy with its ancestral hangings) the unique associations encountered, some of which form the basis of the account that follows, are likely to engross all who chance upon this remarkable family's unique legacy. For those who want to pay a special visit an appointment may be made by writing in advance to the Curator.

A fairy-tale

What follows is an account of the house and its contents which have been lovingly preserved in the same family since 1687: hidden within Southside exists a priceless set of intriguing stories that identify the past and enchant the beholder of the present. For this reason the intrinsic value of the house stimulates the seasoned, but unsuspecting, traveller with an authenticity that is the hallmark of the Pennington-Kemys-Wharton-Tynte-Vaughan-Mellor-Munthe fairy-tale . . .

The Roots of the Family Tree

On Pennington's death, the house passed to his daughter who had married into the family which was to provide the first of the female 'hyphens', -Kemys. Her husband was not the last male to learn that while marriage meant a willingness to share and share alike, it did not necessarily mean that the title deeds of a matrimonial home, when vested in the wife's name, would follow. For the families that the Pennington ladies chose to marry into, this rule would never be broken.

At the end of the last century Catherine Pennington, a great-granddaughter of old Pennington, fell in love with the younger son of the Argyllshire family of Mellors. He swept her off and married her. They went to live north of the border where they would have stayed, happily ever after, had her destiny not interfered. By this time the house was in the hands of a chance niece and it came to Catherine's attention that the male incumbent of Southside nurtured plans to remodel the house. Her Pennington blood quickened and there followed a Dickensian law-suit that she instigated to oust the occupant and which resulted in Southside's reversion to her branch of the family.

In due course, Catherine's granddaughter, Hilda Pennington-Mellor (who economised on hyphens, for the sake of her friends) came to inherit Southside which had, true to form, by-passed a generation and alighted again on another stewardess of the line. Hilda married, as is recounted below, the eminent Swedish doctor – and the author of *The Story of San Michele*, a longtime *classic* – whose surname she assumed in the seventh and, presently, last of the hyphened appendages.

THE FAMILY PEARLS

. . . SOMEONE, SOMEWHERE will always be wearing an article of jewellery that once belonged to *some* forgotten Queen but the actual piece worn by Marie Antoinette when she bowed to the guillotine, found its intriguing way to Southside House where it now features among the royal heirlooms.

This discreet necklace, which slipped from her slender neck on the
chilling day of her execution at 12.15 pm on October 16, 1793 dropped
between the blood-drenched boards of the guillotine's platform and was
seized by the grasping hand of her executioner. This was immediately
spotted by M. Barras, acting Governor of the Bastille, who relieved his
henchman of the right to such an outlandish business perk.

Barras disposed of the goods *so received* by presenting them to his
current flame, Josephine Beauharnais. While their affair raged over a
candlelit dinner, he gently spread the single matchless row of pearls upon
her neck, fastening, with lovers' greed, the pretty clasp upon her nape. As
it turned out, Josephine's neck soon proved more elusive for M. Barras
than had the previous wearer's: on meeting Napoleon she dumped her
suitor but not the pearls, which she kept. Next, she changed her name to
become Mme Bonaparte.

When she confided the provenance of her favourite piece of jewellery to
her husband, he became characteristically tetchy and, despite her
reasoning, *L'Empéreur* ruled it had to go. All shades of sweet talk
foundered; in her flummox, what was poor Josephine to do?

It is clear that Napoleon's Queen
Was referring to army routine,
When for dinner she dressed
Her decoration abreast
But was told: 'Not tonight, Josephine'.

Then entered her stage John Pennington of Southside, a blushing
eighteen year-old whom Josephine came to regard, with good reason, as
very much her English *cup of tea*. John had been enlisted by the British
Plenipotentiary to Paris, Lord Dover (his relation), and seconded to the
Embassy to assist in the evacuation of fugitives from the troubled capital.
More than a handful of Josephine's own relations were among those lucky
to escape. By this coincidence John was bidden to Malmaison where the
grateful Empress had decided to reward the dashing young Englishman
for smuggling so many of her family and friends to a safe haven behind
the white cliffs of 'M' Lord Dover's'.

Master Pennington was swept off his feet to the rose garden, conveniently out of sight of the legendary General (his missing him, the only
disappointment of his life, Pennington later said), and there, between the
bushes, Josephine thrust her precious gift upon him, beseeching him
earnestly –

to choose carefully in the field of love,
lest innocence should be betrayed!

He took her advice, and the necklace, to heart, next to be worn by his future wife, in Southside some years later. There it may still be admired and cause the admirer to wonder if its most illustrious wearer's heartbeat still flickers in the pearls.

Delicately attached to this single strand of pearls is a most unusual loop – six single pearls, at the last count of the late Queen. Many other pearls were once fastened to the string. One by one they were removed as a distraught mother of the little Dauphin bribed the wardress of the Temple prison in return for a fleeting glimpse of her son parading in the yard below her narrow window of captivity and who, with the seventh pearl, was forever removed from her sight.

– THE ROUSSELLE CORRIDOR –

In a discreet back passage lurk seventeen unique works of portaiture by the hand of Rousselle, the Flemish artist. His circle of admiring patrons included one of the family of Southside, the 4th Lord Wharton, who was desirous of a 'corridor of his nearest and dearest', sight as seen, hung wall to wall. These portraits date from the 17thC but would seem to bear their age with enigmatic freshness, such is the standard of Rousselle in his execution of sable brushwork. A 'mirror-image' quality attends the artist's work which lends a three-dimensional focus to the sitters' features, when each is studied in turn. The impression is almost as if they breathe the same air as does the onlooker.

– THE FAMILY DINING ROOM –

From on high the huge bronze candelabra overshadows the massive dining table, especially when all the branches of candles are lit. It was chained to the ceiling in about 1689 and has never strayed from its mooring, although one of Hitler's doodlebugs got damned close to doing the unthinkable, and unpardonable: interrupting an Englishman *over* his dinner.

The handsome Jacobean mantel bolstering the fireplace gives much needed breathing space between the thirty-four, mostly family full-length portraits on display around the walls. There are really too many for the mind to digest at one go: like the table, the old dull grey matter can just about hold twenty, maximum. Of them all, the following notes may assist, en passant –

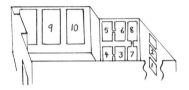

[1]   **MARY WHARTON** – painted 1658,
'Aunt May'* was the heiress that Sir Charles Kemys, Ist Bart., (whose own portrait hangs upstairs), married. She outlived him, as did most of the female line their males. On the exile of Philip, her nephew (Duke of Wharton, K.G., [15] – diagonally facing), she deftly preserved the fortunes of the family;

Note – **For the family *Aunt May* seems to have had an existence well beyond her natural years; as the reader will discover in her activities that span the Elizabethan and Hanoverian eras.**

[2]   **Her statesman brother,** painted in the same year;

[3]   **Sir HASWELL TYNTE, Bart., (1648–1703),** who married:

[4]   **GRACE, Lady TYNTE, (1648–1694)** – painted by *Huysmans*;

[5]   **their son, Sir JOHN, 2nd Bart.,** dressed in his smoke-blue velvet coat. He was nick-named 'Jack' (*the jackpot*) for his choice of bride: an heiress;

[6]   **his ladywife, the Hon. JANE** – portrait by *Kneller*, who was the daughter of **[1]**;

[7]   their daughter, **ANN, Lady KEMYS-TYNTE,** who married:

[8]   **Sir CHARLES KEMYS-TYNTE, 5th Bart., (1710–1785)** – painted by *Hogarth*, depicted with his volume of fashionable reading ('Garden Plans'). A man of wide interests and circle of friends, including Chevalier D'Eon de Beaumont, the transvestite spy (a portrait of whom

hangs in the Hall), and whose *intimate* lifestory is best told by a current member of the family;

[9]   **The Hon. JAMES STUART** – painted by *Van Dyck* [1608];

Young Jamie, the 4th Duke of Lennox & Richmond, was the nephew of King Charles I who presented the full-length portrait to the family as an olive branch following a *cause-célèbre* when Jamie's father and George Wharton, as lads had killed each other in a duel on Highbury Fields, where they were both hastily buried to avoid scandal, at such short notice that there was only one coffin available; so they were laid to rest, as they died, in each other's arms for evermore:

> . . . **and to that end I have sent you the length of my rapyer, wch I will use, with a dagger, and soe meet you at ye farther end of Islington at three of the clock in ye afternoone. . .**
> *Stuart's answer to Wharton's challenge, [10 Nov. 1608].*

The King also presented the rapier which may be seen above the frame.

[10]   **ANN GODWIN,** grandmother of 'the family brat' (*see* **[15]**, *opposite*);

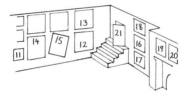

[11]   **ROBERT RATCLIFFE, 1st Earl of Sussex** – the oldest portrait in the house;

[12]   **Marquis of WHARTON,** the statesman remembered for his efforts in popularising the Irish issue:

> *'Lilli-Burlero Bullen-a-la!'*
> Those who like to hum the signature tune of the BBC's overseas broadcasts may be interested to know that it was adapted from Mr. Purcell's 'new Irish tune' [1689] by Wharton for his political song which satirized the papal lieutenant, the Earl of Tyrconnel during James II's expedition.

Of which was said – Burnet's' Account – in 1724:–

> **A foolish ballad was made at that time, treating the Papists, and chiefly the Irish, in a very ridiculous manner, which had a *burden* (sic) said to be of Irish words –**
> > *Lero, lero, lilliburlero*
> **that made an impression on the army, that cannot be imagined by those who saw it not. The whole army, and at last the people, both in city and country, were singing it perpetually. And perhaps never had so slight a thing so great an effect.**

The Irish are a singular nation at times.

The effect on Southside House took another form: whistling *and* humming is frowned upon, except in the closet.

[13] **Lord Wharton's** *first* **Marchioness;**

[14] The replacement 'model' for his Lordship;

[15] **His son, PHILIP, Duke of WHARTON, K.G. (depicted),** whose antics caused the title to become extinct. The infamous 'brat' rocked the Establishment which banished him, although he sounds far better value than the lot of them put together. Enquire of the guide – persistence repays – for the true story about the monkey Philip brought to a Hell-Fire dinner, among many other anecdotes concerning the black sheep of the family;
Note, **[according to the cleaning lady, superstitious, or not] – The picture is not hung crookedly on purpose, it tilts of its own accord depending on the phases of the moon.**

[16] **The** *'Spanish souvenir'* **– by** *Goya***;**
    as Señor Godoy, the Spanish statesman and Lord Dover strolled like old friends through the Prado Museum (the Minister retained the portfolio of Arts), Godoy turned to his guest and said: "Before you leave may I offer you a souvenir of your time in Madrid; of course I regret it is not by a more famous artist, – such as hang here – but do not forget the name *Goya*; one day he will become a famous son of Spain!"

Lord Dover acquired this painting, as well as the ones hanging above and below, during his tour of duty when he assisted in the Negotiations, after Napoleon's fall; Lord Dover was a patron and founder member of the National Gallery in London.

[17] **The 'pageant helper'** – by *Fragonard*; bequeathed to Lord Dover by Marie Walewska **(see 18);**

[18] **The countess, MARIE WALEWSKA [**Val-effsker**], (1786–1817),** the Polish mistress of Napoleon for whom she bore a son, Alexander [– see footnote], – portrait by *Gerard*, when he was much in vogue –

    "Will you allow me to accompany you to Gerard's studio tomorrow morning?" wrote le conte Charles de Flahaut to Anne Potocka in 1811; "Everyone is rushing there to admire Madame Walewska's portrait."

Ten days after their first meeting at the Zamek Ball, Warsaw, when Marie was just turned twenty and NAPOLEON an energetic thirty-seven, he wrote his first *billet-doux* to her –
"I saw no-one but you, I admired only you; I want no-one but you; I beg you to reply promptly to calm my ardour and my impatience." *[17 Jan. 1815]:*

She died of a broken heart, at the tender age of 31 leaving Lord Dover (who befriended her in Paris), this portrait.

Footnote – *Alexander Florian Joseph Colonna.*
Napoleon's illegitimate heir became French Ambassador to the Court of St. James' [1851], married an Englishwoman (his first wife), Catherine Montague, the daughter of Lord Sandwich;

became a Court favourite of Queen Victoria; was credited with the success in his arrangements of the State visit by Victoria and Albert to Paris, and was appointed Minister of Foreign Affairs, under the *Empire* of his cousin, Louis Napoleon Buonaparte III.

[19] The Lord WHARTON, son of Ann [11] – painted, as is the pair, by *J. van Ravensteyn*:

[20] his wife, FRANCES, daughter of the Earl of Cumberland.

Having had as much as is good for one, the patriot will still wish to admire St. George, who is portrayed behind the door, and painted by Burne-Jones. The canvas should be seen before the paint fades completely.

– THE JACOBEAN GALLERY HALL –

When Robert Pennington extended the original farmhouse in 1687, as said before, 'Dutch taste' was all the vogue.

Stout-columned masonry supports the dual Upper Gallery all squeezed into a somewhat bizarre perspective by the prominence of the massive stone fireplace with over-mantel. A Rubenesque mural swirls deliriously around the ceiling and celestial guardians rearrange the cloud formation, giddily, overhead. The *trompe l'oeil* does not stretch to raindrops, but the cherubs occasionally dribble when the roof perennially springs a leak.

A 'minor' royal tie

On the right of the fireplace hangs a gracious portrait of Princess Sturdza, painted by Perignan, who was the grandmother of the Serbian boy-king, Alexander. His mother, Queen Natalie, presented the picture to Hilda Pennington-Mellor on her betrothal to the renowned Swedish author and physician, Dr. Axel Munthe, as a token of her son's childhood friendship, since their meeting in the south of France, at Biarritz, where both families were prone to spend their summers.

History records his horrid assassination soon afterwards, when heathen revolutionary zealots broke through the gates of the Palace in Belgrade. Entering the royal apartments they seized the defenceless 22 year-old and hurled him bodily from an upper balcony to the swine below.

Look-see

Through the archway under the Gallery stands a well-proportioned Adam and Eve: his wilting fig-leaf pre-supposes that the couple had tasted the forbidden fruit, in stark contrast to her feigned expression of innocence.

Frith's *Don Juan* hangs in the stairwell, appropriately close to the marble figment of original sin. The artist is better known for his scenes of racecourses and the like –

"Oh yes," remarked one visitor, to her companion, "I remembers that picture, it's the same one as the card Flo sent us last Christmas, *you know!*"
"*That* one? Was'n't that the donkey-derby, rememba' luv?"
"Now you must be right, come t'think, that's why he painted this one, what the man just told us was the *donkey-hoatie*".

It is but a short trudge up the second flight of stairs to the two rooms on view upstairs. Firstly:

– THE POWDER CLOSET –

The smallest room of the house is located by turning right at the foot of the stairs which leads to the ante-room, in a corner of which the concealed entrance to the Closet may be discovered, through voluptuous folds of heavy brocade. Within the cubicle a retainer would be stationed, to tend to the powdering of wigs which were gently lowered by their wearer through the oval aperture set in the adjacent wallpanel. The other closet, the second smallest room, is not on show, but may be made available in an emergency. Meanwhile, upstairs:

– THE LIBRARY –

Should a rather special custodian in the family be at home, he is more likely than not to be found in his lair. This gives extra significance when knocking at the heavy door of the comfortable library; for, if this special gentleman is 'in', he will doubtless entertain, awash with a stream of wonderful stories about his family's heirlooms. For those who can believe their ears, after hearing him – the true raconteur at work – it may appear that most of Southside's treasure has been stored, at one time or other, in the wishing well, barely visible through the library windows, at the bottom of the garden. (It's also where he keeps his name, well hidden.) Such are the retiring ways of a *major* figure in his own right.

Caught with her hair down

The busts above the bookcases perched in unlikely places about the room, naturally relate to the female line of the family, who retained a monopoly of passing on the estate, as said earlier. Pride of place goes to Hilda Pennington-Mellor who was caught by the sculptor, on one of those rare occasions with her hair down.

– THE PRINCE OF WALES'S BEDROOM –

Prepared for Frederick, Prince of Wales, and also slept in by a successor, the future King Edward VII, the chamber is arranged with all the royal trimmings. The three ostrich feathers in silver sequin, embroidered on royal-blue velvet, are proudly pronounced at the head of the four-poster. A canopy of crimson brocade surrounds the 'tester', (which, given its literal meaning when coupled with the nocturnal reputation of the last royal occupant, may well have thrown a rather different interpretation on a chamber maid's understanding of 'turning down' the sheets).

By enticing the Prince of Wales across the Common from neighbouring Kew, Aunt May had intended that the principal bedchamber be fit for a future king, which it would have been, had fate not intervened in the shape of a cricket ball, which thumped Prince Frederick on the head and from which he never recovered. His death (March 20th, 1751) was mourned in an undeserved doggerel that was the banter of the time –

> Here lies Fred,
> Who was alive and is dead:
> Had it been his Father
> – I had much rather.
> Had it been his Mother
> – Sooner than another.
> Had it been a sister
> – No-one would have missed her.
>
> But since 'tis only Fred,
> Who was alive and is dead:
> There's no more to be said.

England lost the experience of being reigned over by a cultured monarch, unlike his father, George II with whom he quarrelled in 1737 and never repaired the rift. According to Horace Walpole, the king took the news of the death of his firstborn while playing at cards, with the Countess of Walmoden, merely remarking –

Fritz ist todt.

The game went on.

Thus it came about that nine years later, George William Frederick, the Prince of Wales's eldest son, ascended the throne as George III. Presumably Aunt May attended the funeral, not least in the hope of cultivating another member of the family which was no little matter to master; then, or now –

> Aunt May would have had to pick and choose between Prince Frederick's 5 sisters, 2 brothers, 5 sons, 4 daughters, or from the 15 grandchildren.

PORTRAITS in the best guest-bedroom include:

CHARLES, Prince of Wales (later Charles II) a vivid portrait by *Adrian Hanneman* circa 1650, (hanging by the door).

The 1st Lord WHARTON, trusted courtier and in whose charge the future King Charles II spent his time in exile in Holland, along with Robert Pennington, the founder of the family's fortunes at Southside, after the Restoration in 1660; by *Wm Dobson c. 1640*;

His wife, Philadelphia, Lady WHARTON (between window and bed) by *Van Sommers.*

The painting was commissioned by Aunt May to secure her niece's appointment as lady-in-waiting to Elizabeth I whose mother was Anne Boleyn. On sight of the picture, the Queen immediately recognised her mother's ivory comb. Philadelphia was duly received at Court.

Anne Boleyn's sister was Mary, Lady Carey. Sir William Carey had accepted the unenviable task of escorting his sister-in-law to the block but rescued the comb which was used to part the late Queen's hair above her neck so that the executioner could sever her neck at one stroke with his sword. She was spared the axe by right of birth.

A classic example

This picture is an example of the purpose to which portraiture was commonly put, whereby the artist was commissioned to sell the attributes of the sitter with his brush. When means of travel were difficult, and until the invention of the photographic image supplanted the canvas, many a young lady's destiny rested in an artist's eye. Mindful of the market's buoyancy in supplying such painted beauties to an appreciative clientele in the stately homes of England, an enterprising artist would find a ready demand for his works among wealthy patrons. The greatest good fortune of all – both for the artist and the sitter – was to be on display at Court.

Sold down the river

Henry VIII was hood winked on more than one occasion by these framed masterpieces and rashly fell in love with Anne of Cleves, sight unseen, on the strength of Holbein's handiwork (although it might have been Hillyard's, which prompted him). After the veil was lifted on his fourth bride the king saw his dreadful mistake, and, after taking a second look, divorced her. Along with any canvases, she was sold down the river, where she lived mercifully in retirement at Richmond, and afterwards at Chelsea, where she died. She could count her blessings as the only *ex*-Queen (rather than Dowager) to outlive (d. 1557) her tyrannical husband (d. 1547).

In the portrait of Philadelphia, flattering or no, the composition was obviously used to convey to the recipient, Elizabeth I, the significance of the family possession of her martyred mother's ivory comb. By such means were court appointments made, in the Elizabethan age. The comb is now housed in the showcase at the foot of the bed, which also contains Anne Boleyn's vanity case, among a host of other interesting curios on display.

– *THE 'MUSICKE' ROOM* –

To mark the visit of the Prince of Wales in 1735, the family's preparations were extensive and, reflecting the singular importance Aunt May attached to her honoured guest's impressions, it was decided to create a

Musicke Room out of the two reception chambers, at the back of the house. Hanoverian taste was known to include an interest in music and thus a safe form of recreation for 'Aunt May' to adopt and one that dispensed with the need to make conversation, ever a difficult skill, and more particularly one from which the family recoiled, with their limited knowledge of the German tongue! Whether the heir to the throne enjoyed his visit is not known: irrespective of which, Aunt May basked in her success, until she died.

The room's interior is elegant and commodious, in its well-proportioned size. Internal decoration is restrained, the taste of early Georgian period, with gilded pilaster work set on pastel tones. The pronounced set of four casement windows lends a commodious air to the room, and opens onto the pleasing vista of the terraced garden, which was frequented by Byron long after the excitement caused by the royal visit became a forgotten leaf in the visitors' book. John Murray, the publisher, was a regular guest at Southside, often escaping from the summer stench of Mayfair, to his friend's dwelling, set in the 'good air' of Wimbledon village. There in the cool of an early evening the poet would delight both his publisher and the Pennington family, with readings of *Childe Harolde* or his other poems that were set in the latest galley-proofs which Murray brought with him.

A literary sequel occurred in the lifetime of the famous publisher's grandson, also named John Murray, who in the early 'Twenties, combined his visits to Southside with a resolve to publish the memoirs of his extraordinary friend, Dr. Axel Munthe, the noted physician, now living in retirement at Southside with his young wife, Hilda, and their two small sons. His autobiography, entitled 'The Story of San Michele', became an instant best-seller after its publication in 1929 and – if a copy becomes available – makes an ideal read to accompany the tedium of long-haul jet travel.

Of many rare and masterly works of art that the visitor will find bedecking the Music Room, not one should really be missed. Given the profusion of treasures, this is much easier said, than done.

The presence of each article tells an intimate story on which the fascinating association between each era of the family, and the acquisition of an heirloom, hangs together, entangled in the atmosphere that has descended on the house. Unlike museums, where cobwebs are rarely on show, the threads at Southside are spun to enhance the fleeting moment when the shrouds of the past are lifted into the present, and unfolded to the imagination of the beholder. One or other of the vaguely familiar portraits that are suspended around the walls of the Music Room, beckons for a second and then calls for its moment of attention. And so the observations grow, each capturing an ornament and pleasure for the eye.

Perhaps the finest of all Reynolds's self-portraits exists here in its undisturbed frame. The artist was a regular visitor to the house, from Richmond where he lived, and chose this room for one of his works – delicately presenting himself in old age – to hang where he liked. Or the charming portrait of his protégé, Angelica Kauffman, a self-study composed in gouache

'on his easel when he died,'

presented to the family by Sir Joshua's niece, Mrs. Salmon, who also donated the artist's pallette, which hangs next to his protrait.

Another rare portrait which hangs a canvas width apart, bears an equally absorbing temporal association: Romney's vivacious portrait of Emma, Lady Hamilton, which hung at Merton Park, from where it was rescued. It depicts her in the role of 'Lady of the Manor' which, of course, she was, on Hamilton's estate, which lay across the orchard, but is now another tract of suburbia.

Over the fireplace, nearest the door, hangs Raeburn's fine child portrait of Lord Kilmain, near his charming mother, her's by Romney at his expressive best. Over the opposite marble fireplace is 'little Miss Sunshine', by Sant R.A., – the picture of the year, 1880– when it was hung at the Summer Exhibition. The sitter is the coy Hilda Pennington-Mellor, all of three years old and seemingly undaunted by the pride of place in which her family have put her.

Most of the items of furniture and objets d'art were either acquired or collected during the 18thC or the first half of the 19thC, following Waterloo, when peace seemingly reigned through Europe following Wellington's victories over Napoleon, and Englishmen were free to roam the continent unhindered and were allowed to travel –

'without let or hindrance'

– as H.M.'s Foreign Secretary pathetically pleads in every British passport to this day. Objects brought home fell into two categories: those politely referred to as 'acquisitions' were often booty, as for example, Lord Elgin's marbles are popularly misdescribed, whereas those items forming a collection were usually procured in an open market at the going, but rarely the asking price. One such irresistible acquisition, or purchase, on show is the spectacular pair of giant Chinese lacqueur vases which grace the corner of the Music Room: they could have fallen off the back of a caravan, trekking slowly across Siberia's steppes, en route for the Kremlin, where, as a matter of fact, the matching pair fetched up, their being destined as a gift of the Emperor of China for the Tzar.

Radiant features of the room are the ten clusters of cut-glass Waterford chandeliers looped evenly up and down the room. At night they are an arresting sight, when the sheen of candlelight glistens from each cluster that tapers into seven sprouting branches of shimmering crystal irridescence.

It is not difficult to conjure up the entertainment or the faces of the past: through the garden doorway beckons Emma, pacing up the gravelled path from the adjacent home she kept for the two men in her life. Sir William Hamilton and Pennington were the best of neighbours and friends, sharing similar tastes – though hasten it to be said, not Emma. The quartet of Emma, her husband, Horatio Nelson and their neighbour often foregathered in the music room to converse and entertain one another, and who better than Emma to provide –

'my three dearest admirers'

with her 'Attitudes'.

The wooden dias (on which the grand piano now perches) would be set between the centre columns from where Emma played out her conversation pieces: the game was for her enthralled companions to guess correctly which of her classical poses she represented. Such performances became known as 'tableaux vivants', the living pictures of the salon. Picture her appearance through the open window, her robe drenched by the spray of the terrace fountain, the muslin clinging to her limbs, (a fashionable but uncomfortable habit of the time).

Just when the chandeliers appear to grow stronger with the fading light
of dusk, Emma emerges, in step with the soft melodies of the keyboard.
Imperceptibly, the children creep from their mantelpiece frames and
forget their infant shyness as their silent footwork traces Emma's shadow.

Midnight dwells where Merton Park once stood, and Emma is gone.

ROYAL WINDSOR

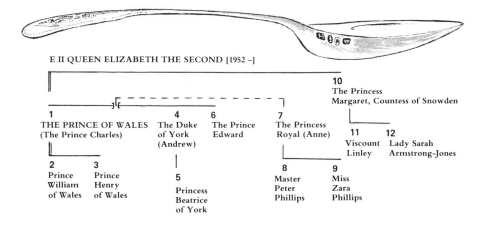

E II QUEEN ELIZABETH THE SECOND [1952 –]

10
The Princess
Margaret, Countess of Snowden

1 THE PRINCE OF WALES (The Prince Charles)	**4** The Duke of York (Andrew)	**6** The Prince Edward	**7** The Princess Royal (Anne)

11 **12**
Viscount Lady Sarah
Linley Armstrong-Jones

2 Prince William of Wales	**3** Prince Henry of Wales	**5** Princess Beatrice of York	**8** Master Peter Phillips	**9** Miss Zara Phillips

THE BLOOD ROYAL LINE OF SUCCESSION

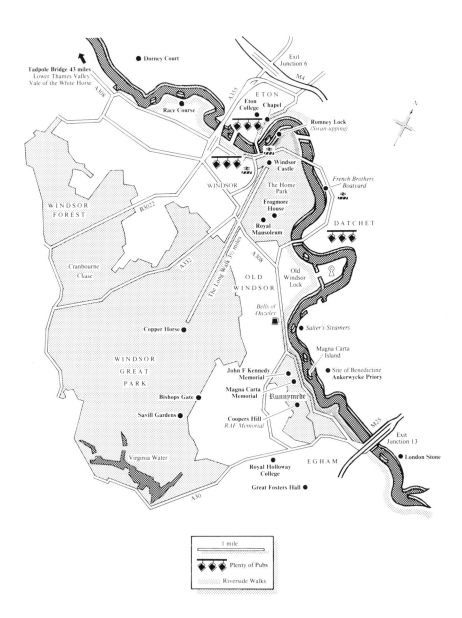

Dorney Court

Exit
Junction 6

Tadpole Bridge 43 miles
Lower Thames Valley
Vale of the White Horse

A308

A355

M4

ETON

N

Eton
College   Chapel

Race Course

Romney Lock
(Swan-upping)

Windsor
Castle

WINDSOR

The Home
Park

French Brothers
Boatyard

WINDSOR
FOREST

B3022

Frogmore
House

Royal
Mausoleum

DATCHET

Cranbourne
Chase

A332

The Long Walk 3½ miles

A308

Old
Windsor
Lock

OLD
WINDSOR

Copper Horse

Bells of
Ouzeley

Salter's Steamers

Magna Carta
Island

WINDSOR
GREAT
PARK

John F Kennedy
Memorial

Site of Benedictine
Ankerwycke Priory

Bishops Gate

Magna Carta
Memorial

Runnymede

Savill Gardens

Coopers Hill
RAF Memorial

Exit
Junction 13

M25

Virginia Water

EGHAM

London Stone

Royal Holloway
College

Great Fosters Hall

1 mile

Plenty of Pubs

Riverside Walks

A Visit to Windsor

THE MOST DIFFICULT DECISION confronting visitors to Windsor is *what* to see within the constraints of time. Many will opt for a coach tour from London, entrusting the day's programme to a guide who also carries admission tickets to all the scheduled places. Some prefer the perceived independence provided by a motor-car. Either way, the highlights of a visit will probably be the tour around the State Apartments. It is prudent to check beforehand that some visiting dignitary has not chosen to stay with The Queen on the very same day, since it is doubly aggravating to find the entrance barred after a fair walk up the Middle Ward. The magnificence of the State Apartments are best tackled earlier than *the hordes*, who combine to reduce the 'stately' progression into a slow-moving shuffle. If the slow-march is to be avoided, choose to get there soon after opening time. A visit to the beautiful Chapel of the Knights of the Garter – St. George's Chapel – is a priority; as is the time to be spent strolling through the precincts of the Castle, with all its impressive views, in and out. Within the time available, Queen Mary's Dolls' House and the Coach House will reward the curiosity of any visitor, grown-up or not. So too, H.M.'s Exhibition of Drawings: Holbein, da Vinci, *et al.*

Windsor Pedestrian Bridge

Then, of course, there is the river. Over Windsor Bridge to Eton High Street on the far side, where a most pleasing walk through the famous College quadrangles may be had, and good food obtained in a wide choice of pubs and restaurants. Where time permits, an excursion on the river – up to Boulter's Lock, or to Mapledurham for the out of the ordinary, or simply a boat trip in itself – will provide the keen photographer with memorable frames of this engaging corner of Royal Berkshire.

Things of interest

An alternative to the spectacular 'Changing the Guard' at Buckingham Palace takes place at Windsor, is easier to see, is quite as colourful, as traditional and as full of pageantry. It is performed at eleven o'clock, day in, day out (except Sundays when the Guards put their feet up). For those who may be planning a future trip, the Royal Windsor Horse Show is a feature of an English Spring Calendar, held in the presence of Her Majesty, in her own back garden, Windsor Home Park. These and other matters of passing interest, are referred to in this section of the book.

Royal Windsor

Windsor on Thames received its royal grant in 1276 when, by Charter of Edward I, the town's inhabitants were accorded the status that befits their existence beside the renowned residence of the Royal Family. Situated on the south bank of the river, Windsor lies some twenty miles upstream of Westminster, although Windsor Bridge is over forty miles distant by river.

The royal association dates back to early Anglo-Saxon kings who took up residence at Old Windsor long before William the Conqueror erected his wooden fortress on the hill near the 'Winding-shore' in 1068. Whilst the town and its environs lie well outside the perimeter of Greater London, the Royal Borough holds a special historical significance for the Capital. Lying within easy reach, it also provides a popular destination for Londoners as well as for most visitors.

The town planners, whose impossible task it is to organise the enormous influx of daytrippers, have ensured that those who arrive by motor inevitably get lost in the detours, between numerous roundabouts before coming to a halt at one of the spaces in the many car parks – if, by chance, a space remains – on the tarmacadamed riverbank just above the bridge, at the bottom of the steep incline of the hill. Owing to the large number of principal places of interest, time will be limited, but do not overlook the pedestrian bridge leading to Eton High Street and College, which is conveniently close to any rendezvous.

Thames Street ascends the gradient and joins the High Street as the main thoroughfare. It is a brisk twenty minute walk from the riverside, though it often seems longer. The majority of shop-fronts which come into view are quite elegant; the shops behind these fronts charge quite elegant prices, too. A worthy few

manage to eschew the varieties of crass merchandise that are passed off as souvenirs. In the cobbled alleyways of Church and Market Streets some fine antique shops are clustered cheek by jowl with other shopwindows full of bric-a-brac. Behind, at Burford House (in St. Albans Street), lived Nell Gwynne and her sons, both given her by Charles II, who took a well-rehearsed shortcut across the far wall, on his visits from the castle.

Hardby are the Royal Mews where, in the redbrick buildings (entered from St. Albans Street) there is an interesting display of royal carriages. The state of the art in harnesses and other riding paraphernalia are well exhibited in the Coach House, together with enchanting carriages, and these attract many a keen eye, of children in particular.

The town is, of course, dominated by the Castle. Even the hill sits in submission to the massive ramparts lining its crest on the brow. On sunnier days the warm honeycomb tone of stone fabric disperses a subtle light on the rooftop townscape nestling below, and its buildings bask in a soft amber glow.

Queen Victoria enjoyed the place. A statue was erected in the year of her Jubilee, 1887, by Boehm, at the top of the High Street, where she now holds court to an over-familiar pigeon: the Castle entrance lies towards her rear.

By proceeding through the Henry VIII Gateway, the expectant
visitor may need to catch a breath or two before attempting
the feast of royal treasure on view within. It was probably a
sensible decision not to keep the Crown Jewels here, among the
Sovereign's other treasures. Besides breaking with tradition,
the former would appear *unutterably* ostentatious alongside the
restrained splendour and exquisite craftsmanship of the monarch's
other heirlooms.

An ideal meeting place for children who lose their parents is
the Guildhall, and the wise will first point this out to their
companions, before one or other becomes lost. The Guildhall, or
Corn Exchange was constructed in 1707. The Dean of Windsor's
son, Sir Christopher Wren, was invited to complete the design

commenced by Sir Thomas Fitch. The great architect incorporated the row of centre columns which are free-standing, one inch short of the ceiling, to prove to the mayor and aldermen that the ante-chamber, where they assembled, was adequately supported by the extant structure.

In the cornices of the upper storey are the statues of –

QUEEN ANNE, Consort of James 1 – 'the wisest fool in Christendom' – and mother of Charles I (her third son) had Prince Henry, her more intelligent firstborn, lived, there might have been no Civil War:

'O Sculptor, your art cannot copy Her, but if you can excel in your carving of her likeness, then *carve a Goddess*',;   *[Latin inscription]*

PRINCE GEORGE OF DENMARK, (Consort of Queen Anne, of England); presented by Wren.

An alternative meeting place is opposite, in the comfort of the Castle Hotel, its car park is free when refreshment is taken within.

Reach the Castle Gates at precisely eleven in the 'forenoon as a detachment of scarlet-coated sentries march past, providing an enviable sight of the Queen's bodyguard, and enter the precincts. There are three major areas to be covered, of which the Lower Ward (now entered) forms the first.

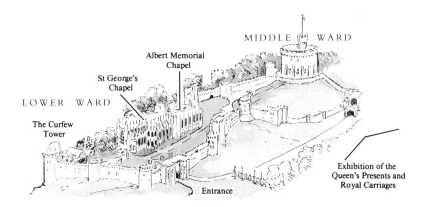

THE LOWER WARD

William the Conqueror chose the site where, over 900 years ago, he built the rudimentary fortification on which the Round Tower now stands. The flanks of outer walls stretch nearly a mile in circumference and contain the largest inhabited castle in the world, although the Vatican, a city within a city (of Rome), can rival its size as an official residence.

The fabric has been enlarged by many of the succeeding monarchs: principally by Henry II in the 12thC, *his* grandson Henry III, and further altered by *his* grandson, Edward III, the great Plantagenet warrior, who was born here in 1312.

Today, the exterior reflects the tasteful extravagance of George IV combined with the talent of his architect, Wyatt. In their joint opinion it was, when they had finished, what a castle should really look like. When the king knighted the architect of the Normanesque addition, the architect likewise embellished his name to appear Norman-French like the castle. He became Sir Jeffry Wyatt*ville.*

St George's Chapel

Whatever preconceptions a visitor may hold about church architecture will be dispelled as soon as the porch of St. George's Chapel is entered. This most radiant example of stonework – transformed into slender, graceful symmetry of line – overwhelms the eye of the intruder, which, having adjusted to the light, will penetrate and absorb the vertical intricacy of the interior. The West window casts a magnificent spell of rich mediaeval glass saints and chivalry ascending to the roof.

> Art historians compare the Chapel with the rival beauty of King's College Chapel, Cambridge, or Henry VII's Chapel at Westminster. In either case, one of England's perfect mediaeval achievements in the Perpendicular style is here at Windsor, the gift of Edward IV. He caused it to be built in 1478 out of jealousy for the lovely college in view across the river meadows, at Eton, which was erected by his kinsman, Henry VI, whom he had deposed in 1461.

> The Chapel is a 'royal peculiar' which means the Dean and his Chapter fall outside the jurisdiction of the Bishopric and the Archbishop of Canterbury may only attend by invitation, (when His Grace becomes merely '*The* Visitor').

> A special privilege of the Chapel lies in its majestic association with the Most Noble Order of the Garter, instituted in 1348 by King Edward III. The senior order of Knighthood in Great Britain, the full complement of Knights is twenty-four and each of the monarch's companions – the Sovereign, is ipso facto, a member of the Knighthood – is individually installed in a time-honoured

ceremony which has been conducted within the precincts, since its inception in the Middle Ages.

HONI SOIT QUI MAL Y PENSE

The actual garter which inspired the Plantagenet king to admonish his finest warriors with these words, originally belonged to the Countess of Salisbury. While attending a Royal Ball in the English town of Calais, she was caught unawares when, by accident, it slipped. The king at once retrieved her garter from the floor and tied it round her knee. He rounded on his snickering knights with these words –

"Evil be
to those
who
evil think"

Behind the richly ornate Choir screen are the lavish darkened stalls, in three tiers, flanked by their coats-of-arms and overhanging banners of the best-behaved knights. The alabaster reredos contains a memorial to Prince Albert, Consort of Queen Victoria.

Royal Tombs

Beyond the High Altar are to be found the royal tombs. The Founder's tomb of Edward IV is beyond a lovely pair of gates (1482) on the north side. Above, in a wooden oriel is the Royal Pew which Henry VIII provided for his Catherine of Aragon, the first wife and which afterwards provided cover for those of his companions that he may have wished hidden from public scrutiny. The King's remains, together with the body of his third bride, Jane Seymour lie in a vault beneath the centre of the stone floor; alongside, reposes the heartless, but not headless body of Charles I, (that organ having been reputedly snatched and eaten by a Victorian nobleman).

In the adjoining *Urswick Chapel* abutting the northwest corner of the Nave the striking sculpture, by Matthew Wyatt (1820) – the talented son of Wyatt*ville* – adorns and embellishes the royal tomb of Princess Charlotte. Considered by one art historian "an unnecessarily prosaic, minor work of art", such comment seems unduly harsh for an effigy that strikes many who chance upon it as a deliciously idiosyncratic work, of pure inspiration. Wyatt's genius may be felt in the softness of the linenfolds turned in stone, in a stage setting sculpted with rare dramatic effect. Half-shrouded, the Princess of Wales seems to ascend from her corpse, released from worldly cares as she ventures from this world in topless dignity. By her side, a mortified lady-in-waiting becomes an angel holding the swaddling corpse of the stillborn infant son.

CHARLOTTE, PRINCESS OF WALES (1796–1817)

Princess Charlotte was the young and popular Queen-elect. Her time would have come to pass in 1830, on the death of her father, the Prince Regent, (George IV). Instead, having married Prince Leopold in 1816, she died in childbirth in the following year, to the regret of the nation's subjects, who freely contributed to the erection of her memorial.

It may be imagined that, having sired seven sons, George III had done his duty. He no doubt felt, on his deathbed in 1820, that he could die in the secure belief that England had its fair share of male heirs on which the throne could devolve.

When the Princess of Wales, his granddaughter, died so unexpectedly, and, worse still, left no heir to the Line, this caused panic in royal circles.

The Prince Regent (the next king) was in his fifties, but married to the unbearable Caroline of Brunswick-Wolfenbüttel – (she being then past child-bearing). This left England to expect of the remaining sons a strenuous joint effort in their respective marital duties to fill the void occasioned by the tragedy of their niece's premature death. Frederick, Duke of York, the next in line, tried hard but failed to produce any surviving issue. The next son, William, Duke of Clarence (afterwards William IV) managed a couple of daughters but they died in their cots. It was left to his younger brother Edward, Duke of Kent and Strathearn to rise to the occasion and, by marrying the scheming and ambitious widow of a German princeling, of Leiningen, in 1818, to sire an only daughter, the shy Alexandrina Victoria, who was, as monarch, to outshine them all.

– THE ALBERT MEMORIAL CHAPEL –

Rebuilt by Henry VII and completed by Wolsey, this private Chapel was converted by Queen Victoria to commemorate her beloved Albert after his death in 1861 at the relatively young age of 42. His memorial tomb, an effigy clothed in full armour, commands centre stage. Meanwhile, the grief-stricken Queen buried his remains privately at Frogmore, in the peace of Windsor Home Park, a short distance away and where she later joined him.

More daunting tombs surround the busy aisle, full of the muddlesome dukes that tie up the Blood Royal. Six of them –

George IV (Duke of York),
William IV (Duke of Clarence),
Edward, Duke of Kent & Strathearn,
Ernest Augustus, Duke of Cumberland,
Augustus Frederick, Duke of Sussex,
and Adolphus Frederick, Duke of Cambridge,

are buried, as was their father, King George III and his Queen Charlotte, out of sight in the vaults beneath.

The Dean's Cloister, beside the Chapel, would make the perfect snapshot but for the cordoned rope that preserves the Right Reverend Prelate some semblance of privacy; instead, photographers may choose Horse Shoe Cloisters, further down the Lower Ward, where the Curfew bell is tolled for visitors who lose their sense of time. On the opposite side stands a row of ancient dwellings, first built for the Military Knights at the same time as the Order of the Garter was founded. Up the hill, the walkway leads in the direction of the State Apartments, beyond the Round Tower, in the middle distance. Around the corner, abutting the North walls of the castle is Winchester Tower where Chaucer reputedly lived when Clerk of the Royal Works (circa 1391), with a view from the North Terrace that must have remained largely the same.

The North Terrace, some 600 yards long with commanding views over the Home Park and Eton on the far bank of the Thames, and surrounding countryside, leads around:

THE MIDDLE WARD

The Round Tower lies at the heart of the Castle, its precincts clearly divided between the Wards. These separated the monarch's functionaries of State – the garrisons, the chapels and the household officers, housed in the Lower Ward; the Upper Ward, where the communal existence of the Court was maintained, and finally the monarch's protected private apartments.

The Middle Ward harbours the impressive Round Tower, part constructed of Caen stone, imported from France and floated up the Thames, as was the flag-pole, which flies the Royal Standard when the Queen is in residence. This was the *fine point* neglected by Lord Melbourne –

> the King is dead: long live the King
>
> *Blackstone: Commentaries [18thC]*

As C.G.S. Greville, the historian, recounted –

> All that I hear of the young Queen leads to the conclusion that she will some day play a conspicuous part, and that she has a great deal of character . . .
>
> The day she went down to visit the Queen Dowager at Windsor, to (Lord) Melbourne's great surprise she said to him that as the flag on the Round Tower was half-mast high, and they might perhaps think it necessary to elevate it upon her arrival, it would be better to send orders beforehand not to do so. *He* had never thought of the flag, or knew anything about it, but it showed her knowledge of forms and attention to trifles.
>
> *Account of the Accession of Queen Victoria. [August 30, 1837).*

He was not the first Prime Minister to learn a thing or two from his – or, (since 1979) her – Queen.

A glimpse of the Queen's private Apartments may be had from Engine Court, beyond the Round Tower, where a lonely sentry stands guard-duty beyond the sweep of the lawn in the Upper Ward.

The official Hoister of the Standard gets an even better view of what goes on in royal circles when he ascends the 220 steps, to the top.

THE UPPER WARD

Beside the Norman Gateway leading up to the Tower stands the principal block of the State Apartments connected to the two wings of the private Apartments, around the Quadrangle. It is here that Windsor may be described as the pre-eminent royal residence of England, a mediaeval palace all but continuously inhabited down to the present day. Of Edward III's prodigious work – by 1377, at his death, he had spent £50,772 – on the royal lodgings, under the direction of William of Wykeham, the surviving Undercroft of the Apartments is the most visually authentic to survive the embellishments and reconstructions of the 17th and 19th Centuries.

> Warning: Do not join the queue for the State Apartments before first queuing to purchase tickets half-way along the North Terrace.

– *THE STATE APARTMENTS* –

THE STATE APARTMENTS number seventeen, each lavishly kept and filled with the best that 'old' money *could* buy. The whole galaxy, of

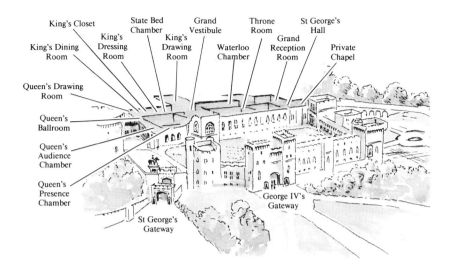

King's Closet · State Bed Chamber · Grand Vestibule · Throne Room · St George's Hall

King's · King's Drawing Room · Grand Reception Room · Private Chapel

King's Dining Room · Dressing Room · Waterloo Chamber

Queen's Drawing Room

Queen's Ballroom

Queen's Audience Chamber

Queen's Presence Chamber

George IV's Gateway

St George's Gateway

UPPER WARD OR QUADRANGLE

priceless art, usually overwhelms the beholder and, as it was intended, impresses beyond belief visiting dignitaries of State. From the side entrance on the North Terrace where pandemonium tends to reign among distressed members of a guided tour, who have become detached from their ticket-holder, access will be gained, slowly – very slowly in the throng – to the magnificent interior of the castle. The contents include, among endless treasures in store – *Note:* Pictures and furniture do tend to get moved around.

GRAND STAIRCASE (1)
Flanking the imposing stairwell are arms and suits of armour belonging to and worn by the sons of James I, the Princes Henry and Charles; Chantrey's statue of George IV; the bullet that killed Lord Nelson (in the display cabinet nearest corridor);

KING'S DINING-ROOM (2)
King Charles II commissioned this the first of Wren's rooms; noteworthy, too, are the carvings by Grinling Gibbons – wherever he carved an unopened pea-pod, it meant he hadn't been paid, which of course is not the case at Windsor; try Chatsworth where he was unlucky – the Brussels tapestries, and a portrait by Mytens of the king when Prince of Wales; the ceiling by Verrio, which depicts the Banquet of the gods, or, as a transatlantic visitor entertainingly put it –

"Some kind of orgy up there."

KING'S DRAWING ROOM (3)
Known as the Rubens Room because of the eminent collection of his paintings, including a fine self-portrait; also hanging is the earliest Van Dyck on show, St. Martin (the patron saint of innkeepers and drunkards, shown dividing his cloak with a beggar, not an inebriate: the lesser saint's day is November 11, the Feast of Bacchus, hence his patronage);

STATE BED CHAMBER (4)
Louis Seize 'king-size' bed –

> Curse not the king, no not in thy thought; and curse not the rich in thy bedchamber: for a bird of the air shall carry the voice, and that which hath wings shall tell the matter.
> *[Ecclesiastes: X.20.]*
>
> – "Oh for the wing of a fairy queen"!

KING'S DRESSING ROOM (5)
Among the fine paintings, Van Dyck's portrait of Charles I's head, composed in the well-known triangular pastiche (head-on, two side-ons) painted to aid Bernini's execution of a bust whilst the sculptor was engaged abroad; the bust was destroyed when Whitehall Palace burnt down (1697);

KING'S CLOSET (6)
In this chamber, the king could have as many closet queens as he wished, but that is not the point. In the few moments available (while being carried along in the tide of the single file) take the opportunity to glimpse at an impressive batch of Canalettos; these are well worth stopping for; the closet, incidentally, does lock;

QUEEN'S DRAWING ROOM (7)
On view, an unrivalled collection of portraits by Sir Anthony Van Dyck, including –
Queen Henrietta Maria (Consort of Charles I) in half-length portrait;
A painting of the three eldest of their seven children: the Princes Charles, and James, both to succeed to the throne, and Henry, charmingly composed;

QUEEN'S BALLROOM (8)
More views by Canaletto, en passant; part of the older wing refurbished by Charles II for his Queen, Catherine, Infanta of Braganza who failed to give him an heir. Thus the throne passed to his brother, James II;

QUEEN'S AUDIENCE CHAMBER (9)
Ceiling by Verrio; the Infanta Catherine represented as Britannia; wall-hangings by Gobelins; tapestries illustrate the story of Esther too loosely for easy comprehension. The decorations continue in:

QUEEN'S PRESENCE CHAMBER (10)
Handsome bust of Handel, by Roubiliac;

QUEEN'S GUARD CHAMBER (11)
Walls strewn artistically, in a martial display designed by H.R.H. The Duke of Edinburgh in tandem with Mr. A.R. Dufty, one-time Master of Armouries, Tower of London with trophies of arms, and various royal portraits; in the centre, a suit of armour made for Sir Christopher Hatton, 1585, worn by the King's Champion at coronations (recounted later, at Westminster). Above the busts of Marlborough by Henning and Wellington by Chantrey, hang two French banners, annually replaced by the present Dukes on June 18th and August 13th, the anniversaries of Waterloo (1815) and Blenheim (1704), in accordance with the condition of tenure of the estates, Stratfield Saye and Woodstock, voted to their ancestors by Parliament: Churchill, a Marlborough relation, is represented by a bust, commissioned of Oscar Nemon, 1953;

ST. GEORGE'S HALL (12)
This impressive chamber, 185 ft. long and 30 ft. wide; formerly used for banquets for the Knights of the Order of the Garter. It has a richly adorned ceiling, boasting their armorial bearings – except for two empty shields, whose bearers were executed for treason; the carved oak throne, formally used, is a replica of the coronation chair in Westminster; the royal portraits and parallel range of busts depict the Soverigns *of the Order*, from James I to George IV; all executed by celebrated artists; (Van Dyck, Lely, Kneller, Lawrence, Nollekens, Chantrey, etc);

– *SAINT GEORGE AND THE DRAGON* –

The patron saint of England, adopted from the early times of the Crusades, became part of the insignia of the Garter, which Edward III's knights first wore, displayed in the form of a pendant attached on a blue riband. The legendary dragon-slayer, represented by the patron saint overcoming his daunting opponent, the triumph of good over evil is based on the folklore of Crusading Christian soldiers. All good Englishmen and true, by longstanding tradition, honour their spiritual mentor on April 23rd.

Artists of every age have relished the spectacle portraying the classic contest between man and beast – more often than not, St. George is astride a dashing white charger while the dragon usually sports a pair of rather inadequate wings.

On view in the Castle is a glowing version painted by Rubens in 1630 shortly after his arrival in England, when he would have been at his most impressionable about English traditions, like many a visitor since. It is almost certain that St. George represents an idealised version of his patron, Charles I, who together with the damsel princess, Queen Henrietta Maria, survey the landscape, with fanciful additions of London's buildings, at which the dragon seems to gaze longingly.

A particularly fine painting may be admired in the National Gallery, London, by the 15thC Florentine artist, Paolo Uccello. His interpretation of the scene includes the suggestive introduction of a damsel in distress, observed slipping her girdle around the dragon's neck, in reckless abandon, to judge from the saint's sedentary response. Mindful of the patriotic fervour her action might have evinced from her admiring knight in shining armour, it is anybody's guess whether and in which order she succeeded in taming both.

– *ROYAL "WALKABOUT" CONTINUED* –

Continuing a 'royal walk-about', the Apartments seems even bigger, grander and more sumptuous as one goes on.

GRAND RECEPTION ROOM (13)

A splendid chamber featuring more Gobelins tapestry hanging on goldleaf'd walls, with the unsuitable theme of Jason and Methea, an unsettling subject for any regular couple in a consumer society, (in pursuit of the modern equivalent of the Golden Fleece), since Jason's endeavours ended in a melancholy suicide:

> One was never married, and that's his hell;
> another is, and that's his plague.
>
> *Robert Burton. Anatomy of Melancholy. 1577–1640*

The furniture is upholstered in Beauvais tapestry, in keeping with the rococo style of the room.

COME TO THE PARTY

The table is laid well in advance of the annual banquet held on 18th June, the anniversary of the famous battle, when much fine porcelain, including French vases from Sèvres, French glass, and other reminders of the vanquished, add to the enjoyment of Wellington's masterstroke. After all, had it gone the other way, it is likely that Napoleon would have changed the locks on Windsor Castle *and* retained the keys.

For those unable to share the evening in the best company, the celebration may always be replicated at home. In addition to a *frenchified* taste – the finest claret (Chateau Latour? Leoville-Barton etc., English-owned, of course) – true vintage Port could also be served. A quick telephone call to the Press Office at Buckingham Palace will elicit the menu in good time to order the basics from Harrods' food hall, or, if their provisions run dry, from Fortnum's. When the meal is over, rather than getting stuck into the washing-up, toast "Old Beaky" (as His Grace, the first Duke of Wellington, and Marquis of Douro, was irreverently labelled by his troops) in his favourite tipple, Warre's Port (pronounced as in the battle). This producer is the oldest (1670) in the eminently respectable line of British shippers who still provide excellent vintages. The Duke would much enjoy in this century, a '27, '34, '45 perhaps?, or one or other of the post-war vintages, a '60, '63 or '66? Currently, the most suitable year for laying down is the '77 which will be nicely ready for the Bicentennial of Waterloo, on June 18th, 2015, or even to see in the Third Millennium, just a decade away?

THE THRONE ROOM (14)

Reserved for important Investitures, this panelled sanctum is decorated in garter-blue where meets the Chapter of the Noble Order; sovereigns are displayed in their Garter robes; the Ante-Throne Room, adjoining, contains Zuccarelli's masterpiece, Isaac meeting Rebecca, (who founded the dynasty, so confusingly deployed in the first Book of Moses) with such profound consequences for mankind;

THE WATERLOO CHAMBER (15)

Covering the 12thC courtyard which was enclosed fifteen years after the battle, this large chamber, 98 ft. by 47 ft., is filled with memorabilia celebrating Napoleon's downfall; it is hung with portraits, predominantly by Lawrence, featuring the men who mattered: Wellington, Blücher, Castlereagh and the like; the unique carpet – it contains no seam – was woven by hand, in Agra (India) for the 'Queen Empress' c.1850.

FROM THE GRAND VESTIBULE, with more war-trophies, another statue of Queen Victoria by Boehm, and the silver-gilt throne that belonged to a certain King of Kandy, to all intents and purposes the visitor may be said to have 'done' Windsor Castle. Thereon out, it is downhill all the way, via the portion of the staircase that leads to the exit. Most would agree that what they have seen on display is an unrivalled collection of art housed in the most famous country home in the world.

The best Private Collection

Finally, and if the legs can stand it, The Print Room contains the Exhibition of Old Master Drawings, loaned by H.M. The Queen from her private collection containing outstanding works by Leonardo da Vinci, Holbein, Raphael, Michelangelo, et al. and which is the most important private collection in the world.

The Private Apartments

What every visitor really hopes to see is the Queen's *Private* Apartments! Never mind the bemusing wealth which is displayed elsewhere, and all the show that goes with it. Where, in the corridors and the rooms visited, are the connecting doors – designed to be easily missed! – which open onto the innermost secrets?

Beyond the party walls of the Grand Reception Chamber and St. George's Hall and Chapel, lie the royal suites. These are entered via the Gateway betwen the Lancaster and York Towers, on the southern wing of the Quadrangle and continue the entire length of the East Terrace, connecting the two. Guests invited so to do should allow sufficient time to inspect the sumptuous rooms, particularly the Crimson and White Drawing Rooms, not forgetting the views or the contents – Chelsea, Dresden, oriental and Sèvres services – of the Dining Room, or the artistic treat afforded in the Grand Corridor, which leads to the Breakfast Room, where the royal family break their fast.

Guests may be said to have truly arrived when the statue of Penelope, (by R.J. Wyatt) is not only reached, but passed. Prince Albert placed it at the entrance to the Queen's Apartments, beyond which threshold Her Majesty was spared standing on ceremony, which is kept strictly to the other end of the castle.

For those who harbour a secret desire to know what goes on in royal circles, the best course – in the absence of an invitation – is to take a leaf out of the book of one or other of the courtiers who have published their experiences, and never to rely on mere gossip columnists. A good book is that of the late Sir Cecil Beaton, from which the following extract is taken –

> On this particular morning during which several matters of state had to be attended to, Her Majesty was a bit late for an audience with a new

ambassador (who arrived in a horse-drawn coach) and had to be shown in by Anthony Eden.

Suddenly Eden said, 'I think Ma'am, we must hurry this through as the Ambassador has been here some considerable time.'

The Queen said, 'Oh yes, we can't keep the horses waiting.'

Beaton: extract – (published) DIARY.

– *QUEEN MARY'S DOLLS' HOUSE* –

WHY QUEUE for the State Apartments, paying an additional price in human suffering, when an agreeable diversion is to be had inspecting a royal residence on quite a different scale? (one-twelfth, to be exact).

Queen Mary's model home was the brain-child of Sir Edwin Lutyens. While showing the King and Queen his working drawings for the Raj's Palace in New Delhi, for which sombre designs he sought their approval, he interspersed their meeting with the unveilingof his pocket-sized water-closet. In next to no time, King George V was ensconced with Queen Mary taking turns to produce a royal flush, after the distinguished architect had demonstrated, (with the utmost decorum befitting such a delicate matter,) how to pull the chain properly. The triumvirate thereupon conceived the idea of building and furnishing a whole house to the scale of the miniature 'loo'. Doubtless, the project proved a welcome diversion for their Majesties from the daily grind of State papers or other trivial government pursuits. Both Queen Mary and Sir Edwin enlisted the unpaid help of the many artists and craftsmen who became involved. It was plain from the start that all the items were to be given free by their creators.

The Dolls' House measures eight feet by five and the contents – charming miniature household effects: miniscule pictures bearing well-known microscopic signatures; choice furniture and furnishings; and, the masterly plumbing; – were all amassed by Queen Mary in the 'Twenties. H.M. Ministry of Works is technically responsible for ensuring the smooth running of all the domestic apparatus. For example, the water-level of the cistern is, or should be, regularly checked for symptoms of abnormal behaviour, such as are defined in the *Draft* Regulations:

> Inspectors should exercise due caution when operating a water-closet vested in the property of the Crown, and, in the event of detecting a malfunction, file a full report, as appropriate in the circumstances. For example:

Nature and official reference:	water cistern no. 3,483.
cause of complaint:	Overspill of bowl.
preliminary conclusion:	(e.g.) (i) blockage from unidentified object.
	(ii) over-plunging of ball-cock.
	Etc.

The Thames Water and Sewerage Authorities can hardly wait for the privatisation of the water that is consumed in the name of their largest and most prestigious domestic user, the Crown. Mindful of water-conservation in the Thames Basin, the existing use of the Dolls' House toilet is barely tolerated: the displacement of the cistern measures an half of a wineglass, (1¾ fluid ounces), but there are at least a thousand dolls entitled to full facilities.

WINDSOR HOME PARK

The combined acreage of the Home Park and the Great Park exceeds 2,000 acres and provides superb views of Windsor Castle. The Home Park lies to the north and northeast of the town, and borders the River Thames on three sides. The celebrated *Herne's Oak* which is alluded to in *The Merry Wives of Windsor* (first performed in the Queen's Gallery, Windsor Castle, 1593), was replanted by Queen Victoria off Queen Elizabeth's Walk after it was struck by lightning in 1863. One of the advantages of English tradition is continuity. Unfortunately, the tree lies in the private area of the park and it is thus difficult to see. Since most of the oaks resemble each other, even Shakespeare might have been deceived.

Frogmore House lies to the south of the Royal Kennels, where Queen Victoria's interfering mother, the ambitious and scheming

Duchess of Kent and her favourite
Pomeranian dog, both lived.
  In the grounds are –

The Royal Mausoleum

Queen Victoria rests here in the magnificent shrine she erected for
her beloved husband, Prince Albert, who is buried alongside. The
Mausoleum, which was designed by Alfred J. Humbert, is open to
the public on a few, very few, days in May, customarily following
Whitsun. Nearby are the celebrated Royal Farms where pedigree
cattle can be viewed, by appointment.

Also buried at Frogmore are the Duke and Duchess of Windsor,
who met by destiny as lovers always will, and changed theirs as an
unhappy result. It is strange that two men who chose such
different paths in public life came to be laid to rest in the same
beautiful sanctuary in the Home Park: the one, who killed himself
by dint of hard work to support the monarchy, shares a grave with
a monarch who abandoned the call of duty for a woman.

Royal Windsor Horse Show

For anyone who finds Bond Street and the fashionable shopping
parlours of the West End a trifle crowded these days, this is an
added reason for obtaining advance tickets to the Royal Windsor
Horse Show, held annually in late spring at Windsor. Many
leading famous London shops attend the four-day event where
they exhibit their wares in a well-organised sector of show-tents.

———————————— TIMELY REFLECTIONS ————————————

What if Albert *the Good* had lived beyond his forty-second year?
Would England be different today? And what if King Edward VIII had
been crowned and had retained it?

ALBERT FRANCIS CHARLES AUGUSTUS EMMANUEL, 1819–1861.

Younger son of the Duke of Saxe-Coburg-Gotha, Albert from his
earliest years was groomed to 'the dangerous grandeur of royalty'.
His parents divorced soon after his birth and he was effectively
brought up by King Leopold of the Belgians and the wise and wily
von Stockmar, a trusted physician, politician, man of the world and
confidante of statesman (Palmerston said of him: "one of the best
political heads . . . ever met with") Thus he was willed to marry his
cousin, Victoria. They lived happily together for twenty one years.

Albert Prince Consort gained the timeless affection of the British
peoples from his example of unstinting hard work, natural grace,
acumen, and commitment to the common good. He raised the
character of the Court, after Hanoverian excesses, and raised
the character of public taste. The Establishment resented him, perhaps
for these reasons.

His industry and zeal, his interest in the Arts, his love of music,
painting and sculpture, and his advancement of the causes of Science
and Philanthropy, set him head and shoulders above his peers. Most of
all he demonstrated a compassion for his adopted countrymen
particularly in his sympathy for the working class.

Prince Albert is best remembered for the Great International
Exhibition, 1851, which was largely of his doing, in his unshakeable
vision of –

> "England's mission . . . to put herself at the head of the discussion of
> civilisation and the attainment of liberty" . . .
>
> *Extract: The Prince Consort's letters.*

One of Prince Albert's last acts in public life was, on his deathbed, to bring
wisdom to prevail in averting war between England and America, following the
'*Trent* Incident' when an English steamer seized two confederate envoys,
Messrs. Mason and Slidell. He rewrote the diplomatic dispatch which Lord John
Russell adopted outright, November 30, thus appeasing American indignation.

On 14 December, 1861, 'beloved' Albert died of typhoid, having packed into
forty years what most do not achieve in twice the time.

Common men shared the profound sorrow of their Queen, in mourning their
loss of a Great Leader.

To-day their ilk may look up to H.R.H. The Prince of Wales, whose
concern for the welfare of all the Kingdom's people, matches that shown
by his illustrious forbear.

The Show combines the best of equestrian events in the world –
the razzamatazz of Philadelphia's Devon Horse Show, with the
regal pageantry of Britain at its well-worn best (The Queen is
patron and the official Hostess of the event). There are horses for
all the courses, as wide apart as the thoroughbred jumpers making
their debut on the eventers' calendar; the regimental splendour of
the Household Cavalry aswirl in the scarlet tunics and gleaming
plumed helmets; a cross-country event staged for four-in-hands
and team pairs, across a seventeen mile course in Windsor Great
Park; or, the steeplechase for Shetland ponies on the last day,
whose nine-year-old riders jockey for position in a miniature
'Grand National'. The finale of the Show is the Musical Drive by
the King's Troop, Royal Horse Artillery, while the massed bands
play below the castle walls.

The Great Park

Windsor Great Park lies to the South of Windsor and is open all
year round, with a restricted route of access (no motor cars
beyond gates). The *Long Walk*, with its double avenue of trees
some of which date back to the 17thC, leads in a straight line for
nearly three miles to *Snow Hill*, crowned by 'Copper Horse' – an
equestrian landmark with George III in the saddle. Several thousand
deer roam in the parkland and, be it noted, red deer are considered
dangerous in October if they are roused in the rutting season.

The great American Lake

Those who come by independent means of transport may also
consider a visit to Virginia Water, with its huge artificial lake
(composed by the Duke of Cumberland, circa 1750 on his return
from the governorship of Virginia) and ruins in the classical
tradition – many of which are genuine. Nearby stands *Shrubbs
Hill*, on which Fort Belvedere formed the retreat of Edward,
Prince of Wales, from unwarranted public exposure of his private
life. It was from there that he left his kingdom for exile and the
hand of the woman he loved.

VISITORS INFORMATION CENTRE

THE VISITORS and Tourists Information Centre is situated at
Central Station, behind Thames Street, in the disused Great
Western Railway terminus, a Victorian structure of some charm.
The staff provide a thoroughly courteous service to visitors in
search of answers to general, and specific, enquiries.

What anyone does with *all* the information is anybody's guess. Visitors will no doubt wish to make the best use of it, though rarely an easy task, as even a judge found out: in a celebrated exchange, during an English trial, an informative · but mercilessly sharp barrister was admonished by a ponderous judge, with the ill-chosen words –

> Judge: Well, Mr. Smith, from all that you have told me, I am really none the wiser.
> Counsel: None the wiser, perhaps, M'Lord, but much the better informed!
>
> *As remarked by F.E. Smith*
> *(the barrister who was to become Lord Birkenhead).*

Duly informed visitors to Windsor who have elected to follow a guided tour, normally by coach from London or the provinces, may find themselves allowed a short time on their own, before regrouping in the Car Park, but "sweek-talked" into seeing the "Royalty and Empire" Exhibition, housed closeby. For those who can do without the inanities of inferior tourist traps, it is an unprepossessing exhibit waxworks, in period costume, attempting to ape Queen Victoria's retinue grouped about a railway platform with unconvincing sound-effects. An unimaginative slide-show extols the virtues of Victoriana. Many may wish to avoid this disappointing attraction. There again, some may not.

Behold the river

Instead, head straight for the river and, with twenty minutes or more to spare, wander across the footbridge that links Eton High Street. Much of interest, and of a different nature to what has been seen in the castle, lies ahead on the opposite bank, set amidst the playing fields of Eton where, according to the Iron Duke, 'the Battle of Waterloo was won'.

Windsor Festival

An annual feast in store for everyone is the Festival, held in late September and early October: concerts – (by permission) – in St George's Chapel, Windsor Castle, Eton and the Theatre Royal. Book early to avoid disappointment.

BOAT TRIPS ON THE THAMES

For idyllic views of Windsor Castle, there are a variety of river excursions available, from the embarkation point on the

Promenade (at Barry Avenue). An inexpensive (£1, 1988) roundtrip to Boveney Lock passes Windsor Racecourse and Eton College fields and boathouses, at Brocas Meadows, lasting thirty-five minutes.

An alternative and more memorable manner of arrival in Windsor is to come by water. Passengers who embark at Boulter's Lock (*one mile north of Maidenhead bridge, which town is well served by British Rail, from Paddington*), may enjoy eight miles of river scenery, their journey culminating in a magnificent view of the Castle ramparts, directly overhanging the Pier at Windsor.

ETON COLLEGE

ONE OF THE SMALLER GLORIES OF ENGLAND may be viewed in the backwaters of the Thames on the stretch beyond Windsor, where the first views of Eton College Chapel meet the eye, . . . faintly at first, then daintily it ascends from the water-meadows in the majesty of its pure Perpendicular form.

The King's College of Our Lady of Eton was founded in 1440 by royal prerogative of the saintly King of England, Henry VI, who also endowed the King's College at Cambridge. The glorious Chapel was completed in 1483 and was intended as the choir of a larger and greater structure. This was not to be, however, for Henry was deposed and his life ended with his cruel murder in 1471.

That Eton survived at all is a minor miracle. Edward IV, who seized his cousin's throne in 1461, wished to obliterate all Henry's good works, notably at Eton, which was too visible a reminder, from the ramparts at Windsor. He sought, and obtained, a papal decree which annexed the deposed king's College to his own institutions at Windsor thereby, effectively, halting its development.

By act of providence he chose to outshine his predecessor's work rather than destroy it. It was he who founded the rival St. George's Chapel at Windsor, regarded as one of the finest examples of medieval architecture in Europe to survive to this day. Thus every visitor may enjoy the beautiful comparisons left to posterity by the two factional heads of the last of Plantagenet rulers. With Edward's passing, Eton was at last secure, and, of all academic institutions in Europe, has enjoyed unparalleled royal favour.

Old School Ties

The school and almshouses have preserved a mediaeval chain while the lovely fan-vaulted Chapel boasts the finest 15thC narrative wall-paintings of their type in Europe. On the opposite side of the School Yard, with the Founder's statue as centrepiece, is Lower School. As the oldest extant schoolroom in England (1500), it is dominated by heavy beams and a central row of wooden pillars inserted to support the scholars' chamber above; whilst, on the west side, is Upper School (1694), comprising part of the Centre block buildings. Situated on the East side is the Lupton Tower (named after the first Provost) whose Gateway leads through to the solitude of cloisters and quadrangles of other college buildings. Not to be missed are the steps leading off the main Cloister from which College Hall is approached. The oak panelling and darkened hall-screen evoke the age-old perceptions of privileged fellowship.

MUSEUM OF ETON LIFE

Alas! regardless of their doom
The little victims play!
No sense have they of ills to come
Nor care beyond to-day

Yet, ah! why should they know their fate
Since sorrow never comes too late,
And happiness too swiftly flies?
Thought would destroy their paradise.
No more – where ignorance is bliss
'Tis folly to be wise.

Ode on a distant Prospect of Eton College – Thomas Gray (c. 1740)

Whether the privileged recipient of a private education goes further in life than less fortunate mortals, is the case in point of a visit to the College

Museum. The list of famous names, some bruised and some bred on the 'playing fields of Eton' is legendary –
umpteen Prime Ministers (including Pitt, Chatham, Walpole, Fox, Canning, Melbourne, Gladstone, including the most famous of all, the 'Iron' Duke of Wellington); illustrious national figures – Fielding, Horace Walpole, Thomas Gray, Shelley, Swinburne, Sir John Herschel, Aldous Huxley, Eric Blair (al. George Orwell) and even Beau Brummell, to mention many too few.

The College museum in the old school house brewery records fascinating vignettes of private schooling, seen through the eyes of the select few. Even flogging is painlessly evoked by the top hat of Dr. 'Tiny' Keate – he was the headmaster who 'chilled the blood off the spine of little boys' backsides' – also preserved is the block he used for flogging the little burghers rightly and wrongly – he once beat an awaiting class of Confirmation candidates mistaking them for the queue of offenders awaiting corporal punishment.

Be reassured that such practices are not officially condoned by an incumbent Provost, who might practise his *Hudibras* –

> Love is a boy, by poets styled,
> Then spare the rod, and spoil the child
>
> *(Samuel Butler)*

The Glorious Fourth

The Fourth of June commemorates King George III's birthday: his many young friends across the river were regularly bidden to a royal 'parley' on the castle walls when His Majesty's field of enquiry would cover all the great issues of their day, including the performance of the school kitchen and –

Which one of you was flogged today?

On the king's passing, Etonians went into mourning (1820) which continued to modern times in the prosaic dress of tail coat and top hat (since discarded). Boys measuring less than 5 ft. 4 in. wore the shorter 'Eton' jacket, broad 'Eton' collar, 'tall' hat, and black tie; the rest wore tail-coats, toppers and *white* tie.

Trousers were – and are – also obligatory.

The boys school represents a high proportion of the English aristocracy and, should the opportunity arise, are generally not averse to talking with strangers (who may wish to practise the Queen's English on a higher level than is sometimes heard on the B.B.C.). In or out of 'half' (termtime), Eton provides a memory to savour long after the shop-windows and buses of busy Windsor are left behind, when the noise of crowded places has subsided out of mind –

> How often you and I
> Had tired the sun with talking
> and sent him down the sky.
>
> *William Johnson Cory [19thC]*.

And in the words of the same poet, himself an Etonian and beak thereafter, who wrote of the sunlit stretches of the Thames

> Oh Thames! my memories bloom with all thy flowers,
> Thy kindness sighs to me from every tree:
> Farewell! I thank thee for the frolic hours,
> I bid thee, whilst thou flowest, speak of me.

ABOVE THE BRIDGE

Above the bridge of Windsor and Eton the river valleys unfold through the soft escarpments of the Chiltern and Cotswold Hills which provide many a choice of excursion upstream. There is no better locality than in the Thames Valley to indulge the dual appetite of scenic and gastronomic pleasure.

Thames-side villages are awash with the 'character' of old England, now mostly to be perceived in the crooked beams and

staircases of any number of hostelries and taverns that beckon
to the eye of the passer-by. Further inland, which always seems
to arrive back at the river course, which twists and turns to
Oxford and beyond, delightful lanes and hamlets link the rolling
countryside –

> Before the Roman came to Rye or out to Severn strode,
> The rolling English drunkard made the rolling English road.
> *[G.K. Chesterton]*

Along the English road

Those who wish to indulge their culinary fantasies within 15 miles of
Windsor will not be short on choice, as any volume of the gourmets'
bibles will vouch. The meccas wherein those with a weakness for high
living may find their salvation are well known:

> such as at Bray (on-Thames) where les frères Roux carved their
> reputation, as chef and patron of the *Waterside Inn*; or at Marlow,
> where the *Compleat Angler* trades as well on its reputation as on the
> immortal treatise of the name, where Izaac Walton wrote it.

Visit stately Cliveden, outside Taplow, the balustraded mansion
(Sir Charles Barry, architect of the Houses of Parliament, 1851) which is
now an hotel – once lived in by the Astors. The Cliveden set lived it up
there 'between the wars'. They were the Establishment Appeasers.

A famous House Party – [8th July, 1961]

Macmillan's Ministry nearly fell, in 1963 – when a prurient public were
titillated by the trappings of wealth and scandal involving beautiful
women, a Russian spy and a compromised minister. The carryings-on
continued to keep the great British public amused for months to come
and particularly the sinister pillow-talk of Soviet attaché, Captain Ivanov
the *terrible* (who struck fear into many a patriotic breast of wenches
working in the Ministry of Defence):

> Lord and Lady Astor had a large party of distinguished visitors to their great
> house at Cliveden . . . There is a fine swimming pool in the grounds . . .
>   On the Saturday, after nightfall, . . . some of the girls were bathing . . .
> when one of them . . . whilst she was in the water, took off her bathing
> costume, threw it on the bank, and bathed naked.
>   Soon afterwards Lord Astor and a party of his visitors walked down after
> dinner to the swimming pool to watch the bathing. '*Miss X*' rushed to get her
> swimming costume. '*Mr W*' threw it on one side so that she could not get at it
> once she seized a towel to hide herself. Lord Astor and *one of his party* arrived
> at this moment, and it was all treated as a piece of fun – it was over in a few
> minutes . . .
>
> *Extract: Lord Denning's Report [1963].*
> **(note** – *Guests' names omitted).*

The house is now an expensive hotel but the Gardens, sloping down to the Thames, are free, open to visitors and should be visited for the setting. Some may wish to refresh their memory of nature at play, in the stylish octagonal gazebo (Leoni, 1740) – with that glorious view of the Thames. Nearby, in some shady dell, the first owner, the libertine Lord Buckingham (a member of the *Cabal*) killed Lord Shrewsbury in a duel (1667), over 'their' lady, Lady Shrewsbury. Her ladyship, dressed as a pageboy, witnessed her husband's death with scarcely concealed relish.

Great Fosters

If the inner needs of the body have been ignored among the many delights on and around Windsor Bridge, and up Eton 'High', take a short drive to an Elizabethan splendour, at Egham, near Runnymede. The Great Fosters Hotel has comfortable four-posters, and a panelled dining-room which is an authentic mediaeval barn, dating from 1455. After all those cold and unused fireplaces in historic buildings, it is doubly welcome to repair to one of the hearty hearths of an open log fire, lit and glowing as it was when Henry VIII adopted the hall as his hunting lodge. (This hotel is still, remarkably and rewardingly, privately owned.)

Please note – To those unfamiliar with the fictional creations spawned by Kenneth Grahame, *Toad Hall* does not exist as a real place.

Many who visit the Thames Valley will be keen to enjoy the countryside further afield. There is no set prescription; the choice is as wide and as varied as the open road –

> "There you are!" cried the Toad, straddling and expanding himself. "There's real life for you . . . The open road, the dusty highway, the heath, the common, the hedgerows, the rolling downs! Camps, villages, towns, cities! Here to-day, up and off to somewhere else to-morrow! Travel, change, interest, excitement! *Kenneth Grahame: The Wind in the Willows [1st published, 1908].*

In addition to the variety of places on offer within striking distance of *Toad Hall* or Toad Tunnel (the latter, near Henley), there is always the pleasure that awaits those who motor through the valleys such as the Vale of the White Horse, finding the idyllic village inn. (see Appendix).

One such choice might be Tadpole-on-Thames, some 90½ nautical miles from Windsor Bridge but half the distance by road:

("Poop-poop").

The Royal Holloway College

Within a mile or two of Windsor, Runnymede and the Great Fosters Hotel, there reposes at Egham an astonishing art collection, now forming part of the inventory of the University of London, and open by appointment only. The collection hangs in the 'Recreation' Hall, and the vastness of the château-style building, a monstrous Victorian pile.

Built for Mr. Thomas Holloway, an enterprising vendor of the patent medicines (which provided him with the bulk of his fortune), his lavish property was turned over to institutional usage as a ladies' college. It was opened by Queen Victoria in 1886, three years after the death of the ingenious inventor of many a 'delectable and efficacious pill'. Holloway endowed the institution, known then as the Royal Holloway College, and endowed it with his remarkable collection of erotic British paintings, some of the best examples of Victorian art. Choice items include –

> Applicants for Admission to a Casual Ward, *by Luke Fildes*;
> The Railway Station, *by Frith*;
> The Marriage Market of Babylon, *by E. Long*;
> The Princes in the Tower, *by Millais*.
> Man Proposes – God Disposes, *by Sir Edwin Landseer* – painted when Queen Victoria's *favourite* painter was going mad, the subject bearing vividly on Sir John Franklin's Arctic exploration in 1847 on which he perished, not, one hopes, at the paws of the polar bears depicted in this strange creation.

Absorbing Windsor, Eton, Runnymede and Mr. Holloway's philanthrophy is liable to saturate the mind. One more painting, another medieval arch, more statues of yesteryear, an additional duchess or king and true satiety is reached. And still there is more to see, to-day, or one day soon.

THE PAVILIONS AT RUNNYMEDE

THE PARCHMENT was on the wall for John, King Henry II's mischievous youngest son, who had lost the Angevin possessions won by his father and, to the affront of his subjects, became the first ex-communicated monarch of England. On Epiphany Sunday, 1215, the Temple accord was struck between King John and his doubting councillors of state, led by the good and great Earl Marshal of England, Pembroke. Peace was agreed on the kingdom's calendar, to reign until Low Sunday, April 26th. The abilities of the king, sharp-witted, energetic but capricious in nature, were on trial by his peers, the same barons who were to stand their ground in the pavilions erected at Runnymede.

The king's conduct did not improve. In the misdeeds of his past lay the active seed of his destruction. His enemies were all about him, above and below the border – King Alexander II (of Scotland) and Louis (of France) schemed and lay seige to his kingdom, assisted by the murmurers of discontent, those on whom he had extracted *scutage* – a levy in lieu of military service – avowedly to restore stability in his territories but causing further distrust when the funds were misspent.

On Low Monday, the day following the Accord's date of expiration, the Barons took the initiative and marched on the king's camp at Oxford, taking the royal garrison of Bedford and encamping at Brackley. The Lord Mayor welcomed them to London, whose citizens joined the cause, nearly two years to the day that King John had pawned his kingdom to the See of Rome by seeking a pardon from the Papal legates. Within the walls of the City of London, the Earles of Arundel, Chester, Surrey, de Ferrers and Pembroke issued their Mandate, on May 24. Once the allegiance of the Capital was known, defections followed from the royal camp. Straightaway John marched to Windsor, a royal stronghold and, in reply, issued the King's Summons, dated 8th June, being returnable within the expiry of three days. A meeting place was nominated at the meadows of Runnymede, where the Barons' list of grievances were to be aired and resolved. The choice of location was strategic, placed between London (a day's march) and the king's troupe at Windsor, which with Dover were the only strongholds in the South of England to remain royalist.

Magna Carta enshrined the basic rights of Englishmen and established the right of a fair trial, which was to go to the root of the development of the Common Law. The royal seal also guaranteed the feudal independence of the City of London, ever the bastion of their own civil liberties. For the Lord Mayor's citizens and the chartered boroughs their "ancient liberties" were propounded and affirmed. Copies of the charter were despatched to the great cathedrals in the realm, at Salisbury and Lincoln where they may be inspected, and at the Public Record Office.

History recounts the king's tale in the aftermath of Runnymede: his renegation of its terms, his desperate and astonishing mobilisation of support in the north, his encounter with the natural elements when he lost nearly all, in the Wash, and his escape to Newark, in Lincolnshire. There he died within the week, and only fifteen months after presiding at the table of the Barons, in their pavilion at Runnymede.

Runnymede

WE GRANT to all freemen of our realm . . . all the undermentioned liberties . . .

TO NONE will we deny or delay right of justice . . . NO FREE MAN shall be taken or imprisoned . . . except by the lawful judgments of his peers or the law of the land . . .

Extracts: Magna Carta, 15th June, 1215

And still when mob or monarch lays
Too rude a hand on English ways,
To whisper wakes, the shudder plays,
    Across the reeds at Runnymede.

And Thames, that knows the mood of kings,
And crowds and priests and suchlike things
Rolls deep and dreadful as he brings
    Their warning down from Runnymede.

Rudyard Kipling

THE SIMPLE MEMORIAL to the signing of Magna Carta was placed at Runnymede by the American Bar Association in 1957 as a mark of homage to the ideals shared in the traditions of the Common Law, some 750 years after the famous acceptance by King John of the rights of his barons. The English have taken it for granted. Visitors from overseas invariably wish to visit the site where English liberties were enshrined, at the first opportunity. British education does not include a compulsory history outing to Runnymede and Cooper's Hill. All too often schoolchildren are allowed to bypass Runnymede for neighbouring Thorpe Park, a theme playground, ignoring their heritage a scant 2000 yards away. (Who could blame *second-rate* teachers)?

The whole area of parkland is owned by the British nation under the auspices of the National Trust. While the general impression does little to stir the sentiment of so historic a site – there are no ripe-looking oak trees under which the signing can be imagined – the meadows provide a suitable picnic spot, if the visitor chooses to linger by the river.

Atop Cooper's Hill, the harmonious Memorial to the Commonwealth Air Forces provides a focal point, while nearby,

the treeline keeps a vigil on the memorial acre – given by the British nation to the peoples of the United States – devoted to the memory of the 35th President, John Fitzgerald Kennedy, which was unveiled in 1965.

Bad King John – et al.

King John is buried in Worcester Cathedral. His eldest son, Henry III, was crowned at Gloucester Abbey on October 28th, 1216, the ten-year old 'golden-haired, pretty, princely youth' whose 56-year reign was to restore his divided kingdom. The Plantagenet bulwark, William Marshall Pembroke, Earl of England, protected his royal protégé through the early uncertain peace, and, with the foes of the country to which he had devoted his service now banished, he died in old age, at Caversham Castle in 1219, confident that his own son, William Marshall the younger, who married the young King's sister, Eleanor, would continue his wise and provident influence at court. The funeral cortege of the architect of Magna Carta was floated on the Thames to Temple Steps where he is buried in the Crusaders' Church in the Temple. There, the young king drew his first adolescent tears in mourning the loss of his, and his realm's, great custodian.

London Stone

Taking leave of Runnymede in the Lower Thames Valley it is time for the visitor to harken to the call of the London Stone, planted below Runnymede Bridge, by Holm Island. The stone marks the former limit of the jurisdiction of the Lords Mayor of London. Downstream awaits the vast array of interesting places associated with England's fascinating past. Those who have become used to the direction of upstream – where vessels passing *'above'* as well as merely *'under'* a bridge – may now appreciate the distinction of downstream terminology; namely, in the less acrobatic movement of vessels which pass *'below'* the such-and-such bridge.

There is no better place to start this journey than at Westminster, to which the reader returns, by turning the page. Firstly, an interlude, to refresh the memory.

A cautionary tale . . .

The famous Clock Tower at Westminster (320 feet high) occupies the site of Edward I's ancient clock tower which summoned the judges of England – and their prisoners – by the death knell to trials held in Westminster Hall for over 500 years, until 1882, when the Royal Courts of Justice were commissioned in the Strand. The tower is known as Big Ben, which is in fact the name of the great bell, named after Sir Benjamin Hall, First Commissioner of Works at the time it was built (1875). The face of each dial is 22½ feet in diameter, enough for a London bus to pass through (if it were going in that direction). The famous bell, weighing 13½ tons, replaced the ancient Great Tom, and God alone knows who Tom was. However, the striking time-piece may be heard all over London on calm days, as was first proved in the 17thC, when a soldier's life was actually saved, because the clock struck thirteen at midnight by mistake.

> John Hatfield, on guard duty at Windsor Castle, was dismissed from his post and court-martialled for being found guilty of falling asleep at his post. Having protested his innocence, declaring that he had definitely heard a clock strike thirteen which was how he remembered he was awake at such an odd hour, a further charge of perjury was levelled at the hapless soldier. Under sentence of death, it was discovered that a detachment of guards at Westminster could verify the fact that Great Tom struck thirteen on that night, whereupon King William and Queen Mary, together signed a royal pardon for their faithful guard. Windsor is twenty miles from Westminster.

BELL OF BOW

ANOTHER BELL IN LONDON is as famous as Big Ben. It is Bow Bell. To be heard from the church of St. Mary-le-Bow downstream, where Cheapside leads from St. Paul's, in the City. According to English folklore, Dick Whittington heard Bow Bell at Highgate milestone (4 miles away, in north London) where he sat resting with his cat. It lifted his spirits, and enjoined him to –

> Turn again Whittington,
> Thrice Lord Mayor of London.

The Great Bell of Bow underscored; Sir Richard Whittington became Lord Mayor of London four times over, in 1395, 1401, 1406, and 1408. According to London tradition those born within the sound of Bow Bell are cockneys. The origin of the name given to a true-born Londoner is obscure but one of its earliest references was in 1250 –

> If I were in my castell of Bungeii-upon-the-water of Wauncie,
> I would not set a button by the king of Cockneie.
>
> *Hugh Bigod, Baron of Henry III.*

This reference may have been to the City of London, colloquially known sometimes as "Cockaigne", now considered old English. The word "cockney" came to mean someone ignorant of the outdoor life, such as a town-dweller. An old wives' tale illustrates the point for what it's worth. When a lass from London Town was restocking her larder from an itinerant grocer, she asked for a sack of barley –

> Merchant – Ay, missus, that be in great demand, begads, the price be high as much fine lace.
>
> Lass   – Be it high as silk, like silk is spun most fine?
>
> Merchant – Ay, I dar say, ay.
>
> Lass   – Tickerty-boo! Any fool could have guessed at that – even I can see that barley's got them threads left hanging out the ends.

A nice tale is also told of a citizen's son out riding in the fields with his father, very many centuries ago. Ignorant of the finer details that nature places in the way of the birds, bees and other animals, he was taken aback when his steed cavorted and snorted at a passing mare:

> "Wot the hoss did, Pater?"
> "The hoss doth neigh, dear boy."

Next a cock crowed, which puzzled the lad still further.

> "Doth the cock *neigh* too?"

Some Cockneys prefer to keep their time by Big Ben: the correct setting of watches is made on the opening chimes that precede the striking hour; the chimes are *said* to harmonise with Handel's opening bars for 'I know that my Redeemer liveth' (*attrib. Fred Pearson [20thC]*).

AT WESTMINSTER BRIDGE

The City of Westminster obtained its Charter of civic government from Queen Elizabeth I in 1585. Westminster was, from
earliest times the seat of national government, and its institutions
the cornerstone of the British Constitution. The Palace of
Westminster, together with the venerable Abbey of Westminster,
form probably the most important contribution to England's
heritage and the advancement of culture in the kingdom.

Houses of Parliament

The Houses of Parliament, one of the largest *Gothic* buildings in
the world, were built in 1843 after a fire swept the site of most of
its Parliamentary structure – Westminster and St. Stephen's Halls
being notable survivors – around which the Victorian architect,
Sir Charles Barry designed his renowned Tudor-style architectural
complex. The exterior stone used was magnesium limestone from
the Yorkshire quarries at Anston whereas the interior is of Caen
stone. From the water, the shimmering facade stretches away to
the points of lateral perspective, heightened and varied by the

vertical counterweights of the three great towers, advancing on the water's edge. The width of the river frontage is 940 feet: a glorious sight at any time of the year or day and whatever the weather.

The loftiest pinnacle is that of Victoria Tower, 336 ft. in height, at the southern perimetre, (as against Big Ben: 320 ft.). Juxtaposed between the two is the Central Spire which provides 300 ft. of ventilation shaft, apparently sufficient for the evacuation of the hot air that is generated by the members of the Upper and Lower Chambers.

The site of the Palace predates the Norman conquest and was the principal London residence of the Anglo-Saxon kings which royal tradition continued until Henry VIII, who removed to Whitehall Palace. In these precincts Edward the Confessor died, having begun his life's dedication to the shrine at Westminster Abbey, and it was here that he entertained his cousin, William, which laid the foundation of the Norman's claim to Harold's throne.

The oldest structure that survives, Westminster Hall is magnificent (but out of sight of the Thames. Proceed on foot past Big Ben, turn left where Churchill greets all-comers in Parliament Square – a noble image [Ivor Roberts-Jones, 1973] – and seek entry through the first entrance admitting the public, all quite easy).

Westminster Hall

The hall is the finest ancient chamber in Europe, built by William Rufus, the Conqueror's son, in 1097. It is noted for its beautiful timber-beamed roof, rebuilt by Richard II with Irish oak ('in which spiders cannot live'). His badge, the white hart is carved in multi-decoration throughout the lofts. It has the dimensions of one of the largest medieval structures in existence.

The home of the Common law

The Courts of Common Law, the King's courts, had their habitat here from before Magna Carta, and finally removed to the Strand with the building of the Royal Courts of Justice in 1882. Long and varied were the legal associations, including the profusion of lawyers in attendance, a fact that shook Peter the Great when visiting the shores 'for the maniac English habits' and prompted him to declare –

> But I have only two lawyers in all my dominions, and I mean to hang one of those when I get home.

Here were enacted the great State trials of England and where the once-proud were condemned, including, among the famous: Sir Thomas More (May 7, 1525), Protector Somerset (1551), Duke of Norfolk (1571), Robert Devereux, Earl of Essex (1603) and Guy Fawkes et al, (1606). Of all the tragic events that took place under Westminster Hall's roof, that of the trial, and condemnation of Charles I on January 27, 1649, is perhaps best remembered –

> The king, who during the reading of the sentence had smiled, and more than once had lifted his eyes to heaven, then said, 'Will you hear me a word, sir?'
>
> *Bradshaw* – 'You are not to be heard after the sentence.'
>
> The King: 'No, Sir?'
>
> *Bradshaw* – 'No, Sir, by our favour – Guards, withdraw your prisoner.'
>
> The King: 'I may speak after the sentence, by *your* favour, Sir . . .'
>
> *Bradshaw* – 'Hold!'
>
> The King: . . . 'I say, Sir, I do –'
>
> *Bradshaw* – 'Hold!'
>
> The King: I am not suffered to speak. EXPECT WHAT JUSTICE OTHER PEOPLE WILL HAVE . . .
>
> *[State Trial of Charles I].*

The Royal Champion

For all monarchs, spanning every accession from the Normans to George IV, there were happier memories too, in the coronation Banquets where the sacred oaths of allegiance were sworn and returned –

> before which, the mailed gauntlet of the Royal Champion, saddled in full armour, was hurtled to the ground, defying all-comers to mortal combat who would gainsay the rights of the sovereign, thrice repeated on horseback advancing down the hall, amidst a blaze of trumpets . . .
>
> *[The King's Chronicler: 14thC].*

Although the Royal Champion is no longer in evidence, his Charger lives on, in the unlikeliest of places.

The Royal Steed

Anyone who intends to be astonished by the size of a noble dashing white charger should pay a visit to the Brewery stables of Whitbread, north of St. Paul's, where the Shire horses, of the lineage of Crécy and Agincourt, lead their lives as dray-horses. Every year the Lord Mayor invites them to his Show and they

reciprocate the kindness by pulling him in his carriage. Each superhorse weighs upward of 1½ tons and thus is capable of carrying half its own weight again such as a knight's in full armour. They were to kings of England what tanks are to-day, armour-plated machines which commanded the battlefields of victorious English armies thundering about Europe. Those who visit the magnificent display of royal armour at the Tower of London can imagine the fine spectacle they presented, with someone like Henry VIII leading the way. They were literally worth their weight in gold – and are so to-day – should the interested visitor be wishing to take home a specimen. Their hulk should be compared with the puny specimen on which Coeur de Lion is astride beside the Peer's entrance to the House of Lords, an otherwise striking sculpture by Marochetti (1851). The Lionheart was mortally wounded by an archer's poisoned arrow at the Castle of Chaluz. Reliefs in the plinth recount the tragedy. His horse, so far as is known, escaped unhurt.

For the acquisitive-minded (which category might include the New York Customs officer, among other brethren), a used shire-shoe weighs half a stone and the diameter exceeds a dinner plate; attracts no duty as a second-hand good, and may be purchased from one of the stable lads. The trifling souvenir fits neatly into a hold-all, the one that is designated 'accompanied baggage' thus need not be weighted at the airline counter.

Meanwhile –

> To Whitbread now deigned majesty to say:
> 'Whitbread, are all your horses fond of hay?'
> 'Yes, please your majesty,' in humble tones
> The brewer answered – 'Also, sire, of oats;
> Another thing my horses, too, maintains,
> And that, an't please your majesty, are grains.
>
> 'Grains, grains,' said majesty, 'to fill their crops?
> Grains, grains, – that comes from hops – yes, hop, hop, hops?'
> Here was the king, like hounds sometimes at fault –
> 'Sire,' said the humble brewer, 'give me leave
> Your sacred majesty to undeceive;
> Grains, sire, are never made from hops, but malt.'
>
> *John Wolcot: A Satirical Poem. [1787). (extracts)*

The daily menu of a Whitebread horse is:

> 25 kilograms of fodder, 2½ kilos of carrots (turnips when not in season),
> ½ a gallon drum of horse-nuts (cob-nuts and 'wild' oats are reserved for their
> holidays in Kent), and 30 pints of water (spritzers of ale are served in pitchers
> on national holidays and after the Lord Mayor's Show).

The Mother of Parliaments

Many may wish to visit the shrine of Parliamentary democracy by attending one of its sittings. The union jack flies from Victoria Tower by day when the House of Commons is in session and the light in the turret of Big Ben is shown by night. Then, a study of the respective organs of government may be more fully investigated. For gastronomes, an invitation to dine at the House carries mixed blessings, but with it, at least, a finer understanding of political tastes –

> Members of the lower House are said to use a brand of sauce which
> goes by the name of 'HP' sauce [Houses of Parliament], surprisingly
> popular in canteens up and down the country. Members of the
> Upper Chamber prefer the taste of two Victorian chemists,
> Messrs Lea and Perrin, of Worcestershire, who made a fortune out
> of adapting their esteemed customer's recipe, which Lord Sandys
> invented to improve the taste of food in India where he spent a
> considerable time.

Of the many places to visit in Westminster, the Abbey and its adjoining Chapter House are a priority, for there, a rendez-vous with antiquity may best be kept. Pay·a visit to the Royal Chapels, too, for which purpose an outline of their significance should be learnt from the helpful vergers. Or wander about the precincts, enjoy the memories engendered by the memorials that virtually obscure the transcript walls in Poets' Corner, or the empty corners of the outlying Cloisters, where still the ghosts of the monks' brooding contemplatative silence reign. The Abbey Bookshop by the west door caters to every range of interest.

─────────── THE FISHERMEN'S TALE ───────────
OF THE FOUNDING OF THE ABBEY

Edric the fisherman, according to the Saxon Chronicler Sulcard, was watching his nets by the gravel bedrock of Thorney Isle at where the Thames bends and broadens downstream, when a stranger hailed from farther shore. Without a fish in sight, Edric agreed to ferry him across the river.

On landing at Thorney Isle, Edric watched in surprise as the stranger tapped the ground with his staff, muttering divine sayings, and lo, there gushed forth springs of pure water from the barren ground. More strangers appeared from nowhere whom Edric swore resembled angels, when of a sudden a voice from heaven was heard, as angels swirled in delirium, all now holding lighted candles.

Edric was commanded to inform his Bishop that on this hallowed ground a church was to be consecrated to St. Peter, whose very voice he heard, and that the keys to the church would be held by the Apostle 'for ever and a day' and in return that Edric would receive a plentiful supply of fishes provided he observed Sundays for reflection and offered his Bishop a tithe of his catch. Bishop Mellitus was called for, and visited the site upon where he saw the holy candlewax rendered in the shape of a cross. So in legend was the Collegiate Church of St. Peter founded at Westminser in 7thC.

As to the fisherman's story, the custom of paying a tithe of fish caught in the Thames continued until 1382 and formed the subject of a bitter dispute in 1231 between the monks of Westminster and the vicar of Rotherhithe (who claimed the salmon caught in his stretch of the parish boundary); the monks taking their protest to law, where they invoked the blessings of St. Peter, whom the vexed judge was unable to summon to court as a witness.

Where 'The Royals' are buried

The Kings and Queens of England, with rare exception, lie buried either in Westminster Abbey or St. George's Chapel at Windsor. Westminster Abbey was the traditional last resting-place of Sovereigns. However, since the Abbey is built on the rockstone promontory of Thorney's Isle, the foundations did not allow space for a crypt. By the time of the 18thC the royal vaults were full and the last Sovereign to join their ranks was George II. Thereafter St. George's Chapel filled the royal needs. For the first-time visitor, a visit to St. George's Chapel is almost to be preferred – with the glory of the castle thrown in – as compared with visiting the Abbey. The Abbey is a labyrinth of *monumental significance* and to appreciate fully (thereby not wasting one's time, or adding to the stifling queues) an approach is worth a little study.

> No-one can understand Westminster Abbey, and few can realise its beauties, in a single visit. Too many tombs will produce the same satiety as too many pictures. There can be no advantage, and there will be less pleasure, in filling the brain with a hopeless jumble in which kings and statesmen, warriors, ecclesiastics, and poets, are tossing about together . . .
>
> *Augustus Hare: Walks in London, vol.II. [1878].*

Those who pay a visit to the shrine of England's princes and sons of her heritage may like to remember that on Wednesday evenings it is open late, when the bustle of the coachloads has gone home and the resplendent architecture, together with the pro fusion of statuary, carvings, tombs and memorials become clothed in the music of twilight and the sweet chords of the great organ at evensong. Then is the moment to linger among the ancient portals, the glorious fan-tracery of the nave and choir, the solemn walkways of the cloister, with thoughts of pure heaven.

When in 1049 Edward the Confessor founded the 'Collegiate Church of St. Peter' at Westminster, on the ancient site of the

Minster at Thorney, in fulfilment of a sacred vow made to Pope Leo IX, and, the greatest church ever built in these isles was consecrated (December 28th, 1065) (eight days before his death), which he had lived to see.

The Norman dynasty which succeeded, and the early Plantagenets, were not buried at Westminster but either where they died – such as William Rufus, of an accident while riding in the New Forest (near Winchester); or Edward II, foully murdered – *cum veru ignito inter celanda confossus* [imagine how it hurt] at Berkeley Castle (near Gloucester), – or, were buried in their French motherland. For ease of reference, the following list of Sovereigns, together with their Consorts, is given in chronological order of date of death. Names in bold type denote burial in Westminster Abbey; nearly all held their Coronation in the Abbey.

KINGS AND QUEENS BURIED IN WESTMINSTER ABBEY:

For ease of reference, the following list of Sovereigns, together with their Consorts is given in chronological order of date of death.
Names in bold type denote burial in Westminster Abbey.

	1042–1066 **Edward the Confessor** aged 62	
	1066 HAROLD II aged 44 (Waltham Abbey)	
	Normans	
Willy, Willy, Harry, Steve,	1066–1087 WILLIAM the Conquer aged 60 (L'Abbaye aux Hommes, Caen)	Matilda of Flanders
	1087–1100 WILLIAM II [3rd son of WI] aged 43 (Winchester Cathedral)	Unmarried
	1100–1135 HENRY I [4th son of WI] aged 67 (Reading Abbey)	1. Matilda of Scotland 2. Adelicia of Louvaine
	1135–1154 STEPHEN aged 50 (Faversham Abbey)	Matilda of Boulogne
	Plantagenets	
Harry, Dick, John, Harry three,	1154–1189 HENRY II aged 56 (Fontevrault Abbaye, Chinon)	Eleanor of Aquitaine
	1189–1199 RICHARD coeur de lion [3rd son of HII] aged 42 (Fontevrault Abbaye)	Berengaria of Navarre
	1199–1216 JOHN [6th son of HII] aged 50 (Worcester Cathedral)	1. Avisa (divorced) 2. Isabella of Angouleme
	1216–1272 **Henry III** aged 65	**Eleanor of Provence**
One, two, three Neds, Richard Two,	**1272–1307 Edward I** aged 68	1. **Eleanor of Castile** [d. 1290] 2. Margaret of France
	1307–1327 EDWARD II murdered aged 43 (Gloucester Cathedral)	Unmarried

1327–1377 **Edward III** aged 65   = **Philippa of Hainault**

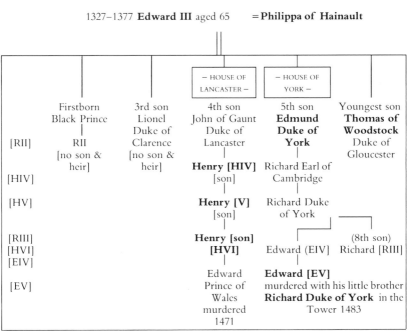

				HOUSE OF LANCASTER	HOUSE OF YORK	
	Firstborn Black Prince	3rd son Lionel Duke of	4th son John of Gaunt Duke of	5th son **Edmund Duke of**	Youngest son **Thomas of Woodstock**	
[RII]	RII [no son &	Clarence [no son &	Lancaster	**York**	Duke of Gloucester	
[HIV]	heir]	heir]	**Henry [HIV]** [son]	Richard Earl of Cambridge		
[HV]			**Henry [V]** [son]	Richard Duke of York		
[RIII] [HVI] [EIV]			**Henry [son]** **[HVI]**	Edward (EIV)	(8th son) Richard [RIII]	
[EV]			Edward Prince of Wales murdered 1471	**Edward [EV]** murdered with his little brother **Richard Duke of York** in the Tower 1483		

1377–1400 **Richard II** (son of Black Prince)   1. **Ann of**
            murdered aged 33   **Bohemia**
                                                         [d. 1394]
                                                      2. Isabelle of Valois

Harry four, five, 1399–1413 HENRY IV aged 46 (Canterbury   1. Mary de Bohun
six – then who?   Cathedral)   [d. 1394]
                                                             2. Joanna of Navarre

            1413–1422 **Henry V** aged 35, victor of   **Katherine of**
                      Agincourt   **Valois**
            1422–1471 HENRY VI aged 49 murdered (St.   Margaret of Anjou
                      George's Chapel, Windsor)
Edward, Edward, 1461–1483 EDWARD IV aged 44 (St. George's   Elizabeth of
Dick the Bad   Chapel, Windsor)   Woodville
            1483   **Edward V** aged 13 murdered   Unmarried
            1483–1485 RICHARD III slain aged 36   Anne of Warwick
                                                        [widow of HV]

    Thereafter in 1485, Henry Tudor, son of Owen Tudor and Henry V's widow Katherine, was proclaimed the first of the Tudor monarchs, and, but for his son Henry VIII and King Charles I, all the succeeding monarchs were buried in Westminster until, with George II's demise in 1760 the royal vaults were full.

Tudor

Henry, Harry,	1485–1509 **Henry VII** aged 53	**Elizabeth of York**
Ned the lad	1507–1547 **Henry VIII** aged 56 (Windsor)	
	Married 1. 1509: Catherine of Arragon (d. 1536)	*Divorced* (1533)
	2. 1533: Anne Boleyn	*Beheaded* (May 19, 1536)
	3. May 20, 1536: Jane Seymour	*Died* (1537)
	4. 1540: **Anne of Cleves** (d. 1557)	*Divorced* July 9, 1540
	5. July 10, 1540: Katharine Howard	*Beheaded* (1542)
	6. 1543: Katherine Parr (d. 1548)	*Survived*

	1547–1553 **Edward VI** aged 15 (son of Jane Seymour)	Unmarried
Mary, Bessy,	1553–1558 **Mary I** aged 43 (daughter by Catherine of Aragon)	Philip II of Spain
James the vain,	1558–1603 **Elizabeth I** (daughter by Anne Boleyn)	Unmarried

Stuarts

	1603–1625 **James I** (nearest relative) aged 59	**Anne of Denmark**
Charlie, Charlie,	1625–1649 **Charles I** *the Martyr*, beheaded Jan.	Henrietta Maria
James again;	30, aged 48 (St. George's, Windsor)	(d. 1669)
	1660–1685 **Charles II** *The Merry Monarch*, aged 55	Catharine of Braganza (d. 1705)
	1685–1701 **James II** [2nd son of CI] died in exile aged 68 (St. Germain, Paris)	Mary D'Este, of Modena (d. 1718)
William and	1689–1702 **William III** [son of CI's daughter,	
Mary, Anna	Mary] aged 51	
Gloria,	1694 and **Mary II** (elder daughter of JII) aged 33	
	1702–1714 **Anne** [daughter of JII], aged 49	married **George of Denmark** (d. 1708)

House of Hanover

Four Georges,	1714–1727 **George I**, aged 67	Sophia Dorothea of Zell (d. 1726)
William and		
Victoria;	1727–1760 **George II** (George Augustus) aged 77	Wilhelmina **Caroline of** Brandenburg-**Anspach** (d. 1737)

Since the reign of George II, all subsequent monarchs have been buried at Windsor, with rare exceptions: – *note.* (see previously) – **Edward IV, Henry VI, Henry VIII** and **Jane Seymour** (3rd Consort) **Charles I:** all buried at Windsor.

House of Hanover, contd.:-

	1760–1820 **George III** (George William Frederick) aged 81	Charlotte Sophia of Mechlenburg-Strelitz (d. 1818)
	1820–1830 **George IV** (George Augustus Frederick) aged 67	Caroline of Brunswick-Wolfenbüttel (d. 1821)
	1830–1837 **William IV** (3rd son of GIII) aged 71	Adelaide of Saxe-Meiningen (d. 1849)

	1837–1901 Victoria (daughter of 4th son of GIII) aged 81 (Frogmore)	Albert, Prince Consort (d. 1861) (Frogmore)
Edward Seven, George the Fifth,	1901–1910 **Edward VII** aged 68	**Alexandra** (d. 1925)
	House of Windsor	
	1910–1936 **George V** aged 70	**Queen Mary** [Princess May of Teck) d. 1953
Edward Eight and George the Sixth,	1936–[1972] Edward VIII aged 78 [Abd. 1936] (Frogmore)	Wallis Simpson (later, Duchess of Windsor, d. 1987)
	1936–1952 **George VI** (younger son of GV) aged 57	

Now we come to modern time   When you know who completes this rhyme!

. . . **Long live The Queen!**

Victoria Tower Gardens

Flanking the Houses of Parliament above Westminster Bridge are the Victoria Tower Gardens, with sweeping views of the riverscape.

> *Observe:* **RODIN'S BURGHERS OF CALAIS** (1915), a replica bronze (Calais, 1865) depicting Queen Philippa's intercession on their behalf to Edward III in 1340, whereby the English possession was saved from being sacked; the sculpture is on a plinth of 17 feet;

> **MRS. EMMELINE PANKHURST**, (1858–1928) and her daughter **DAME CHRISTABEL PANKHURST** (1881–1958) female emancipators a memorial by A.G. Walker (1930)

> Buxton Memorial Fountain, which commemorates **SIR. THOS. FOWELL BUXTON** (1786–1845), campaigner against slavery in the British dominions, designed by S.S. Teulon (1865). Eight of the statues of British rulers which adorned the spire were stolen (four in 1960, the remainder in 1971);

Lambeth Palace and Parish Church

Directly over the water Lambeth Palace snuggles behind its large garden wall which once fronted the Thames. Sir Thomas More would have used Lambeth Pier, on the Albert Embankment, to get to and fro' his home in Chelsea. The Thames Line riverbuses are intending the same route, as soon as local bureaucrats make up their minds that it is a good idea. The pretty church tower (St. Mary's) and the noble Gateway, dressed in red brick (built in 1490 when More was twelve years old, at about the time he was developing his leanings to the church) still stand out as a feature of the South Bank.

Lollards' Tower

A feature of the Palace is the Lollards' Tower, named after the 13thC pastor, but associated with the rabble which followed Wycliff in his uprising, who were imprisoned here. The Lollards Prison housed the condemned souls in a room measuring 13 feet long, 12 feet broad. Eight metal rings (no longer in use) protrude around the walls where the condemned were secured. The one nearest the window got a lovely view. In a room at the top, a secret trap-door let loose unwanted inmates into the Thames, at high tide. For many years, this portion of the Palace buildings was given over to Bishops of no fixed address, while in London.

The Albert Embankment

The Albert Embankment affords an exquisite view of Westminster along its waterside promenade between the two bridges of Lambeth and Westminster, in the fore of St. Thomas's Hospital. At this end of Westminster Bridge, Coade's famous lion turns its tail to the uninspiring bulk of County Hall, with a prominent river frontage (750 feet) and the central colonnade which appears to have been designed for giants, but we mere mortal dwarfs can only contemplate this municipal pomposity. The building was designed by Ralph Knott (1921-3) who did not live for its completion by his partner, Mr. Collins, in 1929. It is to be hoped that this architect passed away in a happier fashion than his distinguished counterparts who designed the Houses of Parliament, opposite; Sir Charles Barry – of a heart disease in 1860 – and Augustus Welby Pugin – nine years before, his mind –

> over-raught with excess of occupation, became unhinged in the year following, committed to Bedlam, died there.
>
> *[Dictionary of National Biography]*.

What price in human sacrifice their lordly halls of fame?

Coade's Lion

The quadruped was the mascot of the Lion Brewery, Lambeth. When it closed down the lion was rescued and was placed in its present position in 1952. On the site of County Hall stood Mrs. Eleanor Coade's Stone Factory. Mrs. Coade acquired the secret formula of the artificial terra-cotta stone after the patent of the inventor, Richard Holt (1720) lapsed, and at the same time acquired Holt's yard. By improving the formula she created a perfect weather-proof fabric, which was used in the adornment of many 18thC buildings.

Good examples survive in the frieze on W. facade of Buckingham Palace, Flaxman's frieze 'tragedy and Comedy' over the portico of the Royal Opera House, the table tomb of Capt. Bligh who is buried at nearby St. Mary's, Lambeth, and the memorials to the St. John family at St. Mary's, Battersea (see Upriver section); Mrs Coade's studios employed two noted sculptors, John Flaxman and John Bacon, (whose works may be seen in Westminster Abbey and St. Paul's Cathedral).

When Mrs. Coade died the factory closed (1840) and with her passing the secret formula was lost. Scientists today are unable to re-invent the composition.

County Hall

County Hall was opened by King George V in 1923 and was long the venerable headquarters of the London County Council disastrously superceded by the Greater London Council. This body was abolished during the second Ministry of the Rt. Hon. Margaret Thatcher, M.P.

Among other abysms of the Authority was its pernicious and wanton neglect of the guardianship of the River Thames.

Londoners are rightly affronted by this pitiful and bad waste. Access to prime portions of the riverbank has been denied to an entire generation. Huge tracts of land fronting the riverway are now closed to public right of way. Downstream development must consider incorporating pedestrian walkways and terraces (perhaps protruding over the water, by buildings already so positioned, with moorings for passing rivercraft to berth) in their grand schemes, so that future generations be permitted to enjoy their birthright and may also then think well of our generation in passing –

> Omne tulit punctum qui miscuit utile dolci
> He has gained every vote who has mingled profit with pleasure.
>
> *Horace: Ars Poetica [66 B.C.]*

Opening up the Highway

One institution, the River Thames Society, a private charity, is more dedicated than any great organ of government to open up the Thames and its banks, from source to mouth. Inter alia, for the public benefit, this Society has campaigned for a pedestrian way from Lechlade to Greenwich and, with the enthusiasm of their thriving membership, this great scheme is nearer than ever to realisation –

> Ille terrarum mihi praeter omnis, Angulus ridet.
> That nook of earth's surface has a smile for me before all other places.
>
> *(ibid): Odes II, vi.13*

Jubilee Gardens

Down–river side, the Jubilee Gardens extend over the site of the 1951 Festival of Britain and commemorate the 25th year of accession (1977) of H.M. The Queen. In the background looms the Shell Centre (designed by Sir Howard Robinson, 1962), another inescapable block of deadly dullness, comprising 43 acres of floor-space on its seven acre site. All is forgiven, however, by those who enjoy the magnificent views of the Capital from the top – 351 feet up, and 26 storeys high – to which the thoughtful owners invite members of the public. Waterloo Station is a few yards away for single-minded viewers.

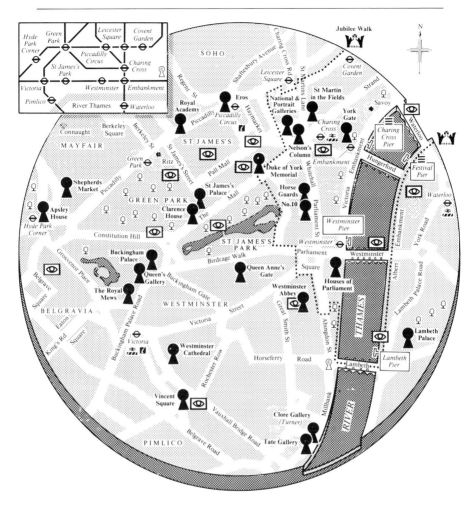

– Passing below –

WESTMINSTER
BRIDGE

*The full majesty of the Capital comes to view.
This, the fourth structure over the Thames –
following London's [1126], Kingston's [12thC]
and Putney's [1729] – is nevertheless regarded
as the second earliest bridge (1750) by reason of
its central location.*

Behold the City

On the left bank, or northern bank, the Victoria Embankment
stretches around the great curve of the river towards the City and
its renowned bridges, and the parallel South Bank leads the Great
Highway towards Docklands, Greenwich and the mighty Thames

Barrier at Woolwich, before it widens in the gaping mouth of its estuary.

The very number of historical monuments, with their links to the fame and fortune of England's past, impose an almost impossible task upon those intent on visiting, or in search of things that should not be missed, especially those with limited time at their disposal.

One of the ways to absorb London's grandeur before deciding on preferred visits and schedules is to embark on a rivertrip, such as the riverbuses now offer through the maze of Central London. From the relaxing decks of a riverboat, the skyline of London presents its profile ancient and modern, sometimes reminding the beholder of a place to be visited, sometimes nudging the onlooker's memory of a place to visit again.

> Who can weary, for example, of a stroll in Dr. Johnson's footsteps down Middle Temple Lane, hidden behind the trees of Temple Gardens? Boswell was a member of Inner Temple and Goldsmith lived in the 18thC enclaves of cobbled courts, and now lies buried beside the Crusaders' Church.

From the vantage point of the river, the famous silhouette of St. Paul's can be picked out. From the balustraded balcony of that cathedral dome, with its splendid view of London, Marshal von Blücher uttered his celebrated remark, after attending a banquet in Oxford –

Was für Plunder!
VOT a place to plunder!
[1814]

The river excursion downstream provides an opportunity to enjoy a new aspect of London, past and present.

By Westminster Pier begins the Victoria Embankment.

THE VICTORIA EMBANKMENT
– Between Westminster and Hungerford Bridge –

Old Scotland Yard

The turrets of Norman Shaw's splendid building (1888) dominate the treelined Victoria Embankment at Westminster Pier. The most famous 'yard' in the world [Scotland Yard] has since been

The great European pillow fight

Plunder was as much a part of 19thC campaigning as it had been in earliest centuries. Even the Iron Duke allowed it on occasions. He accepted it as an organised reward for hard fighting, after a siege for example, but frowned on casual looting and sometimes hanged those who indulged in it. No such orderly notions clouded the military thinking of Field-Marshal Blücher's forces or those of his Prussian descendants. One anecdote, apocryphal perhaps, but with a ring of truth is told by a French hotelier by way of explanation for the lack of pillows in French hotels.

In the Franco-Prussian War the Germanic soldiery prized above all the feather pillows and quilts, the down for which was so laboriously collected over the years by peasant families in their native land. The discovery that hotels in France, catering largely to the British tourist, were equipped with large numbers of feather pillows and eiderdowns was too much for the Teuton to bear. They seized them with relish and sent them home to rest their aching bones upon after their victories.

In the return match of the First World War, the battlegrounds were all in France and Belgium so the French had no chance to reclaim their plundered comforts back. By 1940, pillows were beginning to appear again when the Germans launched their *Blitzkrieg* and found themselves able to snatch even more pillows from all over France.

After the downfall of Hitler, the French troops occupying Germany were eager to see if they could, by way of reparations, get their pillows back. Alas the Prussian area of Germany where most pillows had ended up was in the Soviet sector and the Russians had collared the lot. The French case has been 'bolstered' ever since.

flattened, but denotes the site which was long the foreign soil of the kings of Scotland (since 800 A.D.) –

> . . . ye come to a large plot of ground inclosed with brick, and is called Scotland, where great buildings have been for receipt of the kings of Scotland.   *Stow's Survey [p. 168]*

Margaret, Queen of Scots, and sister to Henry VIII, lodged here when she came to town, obviously for a better view than most of her countrymen were later allowed by Dr. Johnson on his Tour of the Hebrides.

> Sir, the noblest prospect that a Scotchman ever sees, is the high road that leads him to London.   *[10 Nov. 1773].*

Places to visit within walking distance of Charing Cross Pier and Westminster Pier, West End:

– see Appendix for details –

North of the River –

Victoria Embankment Gardens [York Water Gate];

Trafalgar Square [Nelson's Column, statue of Charles I, National Gallery of Art, National Portrait Gallery, St. Martin's-in-the-Fields];

Covent Garden Piazza [Shopping mall and restaurants] – St. Paul's Church;

Whitehall – Horse Guards Parade [Changing of the mounted Guard] – Banqueting House – Downing Street – Cabinet War Rooms;

Westminster – Westminster Abbey – St. Margaret's – Westminster Cathedral – Royal Horticultural Society – Victoria Tower Gardens – Parliament's House of Commons – St. Anne's Gate, leading off St. James's Park – Buckingham Palace [Changing the Guard] – Queen's Gallery – Royal Mews –

Pimlico [3 Tube stops from Westminster, 4 stops from Embankment]: Tate Gallery – Clore Gallery;

St. James's and Piccadilly: St. James's Palace [Changing the Guard] – St. James's Street [Pickering Place] – St. James's Square – Pall Mall [Travellers Club] – Jermyn Street Shopping [Fortnum and Mason's] – Piccadilly [Bond Street – Royal Academy – St. James's Church – Eros] – Regent Street Shopping;

Further afield, by London Transport: The Temple [Middle Temple Hall, Temple Church, Squares, Lanes and Alleyways, Gardens] – St. Clement Dane's – St. Mary-le-Strand – Lincoln's Inn Fields [Sir John Soane Museum, Lincoln's Inn, Old Curiosity Shop] – Royal Courts of Justice – Dr. Johnson's House – Staple Inn;

Bloomsbury: British Museum – Dickens's House – Coram Fields – Coram Foundation – Courtauld Institute (of Art) – Jewish Museum;

South of the River (Festival Pier) –

St. Mary's Church – Tradescant Trust Gardens – Lambeth Palace – Imperial War Museum – Old Vic – Hayward Gallery – South Bank Arts Complex;

Be that as it may, Scotland Yard is more popularly associated with the most famous detective force in the world, now removed to New Scotland Yard a few hundred yards inland of Parliament Square, and immortalised forever in Conan Doyle's fables of the world super-sleuth, Sherlock Holmes.

Sherlock Holmes

The Sherlock Holmes Pub,replete with a replica of the detective's study, lies further along the Embankment, at Northumberland Street, and was presumably so-named for its proximity to Scotland Yard. In any event, its address shares no connection at all with Mr. Holmes's known haunts, (as will be revealed when we get half a mile downstream).

Victoria Embankment Gardens

In the gardens that were created from the tidal stretch recovered by Bazalgette in his grand design of the Embankment – he was knighted for stemming the stench of the sewers as well as the Thames – are the following statues placed between Westminster and Hungerford Bridges.

1 **AIR MARSHAL LORD TRENCHARD**, founder of the Royal Air Force, erected 1961; (William McMillan RA, 1961)

2 **AIR MARSHAL LORD PORTAL**, Chief of Air Staff (1940–45), statue by Oscar Nemon (1975);

3 **GENERAL GORDON *OF KHARTOUM*** (he was hacked to death by the Mad Mahdi's henchmen in the Sudan, but later buried with full military honours, 1885) statue by Sir Hamo Thornycroft [1888]; – behind Queen Mary's Steps (designed by Sir Christopher Wren, 1691) providing the access from old Whitehall Palace to the royal barge stairs;

4 **WILLIAM TYNDALE**, translator of the Bible, martyred 1536 (burnt at the stake at the instigation of Henry VIII's spies, Antwerp) statue by Sir Edgar Boehm, 1884;

5 **SIR HENRY BARTLE FRERE**, 19thC administrator (who negotiated the end of the East African Slave Trade), statue by Sir Thomas Brock (1888);

6 **GENERAL SIR JAMES OUTRAM, Bart.**, hero of the Indian Mutiny, [from the British point of view], statue by Matthew Noble, RA, 1871;

7 **SAMUEL PLIMSOLL** 'the sailors friend', who initiated the (Plimsoll) Load Line, a familiar mark on ships' hulls whereby overloading was banned, sculpture by Ferdinance von Blundston (1929);

8 **SIR JOSEPH W BAZALGETTE**, engineer, bust by George Simonds (1899), memorial on Embankment riverwall, nearest Hungerford Bridge.

Of Whitehall Palace

Whitehall Palace was traditionally the London seat of the Archbishopric of York, until Henry VIII moved in. All that remains of the site are Henry VIII's wine cellars and the elegant building in Whitehall (out of sight) – the Banqueting House. Whitehall Palace was to reach its zenith in the era of the Stuarts. Inigo Jones designed the Banqueting House (1619) as part of the palatial surroundings that would make London pre-eminent in Europe's league of royal residences, (as conceived by Wren).

In the Palladian style, the building was the first of its kind in England and is built of stone floated up the Thames brought all the way by sea from Portland Bill. ("The Gibraltar of Wessex" – Thomas Hardy [1872]).

> To-day visitors may tour the interior, noted for the magnificent ceiling by Rubens, which earned him £3,000 and a knighthood. On the other hand, Inigo Jones received only 8s. 4d. per diem, together with £46 per annum for house-rent.

'The most polite court in Europe'

Whitehall attained unsurpassed splendour in the reign of Charles I:

> . . . and I have no doubt that the celebrated festivals of Louis the Fourteenth *were copied* from the shows exhibited at Whitehall, in its time the most polite court in Europe.
> Ben Jonson was the laureate, Inigo Jones the inventor of the decorations; Lamière and Ferabosco composed the symphonies; the King, the Queen, and the young nobility danced in the interludes.
> *Walpole's Works, iii. p. 271 [18thC].*

Little could James I have imagined that he was raising a palace from which his son was to walk to the scaffold –

"Remember,"

Last word of King Charles the Martyr, (intended for Archbishop Usher, but who had fainted on the spot), shortly before his execution: 30th January, 1649.

A universal groan was uttered by the people, as if by one consent, such as never was heard before.   *Ellis's "Letters", (vol. iii, p. 333.)*

Inigo Jones' plans would have covered 24 acres, to be compared with –
Hampton Court,   8 acres;
St. James's Palace,   4 acres;
Buckingham Palace,2½ acres.
It would have dwarfed the Louvre, and rivalled Versailles.

The coincidence of deaths

Looking at the fine Hall from Whitehall, admire the gracious
windows of the first floor banqueting suite (available for hire for
private functions, since 1987). From the most northerly end the
Martyr King stepped onto the raised scaffold, to meet his Maker
and his end.

Almost exactly a century before to the day (two years more and
two days less, to the pedantic), on the 28th of January 1547,
Charles's great, great, great-uncle, the bluff and terrible King Hal
died at Whitehall too. No ceremony surrounded his end, no crowd
bemoaned his passing. Ironically, fourteen years before his death,
just a few yards from where he lay, he had been secretly married
to his mistress, Anne Boleyn.

Present at those covert nuptials were three witnesses, one –
Norris, Keeper of the Bedchamber – was to follow the ill-fated
young bride to the scaffold.

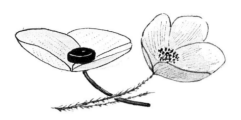

'WE WILL REMEMBER THEM . . .'

In Whitehall itself stands The Cenotaph. This simple monument was designed by Sir Edwin Lutyens, RA, as a stone effigy past which the surviving troops were to parade when they returned to the kingdom to honour their comrades who would never return to homes throughout the Empire. Their wartime leader, before he assumed that role, seemed to prophesy such a structure in the first days of the war.

> . . . we can see the great everlasting things that matter for a nation; the great peaks of honour we had forgotten – duty and patriotism clad in glittering white; the great pinnacle of sacrifice pointing like a rugged finger to heaven.
> *David Lloyd George: Speech, Queen's Hall, London: 19 September 1914.*

On the eleventh hour of the eleventh day of the eleventh month, 1918, being Armistice Day, hostilities ceased between warring nations in the battleground of Europe.

Now he asked –

> What is our task? To make Britain a fit country for heroes to live in.
> *Ibid: 24 November, 1918.*

Those who have fallen in the cause of freedom in two world wars are proudly honoured by the British people, annually on Remembrance Day, the Sunday nearest to Armistice Day. At precisely 11 o'clock, H.M. The Queen of Great Britain and Northern Ireland, Queen of the Dominions and Head of the Commonwealth stands in two minutes' silence before she lays the wreath of poppies to honour the valour of the slain.

> They shall grow not old, as we that are left grow old:
> Age shall not weary them, nor the years condemn.
> At the going down of the sun and in the morning
> We will remember them.
> *Laurence Binyon: For the Fallen. [1920]*

Near the Cenotaph

Further along Whitehall is Horse Guards Parade, where the colourful mounting of the Guard ceremony – symbolising hundreds of years of chivalry – takes place at 11 o'clock daily (Sundays at 10 a.m.), and the Dismounted Inspection at 4 o'clock, day in day out.

Back on the rivertrip, the next building in view is the lofty, palatial mansion block of Whitehall Court (designed by Archer and Green who also built the Café Royal) [1884]), used variously over the years until, recently, opened as the Royal Horseguards Hotel, with splendid views from the riverside bedroom suite windows, at a modest starting price of £145 per night, for double occupancy vision.

In the last War, the American Embassy appropriated one floor, while the Russians took the entire space below, on the 5th floor. The management at the time deployed separate elevators and puzzled staff were given an elementary lesson in Communist principles. Ebenezer Elliot [1781–1849] neatly summed up the

basis of the Soviets' creed well before Marx published his wotnot
and well before he landed (1848) on these shores –

> What is a communist? One who has yearnings
> For equal division of unequal earnings.

(pronounced "Wee-sar.")

The rooms in the hotel continue to enjoy an excellent
reputation in the reliable quality of sound-proofing installation,
regularly overlooked by inferior establishments. Perhaps this is
why the Russians came to stay here. Happy go lucky capitalists.

– Passing below –

HUNGERFORD
BRIDGE

---

which links Charing Cross Station (left) with the tracks that
remain of the London, Chatham and Dover Railway (erected
1866). The pedestrian foot-bridge, as also it is, replaced the famous
Hungerford Suspension Bridge, Brunel's famous masterpiece
(1845) whose chains now occupy the prime position over the river
Avon gorge, on the Clifton Suspension Bridge.

This footbridge is very useful for those who wish to cross the
Thames between Waterloo and the civilisation on the northern
side, or, contrariwise.

South Bank

On the starboard bow the South Bank Arts Complex comes into
hideous view. This Centre of concrete bunkers comprises the
Festival Hall and was built to honour the Festival of Britain (Sirs
R. Hall and L. Martin, architects 1951). The cultural pavilions of
the Arts, the Purcell Room, Queen Elizabeth II Hall and the
Hayward Gallery, enable London to continue its proud tradition

of patronage of the performing arts. There may be many who
would agree with the suggestion made in a letter to *The Times* –

. . . I suggest a "plant a
virginia creeper year" would
greatly enhance London. My
choice of site to begin the
campaign would be the South
Bank Centre.

Yours faithfully,
Norman Stevens,
Royal Academy of Arts,
Piccadilly, W1.

[May 5th, 1988].

London's Clearway

From here enjoy the panorama of the Victoria Embankment
between Hungerford and Waterloo Bridges. Charing Cross Pier,
conveniently situated close to the Embankment Tube line and
Charing Cross station in the Strand, now caters for such travellers
who wish to enjoy the passage by water to:

Cadogan Pier and Chelsea Harbour (*Pier*), upriver,

or downstream to:
Swan Lane Pier, London Bridge City (*Pier*), Rotherhithe's Cherry
Garden Pier, and beyond, to the Isle of Dogs,

in journeys that take the strain out of crossing London.

Statues in the Victoria Embankment Gardens

On the Hungerford Bridge side of the Embankment, the
pedestrian will notice, in the continuation of gardens:

9 **ROBERT BURNS** (1759–1796) Scottish poet (statue by Sir John
Steell, 1884);

10 **IMPERIAL CAMEL CORPS** (1916–1918) comprising the Australian,
British, Indian and New Zealand soldiers (sculpted by Major Cecil
Brown [1920];

11 **LORD CHEYLESMORE** (1848–1925), Officer (Colonel of the
Coldstream Guards), Gentleman (3rd Baron) and civic dignitary,
memorial by Sir Edwin Lutyens RA [1930];

12 **SIR WILFRED LAWSON** (1829–1906), politician, (statue by David
McGill, 1909);

13 **HENRY FAWCETT** (1833–1884), blind politician, (bronze medallion
by Mary Grant, fountain by Basil Champneys (1886);

14 **ROBERT RAIKES** (1735–1811). Founder of the 1st Sunday School in
1780, sculpted by Sir Thomas Brock RA (1880);

Immediately to the rear of this pious gentleman is to be found
an interesting and unique phenomenon. On the left hand side of
Carting Lane there stands a gas-light permanently illuminated by
the methane gas which runs beneath the length of the
Embankment.

Hardby the pier may be seen the Victoria Embankment
Gardens, continuing to Waterloo Bridge. There to be enjoyed,
especially in summer when the plane trees cool the breeze and
during lunchtime as military and other bands strike up from the
modern bandstand.

Victoria Embankment *continued*

– between Hungerford and Waterloo Bridges –

The York House water gate

A century after Cardinal Wolsey's ignominious departure from
public life and the seizure of his residence, York House, Inigo
Jones was commissioned to design the handsome structure seen
today. The Gate was built in 1626 and executed by Nicholas Stone
for Charles Villiers, the Ist Duke of Buckingham (whose arms and
motto are incorporated in the stonework), the self-same adulterer
who slew the husband of his lover at Cliveden. Its position marks
the natural width and level of the Thames before 1866. Soon, the
water gate will be landscaped, again adorned by water, to look as
it was intended.

The glorious sky line

Occasional glimpses of Nelson on his column in Trafalgar Square
may be had as the passing view from the water slides in between
openings in the mass of masonry and rooftops. The familiar figure
of England's favourite Admiral, his good eye facing Merton Park
– the Hamilton residence, upstream – was placed up there, rather

aloofly [184 feet] in 1843. His is the figure that struck Taine, the Frenchman, soon afterwards, as –

That hideous *Nelson, stuck on his column with a coil of rope in the form of a pigtail, like a rat impaled on the top of a pole.*

An understandable example of Gallic exaggeration would certainly not have been tolerated by Dr. Johnson –

London! the needy villain's
  gen'ral home
The common shore of Paris
  and of Rome;
With eager thirst, by folly
  or by fate
Sucks in the dregs of each
  corrupted state
Forgive my transports on a
  theme like this
I cannot bear a French
  metropolis.
Samuel Johnson, London, 1738

A storm in a tea-cup

In any case, the 'villainous' writer would doubtless have been more outraged than ever had the buildings of Waterloo station (1848, rebuilt 1901), just across the water, been completed by the time of his visit. He took too little time to reflect that –

Paris is the City of the Great King, London of the Great People.
Paris strikes the vulgar part of us infinitely the more, but to a
thinking mind London is incomparably the most delightful subject
for contemplation.
Samuel Rogers: Italian Journal [30 August 1814].

Northumberland Avenue leads down from Trafalgar Square –
which celebrates the glorious defeats of the French nation in the
Battles of the Nile, St. Vincent, Copenhagen – set in bas relief at
the base of Admiral Nelson's pedestal – to name but a modest few
of many outstanding English victories. Just by the York Gate in
Villiers Street may be found the curious old cellars (1364)
inhabited by Gordon's wine bar, an ideal 'watering-hole' where
those with a taste for history may linger on; fine wine and 'help-
yourself salads'. Rudyard Kipling lived above, in 43 Villiers
Street, before the turn of the century.

Continuing along the Victoria Embankment

The buildings behind the Gate and the Gardens form a riverside
development called the Adelphi Terrace, built by four enterprising brothers, John, Robert, James, and William Adam in the latter
half of the 18thC. The streets leading to the Strand commemorate
their names, as does the Greek word 'Adelphi' (meaning brothers).

Another tea-cup

In Craven Street nearby, lived Benjamin Franklin (at no. 34) and
as many travellers visit his one-time home as seem to pay their
respects to Mr. Sherlock Holmes, at the public house in
Northumberland Street and where, reputedly, his tea-cup is
replenished daily.

Why Dr. Conan Doyle did not choose 21, Baker Street for Sherlock Holmes

Before writing his first novel (A Study in Scarlet, 1887) Conan
Doyle discussed the character he intended to create with a close
friend, and medical practitioner, Dr. Malcolm Morris (later Sir
Malcolm), whose reaction was sought to the medical points
arising in the science of deduction as well as the consideration of
where Holmes should live. Morris ventured the address of his own
grandfather, John Morris, of 21, Baker Street, adding that he had
the particulars of sale, should Conan Doyle wish to use them to
provide an authentic touch.

Because the house (21, Baker Street) was privately occupied,
Conan Doyle invented the appellation '221B', and further altered
the lay-out slightly – to avoid identification – and any irritation to
the owners that a fictional character *with odd-ball associates* might
engender.

Clues exist to confirm that Sherlock Holmes lived at the southern end of Baker Street, as opposed to the northern end, where the premises of the Abbey National Building Society purport to stand on the invented number – as when Watson answers Holmes –

> 'Do you know where we are?' he whispered.
> 'Surely that is Baker Street, 'I answered, staring through the dim window.
> 'Exactly. We are in Camden House, which stands opposite to our own old quarters.'
>
> *The Adventure of the Empty House.*

Camden House is number 22, Baker Street, from which position Colonel Sebastian Moran (the second most dangerous man in London, it will be recalled) took aim at the wax model of Sherlock Holmes in the hope of killing him. Had the would-be assassin of the great detective chosen number 20 or 22 Baker Street from which to take a pot-shot into 221B, he would – unless he held implicit faith in the range of his air-gun – hardly have chosen that position.

Again, Dr. Watson used the Wigmore Street Post Office to 'send off his telegram' and Sherlock Holmes used the tobacconist, Bradley's, in Oxford Street, which were more convenient to residents of the southern end of Baker Street. Presumably, they would have used the Melcombe Street shops, as opposed to the other ones nearly three-quarters of a mile from 221B, had Conan Doyle intended them to live other than where they did.

The legend lives on

Whatever his address was in fact or fiction and many years after his natural lifespan, letters are still addressed to him and arrive in the London sorting office for the great detective. Many of these missives, incredible though it is to believe, come from people in the Third World with genuine and often insoluble problems.

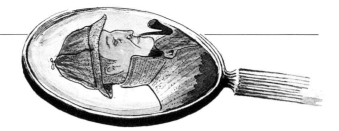

The Unfolding Mysteries of the River Thames

"Well, Holmes! So much for the river Thames. I can warrant that we have conned it, quizzed it, viewed it and studied it sufficiently to say that we pretty well know the Thames."

Holmes rose up and went to the window. He stood looking, out, into the London twilight.

"So you have finally understood the Thames, Watson."
Holmes's voice had a cold, dismissive quality. He turned. He was now outlined by the light relief of dusk falling from the window behind him.

"What you have seen, Watson, is merely the sweet face of the Thames. You have seen the spring and summer and not looked winter in the face."
The light behind dulled. His eyes now invisible, were only detectable by the very edge of the cheek-bone, framing the blackness of his eye-sockets.

"It's down river that spells danger, Watson, so much danger has come from there."

He took a silk 'kerchief from his waistcoat pocket and mopped his brow.
"Saxons, Danes, Vikings, Romans, Dutchmen, Spaniards and Frenchmen. They've all tried, Watson: some of them succeeded, some might yet."

"Good Lord, Holmes," I cried, "Do you mean that this island nation is still in danger from invaders who might come from the mouth of the Thames? What on earth can we do to stop such a catastrophe?"

"There are defences," said the great man, "The Tower, Tilbury and Gravesend, Watson." He nodded, slowly. "Guns at Woolwich, Watson, a network of gunfire."

I was amazed to hear how strongly defended London had been, to what effect, I wondered.
"How effective was it, Holmes? How will we ever know if those defences stopped them? Or was it something else. How will we ever know, Holmes?"

"Elementary, my dear Watson," The great man said quietly. "Read London on Thames (down stream)."

Extract [Chapter I, Volume Two:
LONDON ON THAMES: DOWNSTREAM]
World Exclusive [20thC].

- A WORD ABOUT ENGLISH TITLES -

The titles of the English aristocracy are sprinkled around the stately homes of England with bewildering ease by guides as well as being dropped, endlessly, in official literature. At the mention of a famous name it seems to be assumed that everyone should know exactly Who was Who and, sometimes, one suspects, these names are bandered about merely to impress.

The matter is not of the easiest to grasp. In any visit to an historic house the visitor's mind is required to leap over the centuries, as compressed within the hour or two devoted to the visit in hand. Thus the titled portraits hang about the place like confetti; an avalance of big names get dropped in the background literature or *spiel*. All this tends to obscure the tenuous thread of historical comprehension.

To understand the significance of titles, firstly the importance of the nobility in order of rank:

Hereditary titles:

Duke (First Dukedom 1338, Black Prince, D. of Cornwall; Last non-royal Duke, D. of Westminster 1874)
"Your grace" "Our right trusty & right entirely beloved Cousin"

Marquis (First Marquis 1385, M. of Oxford)
"Your Lordship" "Our right trusty and entirely beloved Cousin"

Earl (Anglo-Saxon origins)
"Your Lordship" "Our right trusty and well beloved Cousin"

Viscount (First Viscount 1440)
"Your Lordship"

Baron (Norman origin)
Baronetcy [established by James I (1603)]
"My Lord"
"Sir A.B."

Non-hereditary titles:
Life Barons (introduced in 1956: known as "lifers")
Note Royal Dukes: the sons of the Sovereign enjoy precedence over all other nobles but their title lapses on their death.

NOBLESSE OBLIGE
Foreign visitors from more democratic lands are often puzzled and not a little over-awed by the titles of some of the owners of the great houses they visit. They may well feel that, if they meet a duke or an earl with a name that has a truly Shakespearean ring to it, they are meeting the direct descendant of one who fought at Agincourt alongside Henry V, or at least was mentioned in the Wars of the Roses.

Things are not that single, as Lord Home (pronounced Hugh-m) pointed out, when, relinquishing his earldom to enter the House of Commons as prime minister, he put down the leader of the opposition – who had taunted him for being the 14th earl – with words to the effect –

Aren't you the 14*th* Mr. Wilson?
[1963].

In Sir Alec Douglas-Home's case, he *was* the direct descendant of the first holder of that title.

Not so some others. Titles once granted could, and frequently did, lapse for either the want of a male heir (being a legitimate heir) or because the individual holder was stripped of social status. The latter process worked by the Act of Attainder, whereby the king issued a Bill of Attainder against the title-holder – usually for an act of treason – who was then stripped of his rank. Another consequence of this was the forfeiture of the attainted's lands and inheritance. Henry VIII used this royal prerogative to great effect upon his courtiers, besides swelling his coffers. The following illustrations make the point:

Earls of Essex (portraits of members of the family of Devereux to be seen in Hampton Court, Southside House and Windsor Castle) –

	Family –	holders –
1st creation	Mandeville	1st earl, d.1144, 2nd: d.1189, 3rd; 4th: d.1213 (A*);
2nd creation	de Bohun	1st earl, d.1274, 2nd: d.1298, 3rd: d.1322 (A*);
3rd creation	Bourchier	1st earl, d.1483, 2nd: d.1539; (A*);
4th creation	Cromwell	1st earl, (Thomas) ex.1540 (B*);
5th creation	Parr	1st earl, (William) d.1571 (A*);
6th creation	Devereux	1st earl, d.1576; 2nd: ex.1601 (C*), 3rd: d.1646;
7th creation	Capel	1st earl, d.1683, 2nd: d.1743; [thereafter title lapsed].

footnotes – A=lapsed, B=executed (attainted), C=re-created, conferred on son. The Act of Attainder was promulgated in 1499 and abolished in 1844.

Occasionally, in the absence of a male heir, the king allowed the title to pass down the female line by remainder. Such an heiress was a prize for the successful suitor (often a commoner with scheming ambition). Take, for example, the Northumberland title (– their seat, Syon House, is a prime riverside attraction –): the current holder's family has borne the noble title for a mere two centuries, only:

Earls of Northumberland:

	Family –	holders –
1st creation	de Mowbray	1st earl, d.1125
	Percy	1st earl, d.1408, 2nd: d.1455, 3rd: d.1461;
	Algernon	4th: d.1489 (D*), 5th: d.1527, 6th: d.1537, 7th: d.1572, 8th: d.1585, 9th: d.1632, 10th [Algernon Percy] d.1668 (E*)

Dukes of Northumberland:

1st creation	Dudley	1st duke, ex.1553 (B*supra);
2nd creation	Fitzroy	1st duke, d.1716;
3rd creation	Smithson	1st duke, d.1786 (F*), 2nd: d.1817; 3rd: d.1847; 4th: d.1865; 5th: d.1867; 6th: d.1899; 7th: d.1918; 8th: d.1930; 9th: killed in action, 1944; 10th: incumbent.

footnotes – D=inherited from Howard family; E=Thereafter, his grandson's earldom was remaindered to his only daughter, who married Sir Hugh Smithson; F=created Duke of Northumberland in 1766, whose descendants adopted the Percy name. (Source: Augustus J.C. Hare, Walks in London [1877]).

As for the Dukedom of Westminster, this title is very 'nouveau': Hugh Lupus Grosvenor, 3rd Marqis of Westminster, was made the first duke in 1874 and, but for royal dukes –

e.g. of Windsor, Edinburgh, Gloucester, Kent, Cornwall, York, or duchesses in their own right e.g. of Fife (1912)

– was the second to last ever created. Of course, Sir Winston Churchill K.G. was offered one but spurned the honour. He was already a Knight of the Most Noble Order of the Garter. What more could he want for?
As to the Orders of Chivalry that is quite another matter (to be canvassed in the forthcoming edition of London on Thames-Downstream).

"Which place first
tomorrow?"

APPENDIX OF PLACES

This Appendix lists a variety of places of interest in and around London in addition to those in Upstream locations. Places or items forming the nucleus of an excursion to a particular location are grouped together where possible; and by alphabetical cross-reference. Riverside neighbourhoods that feature in this Upstream volume are mentioned, in the main, on the page numbers appearing in the circle diagram, and as listed in the Appendix in individual boxes.

Please note –

Admission times:	24 hour clock is used, applying to hours of opening in British summertime; in winter, places usually open later and close earlier.
Days of admission:	The seven weekdays, commencing Monday [M] Tuesday [Tu] Wednesday [W] Thursday [Th] Friday [F] Saturday [Sa] Sunday [Su] are listed in sequence, following the hours of opening given for those particular days. Different times of opening, if applicable to other days, are stated separately.
Days of closure:	On Good Friday, Christmas Eve, Christmas Day, Boxing Day, New Year's Day, May Day, Spring and Summer Bank Holidays, and variously, most places shut: **visitors should check** dates and admission times generally, before embarking on a visit.
	When a place is closed, this is denoted by leaving a blank space on the day(s) in question –
	Example. (Banqueting House) 1000–1700 – Tu W Th F Sa, = closed on Mondays 1400–1700 Su = different hours on Sundays
Admission charges:	Admission charges vary and are not listed. Places denoted by an asterisk [*] provide free admission (although the visitor is not forbidden from leaving a small contribution behind if he or she has enjoyed the time so spent).
Facilities for handicapped persons:	Information which may be very relevant to such persons' ability to enjoy their visit to a given place or location is not included in the Appendix: facilities vary greatly and sometimes do not exist (– try viewing the Crown Jewels, after all those cobbled walkways in the Tower of London, by wheelchair). Readers in need of information, and guidance, should contact the place or building intended to be visited by telephone beforehand.
Sundry information:	About places of refreshment: establishments so listed are provided by way of information only.
Telephone numbers:	Where London numbers are given (i.e. 7 digits), the additional prefix [01-] should be dialled when calling from outside the metropolis. Telephone numbers can change or be out of order: check with Directory Enquiries: 142 – London, 192 – countrywide.

Albert Memorial Chapel, Windsor Box
All England Lawn Tennis and Croquet Association, Wimbledon Box
ALL HALLOWS BY THE TOWER Byward Street EC3
T.481–2928 *historic church, undercroft museum*
   0900–1730 M Tu W Th F Sa Su [service: **1100**]
APSLEY HOUSE 149 Piccadilly W1 T.499–5676 *Town residence of 1st Duke of Wellington*
   1000–1800 – Tu W Th – Sa, 1430–1800 Su
ASHBURNHAM HOUSE Dean's Yard Westminster SW1
T.222–3116 *historic home of Earls of Ashburnham*
During Easter holidays only: **1000–1600 M Tu W Th F – –**
BANK OF ENGLAND Threadneedle Street City EC2
Admission by prior written arrangment
BANQUETING HOUSE Whitehall SW1T.930–4179 *sole existing portion of Whitehall Palace designed by Inigo Jones,* ★ *Rubens ceiling*
   1000–1700 – Tu W Th F Sa, 1400–1700 Su
Barnes, Thames-side village, page 53
ST. BARTHOLOMEW THE GREAT ★ Smithfield EC1
T.606–5171/1575 *oldest [1123] church in London*
   0900–1630 M Tu W Th F Sa Su [services **0900, 1100, 1830**]
Battersea, Thames-side village

--------------- BATTERSEA ---------------
   (and see neighbouring Chelsea) – 24, 36–45
Access: tube, Sloane Square and bus, 19 or 137
BR, Battersea Park
Boat, riverbus to Cadogan Pier and walk over bridge
BATTERSEA DOGS' HOME ★ Battersea Park Road SW18
T.622–3626 *Prospective owners of lost dogs welcomed (note Sunday viewing restricted to owners seeking their dog(s))*
   1030–1615 M Tu W Th F Sa, 1400–1600 Su [see note]
BATTERSEA PARK ★ Battersea Park Road SW11 *198 acres facing Chelsea* **Dawn to Dusk**
BATTERSEA PARISH CHURCH, ST. MARY'S, ★ Battersea
Church Road SE11 *historic church*
(Keys by arrangement with The Vicarage)
BATTERSEA LEISURE PARK Battersea Power Station SW8
T.720–3000 *leisure complex due open 21/5/90*
OLD BATTERSEA HOUSE Vicarage Crescent SE11
(visit by arrangement: write – De Morgan Trust 21 St.
Margaret's Crescent SW15 *small collection of ceramics and paintings*

HMS BELFAST River Thames (Nr London Bridge) *Former Royal Naval cruiser now a floating museum*
   1100–1750 M Tu W Th F Sa Su (**–1630**, Winter)
Blind, National Library for, p.246
Boat trips on the river Thames,
Central London: pp 16, 17, maps inside front cover
Upstream services: pp 70, 71 et seq. [from and to – Hampton Court, Kingston-upon-Thames, Richmond]
Bow Bells, City Church of St. Mary-le-Bow
Bridges, *Banner Maps,* front & back of book
ST. BRIDE'S ★ Church Fleet Street EC4 T.01–353–1301 *notable City church by Wren*
   0830–1730 M Tu W Th F Sa, –2030 Su [music recitals **1315: Tu W F**]
British Heritage Motor Museum, Syon Park
BRITISH MUSEUM ★ Great Russell Street Bloomsbury WC1
T.636–1555 (recorded information T.01–580–1788) *National collections of archaeology, prints, drawings, coins, medallions, ethnography, et cet., inc. Elgin Marbles*
   1000–1700 M Tu W Th F Sa Su, 1430–1800 Su
BROMPTON ORATORY ★ Brompton Road Knightsbridge SW7
T.589–4811 *sumptuous Roman Catholic place of worship*
   0630–2000 M Tu W Th F Sa Su [Solemn Mass in Latin **1100**]
BUCKINGHAM PALACE London SW1
Admission by prior Invitation only
[Press Office: T.930–4832]
see, also – Ceremony of the Changing of the Guard – Queen's Gallery – Royal Mews
Signing the Visitors' Book – Visitors to London may like to sign the book at Buckingham Palace by enquiring of the police officer on duty in the [right-hand] Gate House. Please *note* – Maximum six persons at any one time; not permitted when forecourt is busy; sole discretion reserved by duty officer.
Butterfly House, Syon Park
CABINET WAR ROOMS Clive Steps King Charles Street SW1
T.930–6961 *Churchill's war-time bunker*
   1000–1750 – Tu W Th F Sa Su

CAFÉ ROYAL 68 Regent's Street, W1 T.437–9090 *sit in style, where the likes of Augustus John and Oscar Wilde entertained! Ask (if you dare) how Enid Bagnold 'went through the gateway to life' (in an upper room).*
Cannizaro House and Park, Wimbledon Box
CENTRAL CRIMINAL COURT Old Bailey Street, City of London EC4 T.248–3277 *(referred to as 'Old Bailey', forum for major criminal trials conducted before a jury)*
   Public Admission – 1015–1545 M Tu W Th F – –, excepting luncheon recess **1300–1400** [or longer]
Ceremony of the Keys, Tower of London Box
Chamber of the Pyx Westminster Abbey Box
Changing the Guard, ceremonies of:
   at Buckingham Palace: **1130** DAILY (Summer), Alternate Days in Winter;
   at St. James's Palace: **1100** DAILY (Summer), Alternate Days in Winter;
   at Whitehall: **1100** DAILY (**1000 SUN**) & **1600**
   at Windsor: **1100** DAILY (**1000 SUN**) & **1600**
CHAPEL ROYAL St James's Palace SW1 *Private royal chapel designed by Inigo Jones (1623)*
   – – – – – – Su (services: **1045** for Sung Eucharist at **1115**)
Chapter House Westminster Abbey Box
CHARTERHOUSE, (The London), Charterhouse Square, EC1
14thC monastery, Tudor mansion, converted to school charity (1611); Written appointments: Clerk to the Governors, Sutton's Hospital in Charterhouse
   1445: Wednesdays only (April–July); Tube: Barbican

--------------- CHELSEA ---------------
Access: tube, Sloane Square, bus down King's Road
Boat, riverbus to Cadogan Pier
CARLYLE'S HOUSE 24 Cheyne Row SW3 T.352–7087 *Thomas Carlyle (19thC Scottish writer) lived here, now a museum*
   1100–1700 – – W Th F Sa Su (April–October)
CHELSEA OLD CHURCH ★ Chelsea Embankment SW3
T.352–5627 *historic parish church, fine monuments*
   1000–1300 M – W Th F Sa Su, 1330–1700 – – W Th F Sa Su [**–1900**]
CHELSEA PHYSIC GARDEN 66 Royal Hospital Road SW3
T.352–5646 *historic garden [est. 1673]*
   1400–1700 – – W – – – Su (teas, Su) [summer opening only]
CHELSEA ROYAL HOSPITAL ★ Royal Hospital Road
Chelsea SW3 T.730–0161 *Home of the famous red-coated Chelsea In-Pensioners (est. 1682);* ★ *Great Hall, Council Chamber*
   1000–1200 and **1400–1600 M Tu W Th F Sa, 1400–1600 Su**
Chapel: (Sunday Services: **0830, 1100**)
GARDENS ★ & RANELAGH GARDENS SW3
   1000–Sunset M Tu W Th F Sa, 1400–Sunset Su
NATIONAL ARMY MUSEUM ★Royal Hospital Road Chelsea *comprehensive exhibition and history of British Army*
CROSBY HALL ★ Cheyne Walk Chelsea SW3 T.352–9663
magnificent old City hall [15thC hammerbeam roof]
   1000–1200 & **1430–1700 M Tu W Th F Sa, 1430–1700 Su**

Cherry Garden Pier, Rotherhithe, Banner Map 1
Children as companions in London, separate boxed information
Chiltern Hills, Excursions in the Thames valley
CHISWICK HOUSE Burlington Lane Chiswick W4 T.995–0508
3rd Earl of Burlington's Palladian villa
   0930–1300 & 1400–1830 M Tu W Th F Sa Su [**–1600,** Winters: — **W Th F Sa Su**]
City Information Centre, St. Paul's Churchyard, EC4 T.606–3030
x.1456/7 *General information about City events, livery halls, City churches etc.*
   0930–1700 M Tu W Th F [**Sa–1600,** summer, **–1230,** winter)
ST. CLEMENT DANES Church Strand WC2 T.242–8282 *church of the R.A.F., 'Oranges and lemons say the bells of St. Clement' – nursery rhyme [Bell peal: **0900, 1200, 1500 & 1800**]*
   0800–1700 M Tu W Th F Sa Su (Sunday services: **0830, 1100**)
Clore Gallery, Tate Gallery
Cotswold Hills, Excursions in the Thames valley
COLLEGE OF ARMS Queen Victoria Street City EC4 T.248–2762
official heraldic authority for English families and institutions (est. 1484) – trace your family blood by contacting the Officer in Waiting –
   1000–1600 M Tu W Th F – –

Coram Fields, Thomas Coram Foundation
COURTAULD INSTITUTE GALLERIES Woburn Square Bloomsbury WC1 *Most important collection of Impressionist and Post-Impressionist paintings*
1000–1700 M Tu W Th F Sa, 1400–1700 Su
Covent Garden Piazza – Banner Map 2
Dean's Yard, precincts of Westminster Abbey
DICKENS HOUSE 48 Doughty Street Bloomsbury WC1 T.405–2127 *Charles Dickens [1812–1870] writer, lived here [1837–39], now a museum of his memorabilia*
1000–1700 M Tu W Th F Sa –
Dr. Johnson's house, *see* Johnson
Docklands, Thames-side neighbourhood – Banner Map 1
Docklands Light Railway – Banner Map 1
Dolls' House, Queen Mary's, – Windsor Castle Box
DULWICH PICTURE GALLERY College Road Dulwich SE21 *London's first public art gallery (fou. 1814) housing a very fine collection of Dutch, Flemish and Italian art, and English portraiture* [Travel: BR West Dulwich via Victoria, then ask]
1000–1300 & 1400–1700 – Tu W Th F Sa, 1400–1700 Su
ELTHAM PALACE★ Eltham SE9 T.854–2242 × 4232 *Great Hall [1480] of Tudor Palace survives*
1100–1900 – – – Th – – Su (winter: **1100–1600**)
Exhibition of The Queen's Presents, Windsor Castle Box
FORTNUM & MASON LTD, 181 Piccadilly, SW1 T.734–8040 *H.M. The Queen's Grocer*
Foundling Hospital, see Thomas Coram Foundation for Children
Frogmore, Royal Mausoleum, Windsor Great Park – Windsor Box
Fulham, Thames-side village Banner Map 3
GEFFRYE MUSEUM★ Kingsland Road East E2 T.739–9893 *collection of furniture and woodwork in period setting*
1000–1700 – Tu W Th F Sa, 1400–1700 Su
GEOLOGICAL MUSEUM★ Exhibition Road Kensington SW7 T.589–3444 *comprehensive collections of mineral science*
1000–1800 M Tu W Th F Sa, 1430–1800 Su
GRAY'S INN★ [HALL, WALKS] High Holborn WC2 T.242–8592 *historic Inn of Court*
Walks: **1200–1430** [summer] **M Tu W Th F Sa Su**
Greenwich Tourist Information Centre Cutty Sark Gardens SE10 T.858–6376
0930–1900 M Tu W Th F Sa Su [winter: **1000–1700**]
GROSVENOR CHAPEL★ South Audley Street Mayfair W1 *fine 18thC place of worship belonging to the Duke of Westminster (Grosvenor family)* (enquiries: 24 South Audley Street) *Sunday services:* **0815, 1030, 1100**
GUARDS CHAPEL★ Wellington Barracks Birdcage Walk SW1
1000–1600 M Tu W Th F – – (**0930–1300 Su:** service **1100 M.**)
GUILDHALL★ Gresham Street City EC2 T.606–3030 (Keeper's Office)
1000–1700 M Tu W Th F Sa –, **1000–1700 Su** [summer only]
note– **GUILDHALL LIBRARY★**
0930–1700 M Tu W Th F – –
15thC Civic hall of the Corporation of the City of London
GUILDHALL CLOCK MUSEUM★
0930–1700 M Tu W Th F – –
exquisite collection of timepieces on loan from the Worshipful Company of Clockmakers
HAM HOUSE Ham Street Petersham Surrey T.940–1950 *17thC Riverside mansion in enviable/setting park*
1100–1700 – Tu W Th F Sa Su [all year]
HAMPTON COURT PALACE Hampton Court East Molesey Surrey T.977–8441 *16thC residence of Cardinal Wolsey and (after) Henry VIII in magnificent Thames-side setting*
0930–1800 M Tu W Th F Sa – [–1700, winter**], 1100–1800 Su [1400–1700,** winter**]**
Gardens★ (dawn to dusk)
Kitchens and Cellars (above hours, March–October)
Mantegna Gallery (above hours, March–October)
Maze (above hours, March–October)
HAMPTON COURT QUEEN'S CHAPEL
services: Sunday **0830, 1115, 1415**
Horse Guards, Ceremony: Changing the Guard
Horse Rangers Association, The Mews, Hampton Green, Surrey *Friendly charity housed in Tudor Mews [1558]*
HARRODS Department Store Knightsbridge SW1 T.730–1234 *World-famous departments (230) store on 20 acre site; services include tourist information 4th floor*
0900–1800 M Tu – Th F Sa –, 0930–1900 – – W – – – –
Harrods Luxury Sightseeing Tours T.581–3603 e.g. London Panorama [2 hrs] **1000, 1300, 1600 M Tu W Th Fr Sa Su** (on-board refreshments)

─────────── **HAMPSTEAD** ───────────

Hampstead, fashionable north London suburb
BURGH HOUSE New End Square NW3 T.431–0144 *Hampstead Museum of Local History*
1200–1700 – – W Th F Sa Su
FENTON HOUSE Hampstead Grove NW3 T.435–3471 *17thC house, museum of ceramics and musical instruments, worthy of detour in an excursion to Hampstead, North London*
1100–1800 M Tu W – – Sa Su (Apr–Oct)
FREUD MUSEUM 20 Maresfield Gardens Hampstead NW3 T.435–2002 *Austrian psychoanalyst's London residence now a museum*
1200–1700 – – W Th F Sa Su
HAMPSTEAD HEATH 825 acre heathland, 443 feet above sea-level [Swimming, summer: Highgate Pond: men, Kenwood Pond: women, Hampstead Pond: mixed company]
IVY HOUSE North End Road NW3 *residence of Anna Pavlova (1912–1931)*
1400–1800 – – – – – Sa –
KEATS' HOUSE★ Wentworth Place Keats Grove NW3 T.435–2062 *Residence (1818–20) of John Keats [1795–1821] now a museum*
1000–1300 & 1400–1800 M Tu W Th F Sa, 1400–1700 Su
KENWOOD HOUSE★ Hampstead Lane NW3 T.348–1286 *18thC mansion of Lord Chief Justice Mansfield, Adam interior, fine collection of paintings inc. Vermeer, Rembrandt, Gainsborough, Romney, Lawrence, Reynolds; magnificent parkside setting; donated to the nation by the 1st Lord Iveagh [Iveagh Bequest] (Guinness family)* [Tube: Archway, then bus 210]
1000–1900 M Tu W Th F Sa Su [–1600, winter**]**
Summer evening lakeside concerts:
English Heritage Special Events T.734–1877
[1,300 deck chairs, 8,000 grass seats]

HIGHGATE CEMETERY Swains Lane N6 T.340–1834
1000–1600 Hourly tours **M Tu W Th F Sa Su [–1500,** winter**]**
Entertaining tours round crowded Victorian cemetery
HOGARTH'S HOUSE★ Hogarth Lane Great West Road W4 T.994–6757 *home of 18thC artist William Hogarth [1697–1764]*
1100–1800 M – Tu W Th F Sa – [–1600, winter**], 1400–1800 Su [–1600,** winter**]**
[Tube: Turnham Green, Car Park: Fleming House, adjacent]
HONOURABLE ARTILLERY COMPANY★ of the City of London, Armoury House, City Road EC1 *oldest military body in the realm (est. 1537)* admission by prior written application
HORNIMAN MUSEUM★ London Road Forest Hill SE23 T.699–2399/1872/4911 *Home of F.H. Horniman, tea merchant, now an eclectic museum*
[BR: London Bridge – Forest Hill, E. of Dulwich, South-east London]
1030–1800 M Tu W Th F Sa –, 1400–1800 Su
Hotel Value: **KNIGHTSBRIDGE GREEN HOTEL 159** Knightsbridge SW1 T.584–6274 [Telefax 01–225–1635] *excellent accomodation in the heart of the Capital – opposite Harrods – example tariff: suite (double room, bathroom and reception room, £85.00 per night)*
HOUSES OF PARLIAMENT Palace of Westminster SW1 T.219–3000 *Seat of the British institutions of government, rebuilt 1848*
HOUSE OF COMMONS★ T.219–4272
[Prime Minister's Question Time: **1515:** Tu, Th] *note–* ticket admission: available from M.P. or Consulate (non-residents) Left hand queue, St. Stephens Entrance, for Strangers' Gallery
HOUSE OF LORDS★ T.219–3107 [Shorter queues, higher standards of debate] Right hand queue, St. Stephen's Entrance, from Strangers' Gallery
WESTMINSTER HALL,★ Palace of Westminster SW1 T.219–3000 *historic 11thC hall built by William the Conqueror's son, William II [1099]*
Visit by prior arrangement with a Member of Parliament
★IMPERIAL WAR MUSEUM Lambeth Road SE1 T.735–8922 *post-1914 war museum*
1000–1750 M Tu W Th F Sa, 1400–1750 Su
Isabella Plantation and Woodland, Windsor Box
Isle of Dogs, Thames-side neighbourhood Banner Map 1
Isleworth, Thames-side neighbourhood, Banner Map 4
Ivy House, Hampstead Box

233

DR JOHNSON'S HOUSE Gough Square City EC4 T.353–3745
18thC residence [1749–59] of Dr. Samual Johnson now a museum
1100–1730 M Tu W Th F Sa – [–1700, winter]
JEWISH MUSEUM* Woburn House Tavistock Square
Bloomsbury WC1 T.388–4525 *collection of Judaism and Jewish
history*
1000–1600 – Tu W Th – – –, (1000–1245 F – Su)
Keats' House, Hampstead Box
KENSINGTON PALACE State Apartments Kensington Gardens
W8 T.937–9561
*residence of William III & Mary II [1689–1702] now the residence of
TRH Prince and Princess of Wales*
0900–1700 M Tu W Th F – –, 1300–1700 Su
Kenwood House and Park, Hampstead Box
Kew, Thames-side village Upstream Banner Map 4
KEW BRIDGE ENGINES MUSEUM Green Dragon Lane
Brentford Middlesex T.568–4757 *Steam-pumping engines exhibition*
1100–1700 M Tu W Th F Sa Su
KEW GARDENS, Royal Botanic Garden at Kew, Surrey
T.940–1171 *World's foremost botanical garden and research centre set in
a gorgeous setting beside the river Thames*
Gardens: **0930–1800 M Tu W Th F Sa Su** [–dusk [1600]: winter]
note– Guide lecturer service available to tour Gardens,
Glasshouses, Museums [6 weeks' advance notice]
Glasshouses: **1000–1600** ibid
Queen Charlotte's Cottage: **1100–1730 – – – – – Sa Su** [summer
only]
Kew Palace: **1100–1730 M Tu W Th F Sa Su** [summer only]
[Access: Tube to Kew Gardens via District Line (14 stops from
Victora)]
Kew Parish Church: ST. ANNE'S, Kew Green, Surrey
Dainty 18thC Church where Gainsborough lies buried
Kingston-upon-Thames, Thames-side village town Banner Map 4
KNELLER HALL, Royal Military School of Music, Kneller Road,
Whitton, Middlesex. Open air musical concerts in summer on
Wednesday evenings
*London residence of Sir Godfrey Kneller Court painter, now an
institution;*
KNIGHTSBRIDGE CROWN COURT I, Hans Crescent,
Knightsbridge, London SW1 T.[01] 589–4500
(criminal jury trials, conveniently close to Harrods department
store) *note–* useful to attend if queues prohibitive at Old Bailey
Lambeth, Thames-side village – Banner Map 2
LAW COURTS* Strand WC2 T.936–6000
Courts in session: **1030–1300 & 1400–1600 M Tu W Th F – –**
central court-house of High Court of Justice, civil jurisdiction
(Court Dress Exhibition) Law Terms:
Hilary – Jan–Mar   Trinity – June–July
Easter – April–June   Michaelmas – Oct–Dec
note– no sittings in Vacation periods
LAUDERDALE HOUSE* Waterlow Park Highgate N6
T.348–8716 *mid 17thC mansion reputedly visited by Nell Gwynne,
now a community centre, adjoins Waterlow Park ['a garden for
gardeners'], 27 acres*
1100–1600 M Tu W Th F, 1330–1700 Sa, 1200–1700 Su
[Tube: Archway, then bus 143, 210, 271 or walk]
LEIGHTON HOUSE* 12 Holland Park Road Kensington W14
T.602–3316 *residence of Lord Leighton [1830–1896] now an art
museum of Victorian works of art*
1100–1700 M Tu W Th F Sa –
LINCOLN'S INN,* Hon. Society of, London WC2 T.405–6360
historic Inn of Court, in scenic surroundings
Porter's Lodge: cnr Lincoln's Inn Fields, for admission to:
Old Hall, Chapel, New Hall, Library, 17thC quadrangles
Living Steam Museum, Kew Bridge Engines Museum –
LINLEY SAMBOURNE HOUSE 18 Stafford Terrace Kensington
W8 T.994–1019 *home of late Victorian, Edward Linley Sambourne
[1844–1910] now a cute little museum*
1000–1600 – – W – – – – & 1400–1700 Su (summer only)
London Bridge – Banner Map 1
London Bridge City Pier – Banner Map 1
LONDON LIBRARY II St. James's Square SW1
Write – nomination for subscribing membership
*One of the largest and most comprehensive private subscription libraries in
the world (founded by Thomas Carlyle in 1841)*
London Planetarium, Madame Tussaud's waxworks –
LONDON SILVER* VAULTS Southampton Buildings Chancery
Lane WC2 *where to acquire the finest old English silver and plate*
0900–1730 M Tu W Th F –, 1000–1230 Sa
LONDON TOURIST BOARD General Enquiries T.730–3488

LONDON TRANSPORT MUSEUM Covent Garden WC2
T.379–6344 *entertaining display of transport development*
1000–1800 M Tu W Th F Sa Su
LONDON ZOO Regent's Park Zoo Regent's Park NW1
T.722–3333 *the famed Gardens of the Zoological Society of London
(founded 1826)*
[Travel: tube to Camden Town, Northern Line, or Baker Street
then bus 74]
0900–1800 M Tu W Th F Sa Su [–1900 Su] (winter: **1000**–dusk)
LLOYD'S OF LONDON* Lime Street City EC3 T.623–7100
exhibition and Visitors' Viewing deck: **M Tu W Th F – –**
World's leading insurance market headquarters
MADAME TUSSAUD'S* Marylebone Road NW1 T.935–6861
waxworks of prominent persons, Chamber of Horrors, etc.
1000–1730 M Tu W Th F Sa Su
ST. MARTIN-IN-THE-FIELDS* Trafalgar Square WC2
T.930–0089 *Royal parish church [James Gibb, 1726]*
f110730–1930 **M Tu W Th F Sa Su** [Sunday services, telephone for
details] regular lunchtime concerts: T.930–1862
ST. MARY-LE-BOW* Cheapside City EC2 *Wren's beautiful City
church and Norman (900 year-old) Crypt, in the belfry hang the world-
famous BOW BELLS (true cockneys are born in sound of)*
0900-1600 M Tu W Th F – –
MARBLE HILL HOUSE* Richmond Road Twickenham Middlesex
T.892–5115 *18thC riverside mansion built for George II's mistress, the
Countess of Suffolk and later lived in by George IV's mistress,
Mrs. Fitzherbert*
1000–1700 M Tu W Th – Sa Su (–1600: winter)
[access: see Twickenham]
Summer evening riverside concerts: 5,000 grass tickets (no deck
chairs) (write enquiries for advance tickets)
MARBLE HILL PARK:* Dawn–Dusk Stable Block Cafeteria,
licensed – good value: T.891–2900
MIDDLE TEMPLE HALL Temple City EC4 T.353–4355
1000–1130 & 1500–1600 in term (see Courts: term periods)
MONUMENT Monument Street City EC3 *City monument
commemorating Great Fire of 1666, 311 steps to viewing deck*
0900–1600 M Tu W Th F, 1400–1800 Sa Su
Mortlake, Thames-side village
MUSEUM OF GARDEN HISTORY St. Mary at Lambeth
Lambeth Palace Road SE1 *church displays of garden history by the
Tradescant Trust (named after pioneer father and son, gardeners to
Charles I)*
1100–1500 M Tu W Th F –, 1030–1700 Su (closed winter)
MUSEUM OF LONDON* London Wall City EC2 T.600–3699
First-rate museum
1000–1800 – Tu W Th F Sa –, 1400–1800: Su (–1700, winter)
MUSEUM OF MOVING IMAGE South Bank SE1 T.928–3535
Modern, spectacular presentation of history of cinema and TV
1000–2000 – Tu W Th F Sa Su [–1800]
MUSEUM OF RICHMOND Richmond-Upon-Thames Box
MUSEUM OF THE ORDER OF ST. JOHN St. John's Lane
Clerkenwell EC1 T.253–6644 *conducted tours of the Priory and
Gatehouse and memorabilia of the Knights Hospitallers of the Order of
St. John of Jerusalem (12th–16thC)*
1000–1800 – Tu – – F Sa –
National Art-Collections Fund see post-appendix
National Army Museum Chelsea Box
NATIONAL GALLERY* Trafalgar Square WC2 T.839–3321
Unrivalled collection of Euopean painting (13th–20th centuries)
1000–1800 M Tu W Th F Sa, 1400–1800 Su
National Library for the Blind, see post Appendix
NATIONAL PORTRAIT GALLERY* St. Martin's Place
(Trafalgar Square) WC2 T.930–1552 *Stunning collection of portraits
of famous British men and women in history to the present day*
1000–1700 M Tu W Th F, Sa [1800], 1400–1800 Su
NATIONAL POSTAL MUSEUM* King Edward Building King
Edward Street City EC1 T.432–3851 *Permanent exhibition of stamps
of Great Britain and the world*
1000–1630 M Tu W Th F [–1600] – –
NATIONAL SOUND ARCHIVE 29 Exhibition Road SW7
T.589–6603 *Voices of the past stored for posterity*
0930–1630 M Tu W Th [–2100] F – –
NATURAL HISTORY MUSEUM* Cromwell Road South
Kensington SW7 T.589–6323
1000–1800 M Tu W Th F Sa 1430–1800 Su
NATIONAL MARITIME MUSEUM Greenwich SE10 *Britain's
maritime heritage excellently presented*
1000–1800 M Tu W Th F Sa, 1400–1800 (–1700 winter)
(ticket includes admission to Old Royal Observatory)

OLD BAILEY* Newgate Street City EC4 T.248–3277 *Central Criminal Court(s) where major trials are conducted on indictment before a jury [if queues, see Royal Courts of Justice, Knightsbridge Crown Court] – no cameras –*
1015–1454 M Tu W Th F – – [luncheon recess: 1300–1400]
OLD OPERATING THEATRE St. Thomas Street Bermondsey SE1 T.407–7600 *1821 operating theatre 'discovered' [1956] and restored as a museum*
1230–1600 M – W – F – –

PETTICOAT LANE Middlesex Street Aldgate E1 *famous East End street market* **0900–1400 – – – – – – Su**
PIERS
    CADOGAN   CHELSEA   HARBOUR   CREMORNE   CHARING CROSS   CHERRY GARDENS   FESTIVAL   KEW   KINGSTON   LONDON BRIDGE CITY   PUTNEY   ROYAL PIER (HAMPTON COURT)   RICHMOND PIERS   SWAN LANE   WEST INDIA   WESTMINSTER – Banner Maps & Contents Pages

OLD ROYAL OBSERVATORY Greenwich Park SE10 *Flamsteed House [17thC] museum: history of Time, nearby: centre of the world's meridien (one foot in the Eastern, one in the Western, hemispheres)*
1000–1800 M Tu W Th F Sa, 1400–1800 Su (–1700 winter)
ORLEANS HOUSE GALLERY* The Octagon Room Lebanon Park Road Twickenham T.892–0221 *various temporary exhibitions and the Ionides display of local topography in old wing [James Gibbs 1720] of demolished house, woodland gardens beside the Thames*
1300–1700 – Tu W Th F Sa, 1400–1630 Su
[access: see Twickenham]
OSTERLEY HOUSE [AND PARK] Osterley Middlesex T.560–3918 *Seat of the Earls of Jersey [Adam interior] donated to the nation in 1923 Mansion built for Sir Thomas Gresham [16thC], founder of the Royal Exchange*
1400–1800 – Tu W Th F Sa Su (1200–1600 winter)
[Park: **1000–dusk**]
Palace of Westminster, Houses of Parliament
ST. PAUL'S CATHEDRAL Ludgate Hill City EC4 T.248–2705
0800–1800 M Tu W Th F Sa Su [–Subject to services. (Su Services: 0800, 1030, 1130, 1515)]
Crypt, Whispering Gallery: **1000–1515 M Tu W Th F Sa –**
Pembroke Lodge, Richmond Park
PERCIVAL DAVID FOUNDATION OF CHINESE ART* 53 Gordon Square Bloomsbury WC2 T.387–3909 *Sir Percival David's bequest of Sun, Yuan, Ming and Ch'ing porcelain [a.d. 962–1912]*
1030–1700 M [1400–] Tu W Th F Sa [–1300] –
Peter Pan Statue, Kensington Gardens
Petersham, Thames-side village and water-meadows Banner Map 4

O P E N TO THE PUBLIC FOR PRIVATE HOSPITALITY – ON A FUTURE OCCASION?
*Many visitors to the grand places open to the public are unaware that these historic surroundings may be hired for use as a private venue for a social or business function. The following list spoils the reader for choice: * Eaton Catering is a recommended caterer by many of these – and dozens more – establishments, and will be happy to undertake arrangements for booking and serving of functions held in such lovely places: Enquiries, Eaton Catering, 7 Willow Stret EC2 T.739–0993.*

BANQUETING HOUSE Whitehall
HAM HOUSE nr. Richmond
KENWOOD HOUSE Hampstead
CARLTON HOUSE TERRACE (ICA)
NATURAL HISTORY MUSEUM
RIVER THAMES: Livery Barge Regalia, Catamaran Cruisers T.623–1807; Catamaran Cruisers T.839–3572
ROYAL ACADEMY Piccadilly
STATIONERS HALL City
OSTERLEY HOUSE near Heathrow
TOWER BRIDGE City
VICTORIA AND ALBERT MUSEUM
Come to think of it, why not hire an orchestra or military band for the soiree?
LONDON SYMPHONY ORCHESTRA LTD T.588–1116
PHILHARMONIA ORCHESTRA T.580–9961
SAVOY ORPHEANS T.836–1533
ROYAL MARINE BANDS T.898–5533 (Enquiries)

Planetarium, Madame Tussaud's
POLLOCK'S TOY MUSEUM 1 Scala Street London W1 *Benjamin Pollock's Victorian replica shop [adult interest]*
1000–1700 M Tu W Th F Sa –
Pope's Grotto Cross Deep – Twickenham Box
Porter Tun Room, Whitbread Brewery
PORTOBELLO ROAD Street Market Notting Hill and Ladbroke Grove W11 *cosmopolitan street market, predominantly antiques; street name commemorates great British capture of Puerto Bello [Admiral Vernon: Caribbean, 1739]*
0900–1700 (M Tu W Th [–1300] F) Sa –
PUBLIC RECORD OFFICE* Chancery Lane WC2 T.876–3444 *National archives inc. Magna Carta.*
note– Telephone for Exhibition information.
0930–1700 M Tu W Th F – –
Putney, Thames-side village – Banner Map 3
The **QUEEN'S GALLERY** Buckingham Palace Road SW1
1100–1700 – T W Th F Sa, 1400–1700 Su [also open on Bank Holidays] *'An exhibition of famous artists' works'*
RAF MUSEUM* Hendon NW9 T.205–2266 *Exhibits of British Military Aviation hardware*
1000–1800 M Tu W Th F Sa, 1400–1800 Su
And see – **BATTLE OF BRITAIN MUSEUM**
[Access: Tube to Colindale [Northern Line]
RANGER'S HOUSE* Chesterfield Walk Blackheath SE10 T.853–0035 *4th Earl of Chesterfield's 18thC home*
1000–1700 M Tu W Th F Sa Su
[Access: BR Greenwich, River launches to Greenwich]
REGENT'S PARK ZOO Regent's Park NW1 T.722–3333 *Gardens of the Zoological Society of London founded by Sir Stamford Raffles (Singapore fame) and Sir Humphry Davy (safety harness fame) [1826]*
0900–1800 M Tu W Th F Sa Su
[Access: Tube to Baker Street, bus 74, or Camden Town, then walk; Waterbus: from Little Venice, summers only]
RICHMOND THEATRE Little Green Richmond Upon Thames Surrey T.940–0088 *Victorian theatre with notable performances of Pre-West End productions and renowned Christmas pantomimes*

RITZ, THE
Piccadilly W1 T.493–8181 (Telefax: 493–2687) *Opulence within – Norwegian granite stone exterior dressing of early steel-framed structure [Mewes & Davis, 1906] – splendid restaurant ceiling! For a 'tee'-total experience: ask for Michael to serve up the best 'Pussyfoot' in town (cost £3 1988)*
River Thames Society see post-Appendix
Rotherhithe, Thames-side village [map 1: East End]
ROTUNDA MUSEUM OF ARTILLERY* Repository Road Woolwich SE18 T.854–2242 *Royal Artillery's collection of guns, tanks and so forth, housed in the 1814 Pavilion moved from St. James's Park [1819]*
1200–1700 M Tu W Th F – – 1300–1700 Sa Su
Nearby – Royal Artillery Barracks: 1000 ft frontage rivalling Leningrad Winter palace
[Access: BR to New Cross, bus 53; river launch to Thames Barrier, and taxi]
Round Pond, Kensington Gardens
ROYAL ACADEMY OF ARTS Burlington House Piccadilly W1 T.734–7438 *renowned venue for remarkable loan exhibitions shown in the galleries*
1000–1800 M Tu W Th F Sa Su
ROYAL BRITAIN EXHIBITION Barbican Centre City EC1 T.588–0588 *'a kaleidoscope of royal history, presented with flair using modern technology' – a must to visit*
Royal Ballet Junior School – Richmond Park
Royal Botanic Gardens, Kew
ROYAL SOCIETY OF ARTS 8 John Adam Street Adelphi Strand WC2 *RSA founded 1754 to foster 'art, manufacture, and trade' Admission on prior application*
ROYAL COURTS OF JUSTICE* *['High Court' trials of civil litigation – inc. libel and slander actions before a jury]* and see Central Criminal Court, Law Courts
ROYAL FESTIVAL HALL Belvedere Road SE1 T.928–3641 *Free lunch-time music, inexpensive evening concerts and the like*
Royal Holloway & New Bedford College Surrey – Windsor Box
ROYAL HORSEGUARDS HOTEL SW1 T.839–3400 *Riverside hotel: excellent views from the hotel's south-facing bedrooms*

RICHMOND UPON THAMES

TOURIST INFORMATION CENTRE Central Library: T.940–9125 (office hrs) [Richmond Festival: June – Walking tours etc]
Access – See Contents Pages

View – The Green – Riverside – The Terrace – Richmond Hill – Richmond Park –
RICHMOND PARK (2500 acres) 0730–Dusk
Cafeteria/Restaurant – Pembroke Lodge T.940–8207
[½ mile south of Richmond (Hill) Gate]
Riverside pub – *White Swan* Old Palace Lane R T.940–0959
MUSEUM OF RICHMOND Old Town Hall Whittaker Ave T.332–1141 *'the life and traditions of Richmond, Kew, Petersham and Ham'*
1330–1700 – Tu W Th F Sa – [–2000 W, –1800 Th F]
Note – Saturdays, also 1000–1230 and Sundays in summer: 1300–1600
ST. MARY'S Parish Church Paradise Road Richmond
WHITE LODGE Richmond Park T.876–5547 *George II's hunting lodge, now home of the Royal Ballet.*
1400–1800 M Tu W Th F Sa Su [*note:* August only].

ROYAL HORTICULTURAL SOCIETY Vincent Square Westminster SW1 *Society founded 1805: regular flower shows*
ROYAL MEWS Buckingham Palace Road SW1 *Royal carriages and equipage*
1400–1600 – – W Th – – – [closed Ascot week, 3rd in June]
Royal Mews, Windsor
ROYAL HOSPITAL – Chelsea
ROYAL NAVAL COLLEGE* Greenwich SE10 *Former Royal Naval Hospital (Wren, 1698) who incorporated the earlier wing (J. Webb, 1641)*
Noted ceiling in the Painted Hall [Sir. J. Thornhill] and chapel
1430–1700 M Tu W – F Sa Su
[Access: BR to Maze Hill, river launch to Greenwich Pier]
ROYAL SCHOOL OF NEEDLEWORK 25 Prince's Gate South Kensington SW7 *(interesting embroidery shop)*
1030–1230 – – W – – – – *note* first Wednesday in the month, only.
Royal Shakespeare Company Theatre – Barbican
ROYAL SOCIETY 6 Carlton House Terrace SW1 *Headquarters of the distinguished scientific body [760 fellows, first incorp. 1662] very interesting collection of the distinguished Fellows*
Admission by prior appointment
Runnymede – Windsor Box
SAATCHI GALLERY of modern art 98A Boundary Road London NW8 T.624–8299
SAVOY CHAPEL* Savoy Hill WC2 *historic chapel of the Royal Victorian Order (an honour of knighthood in the personal gift of the monarch)*
1130–1730 – Tu W Th F – – [closed August and September]
SAVOY HOTEL Strand (front)/Embankment (rear) WC2 T.836–1533 *famed riverside hotel for celebrities and others who appreciate legendary service*
SCIENCE MUSEUM* Exhibition Road South Kensington SW7 T.589–3456 *historical perspectives of science and industry*
1000–1800 M Tu W Th Fr Sa, 1430–1800 Su
SIMPSON'S IN THE STRAND WC2 T.836–9112 *old-fashioned restaurant famed for its cuts of meat served on the trolley.*
SIR JOHN SOANE's MUSEUM 131 Lincoln's Inn Fields, WC2 T.405–2107 *Home of Soane, architect [18thC] presented as he left it, in mint condition and with distinguished contents*
1000–1700 – Tu W Th F Sa – [Public lecture tour: Sa 1430]
SOSEKI MUSEUM* 80B The Chase Clapham SW4 *London home of Soseki Natsume, novelist [19thC] with memorabilia japanois*
1000–1200 & 1400–1700 – – W – – Sa, 1400–1700 Su
[access – tube to Clapham Common]
SHAKESPEARE GLOBE MUSEUM 1 Bear Gardens Bankside SE1 T.928–6342 *a presentation of London associations with Shakespeare*
1000–1800 – Tu W Th Sa, 1400–1800 Su (telephone confirmation of opening times suggested)
SHAKESPEARE GLOBE CENTRE Bankside SE1 T.620–0202, *mock-tudor theatre and entertainment centre planned for 1992*
SOUTHSIDE HOUSE South Side – Wimbledon Box
Southwark, Thames-side Borough – Banner Map 1

SOUTHWARK CATHEDRAL London Bridge SE1 T.407–2939 *finest Gothic ecclesiastical structure in London after Westminster Abbey, shrine of John Gower, poet 14thC, Edmund Shakespeare, brother of the Bard, John Harvard (Chapel) baptised here [1607], who founded the University in Massachusetts, astonishing cluster of architectural delights*
0830–1700 M Tu W Th F Sa [services:] **1100, 1500**
Choral evensong **1730 – Tu – – F – –**
Organ recital **1310 M – – – – – –**
STAPLE INN High Holborn WC1 T.242–0106 *Picturesque Inn of Chancery Hall and cobbled courtyard (occupied by the Institute of Actuaries) 16thC [abol.1884]*
Swan Lane Pier, access to the City – Banner Map 1
SYON HOUSE AND PARK (including the Butterfly House and Heritage Motor Museum
Park Road Brentford Middlesex T.560–0881
House: **1200–1815 M Tu W Th – – –** (summers only)
Grounds: **1000–dusk**, all year
TATE GALLERY★ Millbank SW1 T.821–1313 [821–7128: recorded information] *National collection of British art*
1000–1750 M Tu W Th F Sa, 1400–1730 Su
TATE GALLERY RESTAURANT Millbank SW1 T.834–8754 *Best value wine list in London*
Teddington, Thames-side village
TEMPLE CHURCH Temple City EC4 T.353–1736 *Crusaders' round church [1185]*
1000–1600 M Tu W Th F – –
Sunday services: **0830, 1115** [except August & September]
Temple Hall, Middle Temple Hall
TEMPLE GARDENS Victoria Embankment City EC4 T.353–8462 [Inner Temple] 353–4355 [Middle Temple] *Dawn to dusk note private sanctuary of the legal profession: no uncouth children (or adults) historic site of the Wars of the Roses, good specimens of white (Yorkist) & red (Lancastrian) blooms*
THAMES BARRIER VISITORS CENTRE Woolwich SE18 *apparent water-tight defence to the capital from floods best approached by river launch.*
1030–1700 M Tu W Th F Sa Su (–1730 Sa Su)
Thames Bridges, sprinkled about the text, see Maps 1, 2, 3, 4 etc
Tourist Information, Information – Post-Appendix
THOMAS CORAM FOUNDATION FOR CHILDREN [Foundling Hospital Art Treasures] 40 Brunswick Square Bloomsbury WC1 T.278–2424 *18thC legacy of Capt. Coram, grand old mariner and philanthropist [Handel MS: Messiah, Founder's portrait by Hogarth, etc]*
1000–1600 M Tu W Th F – –
see – Coram Fields: **0900–dusk M Tu W Th F Sa Su** [note. no adult admittance unless accompanied by a child]
THEATRE MUSEUM Flower Market Building Covent Garden WC2 T.836–7891 *Theatrical memorabilia [good cafe but no smoking]*
1100–1900 – Tu W Th F Sa Su [note Theatre ticket office facility: useful, and helpful staff]
TOWER BRIDGE River Thames SE1 T.430–3761 *Walkway: 60ft above sea level, views, Steam engine museum, Bermondsey bank*
1000–1730 M Tu W Th F Sa, 1400–1700 Su

TOWER OF LONDON
Tower Hill River Thames EC3 T.709–0765
0930–1745 M Tu W Th F Sa, 1400–1745 Su (winter
0930–1630 weekdays)
note. Jewel House (Crown Jewels) closed February
St. Peter ad Vincula church services: sunday **0915, 1100**
The Ceremony of the Keys [performed nightly],
2135–2205 M Tu W Th F Sa Su
Application for tickets to attend Locking up the Tower:
H.M.'s/Resident Governor,
H.M.'s Tower of London EC3
n.b. state preferred dates (10 days in advance), names in party (maximum seven) and enclose stamped return envelope.
Locking up the Tower.
Sentry: HALT! Who comes there?
Chief Warder: The Keys.
Sentry: *Whose keys?*
Chief Warder: Queen Elizabeth's keys.
Sentry: ADVANCE Queen Elizabeth's Keys, All's Well.
. . . Guard and Escort present arms in honour of the keys . . .
Chief Warder advances two paces in front of the escort, removes his hat, says: God preserve Queen Elizabeth.
Assembled: Amen.

TRAVELLERS CLUB Pall Mall SW1 T.930–8688 (prior appointment) *Private Gentleman's club [fou.1819], Italian Renaissance style [Barry, 1832] on limited view to the curious*
1000–1200 & 1400–1730 M – – – F – –

--- **TWICKENHAM** ---

Upstream *10* miles southwest of Central London
Access: – by river, Richmond Pier, cross bridge
– by road, A316
– by rail, BR from Waterloo [½ hour] St. Margaret's Station, walk to riverside
– by London underground, to Richmond, walk across bridge
– by London Transport Bus, Number 33 from Kensington High Street
Information: T.892–0032 (District Library, Garfield Road).

Places of interest: and general information
MARBLE HILL HOUSE★ Richmond Road Twickenham T.892-5115
1000–1700 (–1600, Nov–Mar), Closed Friday;
MARBLE HILL PARK Open throughout year, dawn–dusk.
THE STABLEBLOCK Cafeteria, Marble Hill Park Open daily, April to September; licensed.
[note– inexpensive food, lovely setting]
HAMMERTON'S FERRY, Riverside, Twickenham *Eccentric ferry service to Ham House*
HAM HOUSE Ham Street Petersham T.940–1950
1400–1800, Closed Mondays.
ORLEANS HOUSE GALLERY,★ The Octagon, Lebanon Park Road, Twickenham T.892–0221
1300–1700 Tues–Sat, 1400–1630 Sun & Bank Hols, Closed Monday.
ST. MARY'S★ Parish Church, Church Street, Twickenham T.892–2318 (appears engaged in prayer?)
STRAWBERRY HILL Waldegrave Road Twickenham T.892–5633/0051
Admission by tour on Wed & Sat, only, by prior appointment
POPE'S GROTTO Cross Deep, Teddington T.892–5633
Admission by key on Sat, only by prior application
YORK TERRACE, Riverside, Twickenham
Open: dawn–dusk
Plenty of Pubs, including: *EEL PIE TAVERN* 9 Church Street Twickenham T.891–1717
WHITE SWAN Riverside Twickenham T.892–2166
TWICKENHAM GROUND, Rugby Football Union, Whitton Road, Twickenham T.892–8161

Vauxhall, Thames-side neighbourhood
VICTORIA AND ALBERT MUSEUM South Kensington SW7 T.938–8500 (recorded information: T.581–4894/6 *outstanding museum of art of mankind note.* Pirrelli Restaurant
1000–1750 M Tu W Th F Sa [Su, 1430–1750]
VICTORIA TOWER GARDENS Victoria Embankment SW1
usually open **dawn to dusk**
VINTNERS' HALL Kennet Wharf Lane City EC4 T.238–1863
by appointment (Court Room [1446: pannelling 1576]
WALLACE COLLECTION★ Manchester Square Marble Arch W1 T.935–0687 *much overlooked but magnificent art collection of European schools*
1000–1700 M Tu W Th F Sa, 1400–1700 Su
Wandsworth, Thames-side neighbourhood (Borough of) – Map 2
Wapping, Thames-side district (Map 1)
Wellington Museum – Apsley House
WESLEY's HOUSE & CHAPEL City Road City EC1 T.253–2262 *18thC home [1779–91] of Founder of Methodism [1703–1791] and "the mother church of world Methodism"*
note – see Charterhouse, nearby, where he was educated (open Wednesday afternoon tours)
House: **1000–1600 M Tu W Th F Sa –**
Chapel:★ **0800–1600 M Tu W Th F – –** (Sunday services **1100** followed by snack lunch)
Westminster, Thames-side City see Contents and disc Map

WESTMINSTER: COLLEGE GARDEN (by front entrance to Westminster Abbey) SW1 *lunchtime summer concerts: August & September*
WESTMINSTER HALL Parliament Square – Houses of Parliament Whitehall – Banqueting House; – Changing the Guard;
WHITBREAD BREWERY Chiswell Street City EC1 *By appointment: Porter Tun Room, Speaker's Coach etc.*
WHITBREAD STABLES Garrett Street City EC1 T.606–4455 x2534
1100–1500 M Tu W Th F – – [Other times, by appointment]
York House & Terrace, – Twickenham Box
York Water Gate, Victoria Embankment (music, summer evenings) *historic arch designed by Inigo Jones 17thC*
Zoo, Regent's Park (London)

Walking along the banks of the Thames –
varied: [see Banner Maps 1 [inside front cover]
[see Banner Maps 3 & 4 [inside back cover]
3 miles Hampton Court – Kingston-upon-Thames
Towpath (northside) to Kingston Bridge – cross to east bank to continue: [BR Kingston]

4½ miles Kingston Bridge to Richmond
Townside bank of Thames (eastside) continue northwards to Ham, and Petersham – Hammerton's summer ferry to Twickenham bank) – and on to Richmond. [BR Richmond, tube]
3 miles Richmond and Twickenham
Cross Richmond Bridge westwards to Twickenham bank – turn south (left) along towpath to Marble Hill Park and Riverside, Twickenham [BR Twickenham]
To Teddington – via Twickenham – 2 miles – or via Kingston, cross river by Teddington footbridge at Teddington Lock.
8½ miles Richmond – via Kew, Chiswick, Hammersmith – to Putney Bridge
Continue northwards from Richmond on towpath passing under Twickenham Bridge past Old Deer Park, Kew Gardens, to Kew Bridge [BR] – Strand-on-the-Green (north bank) – thereafter "long haul" to Mortlake, Barnes and Putney (southbank), or to Chiswick and Hammersmith (north bank)
10 miles Putney Bridge to Westminster [5½ miles overland]
Towpaths interrupted – dexterous use of bridges to cross banks – consult London Tourist Board Information services – contact the River Thames Society – pioneer the route from the decks of a river steamer before pedestrian exersion?
note. All distances approximate.

WESTMINSTER ABBEY Parliament Square SW1 T.222–5152

The ensemble: most exceptional architectural building and shrine to man's vaingloriousness.

Cloisters* & Nave*	0800–1800	M	Tu	W	Th	F	–	[Su: between services]

"historic monastic Cloister and Milling green" see – where the monks played solitaire, Tomb of Unknown Warrior, "over 5,000 memorials in the Abbey"

Chapter House, Pyx Chamber & Muns Room	1000–1800	M	Tu	W	Th	F	Sa	– "home of Parliament" (1257–1547)
Jerusalem Chamber, & Jericho Parlour, Little Cloister	see "Super Tours"	[–	–	–	–	–	–	– by guide only]
College Garden*	1000–1600	–	–	–	Th	–	–	– "oldest garden in England"

see – old trickling fountain in hushed surroundings

Transepts (Poets' Corner)	0900–1645	M	Tu	W	Th	F	Sa	– "famous names everywhere you look"

see – Chaucer's Tomb

Royal Chapels	0900–1645	M	Tu	W	Th	F	Sa	– nb – Sa: 0900–1445, 1545–1745

"resting place of nearly every king and queen from St. Edward the Confessor until George III" see – Henry VII Chapel Coronation Chair Tomb of Queen Elizabeth I

***Whole Abbey* [free]	1800–1945	–	–	W	–	–	–	–

Services:

Matins	0730	M	Tu	W	Th	F	[Sa]	– [Sa, 0900]
Holy Communion	0800	(M)	Tu	W	Th	F	Sa	Su (and Bank Holidays)
Matins	1030	–	–	–	–	–	–	Su
Holy Communion	1230	M	Tu	–	Th	F	–	[Su, 1140]
Lunch hour service	1230	–	–	W	–	–	–	–
Evensong	1700	M	Tu	W	Th	F	[Sa, Su, 1500]

nb usually preceded by ½-hour organ recital
"choose a service when the sound of the beautiful organ sound accompanies the Choristers
Notes – Photography is not permitted without leave of the Vergers
– Super Tours bookable at 20 Dean's Yard SW1 T.222–7110
– For private prayer: St. Faith's Chapel [behind the red curtain, Poet's Corner']

238

WILLIAM MORRIS GALLERY* Lloyd Park Walthamstow
Forest Hill East London E17 T.527–5544 x4390 *attractive Georgian
boyhood home of Morris [1834–] now a museum of memorabilia to the
poet, founding father of socialism, Arts and Crafts movement, including
good collection of Pre-Raphaelite and Edwardian paintings*
1000–1200 & 1400–1700 – Tu W Th F Sa, – [note – 1st Sunday in
month: open **1000–1200 & 1400–1700**]
Access: Walthamstow tube, central line.

WINDSOR AND ETON
[Access: by road – M4 motorway exit junction 6 (21 miles from
London, by BR from Waterloo or Paddington, by boat: from
Maidenhead)
TOURIST INFORMATION CENTRE [T.(0753) 852010] or
Windsor & Eton Central Station, off High Street
WINDSOR CASTLE Windsor Berkshire [General Eqnuiries
T.0753–868286]
Castle Precincts: 1000–1900 M Tu W Th F Sa Su
[–1615: winter] Monday
note– Closed on Garter Day (mid June)
The State Apartments: 1030–1700 M Tu W Th F Sa Su
[–1500: winter]
note– Closed 5th–26th June and at short notice
St. George's Chapel: 1045–1600 M Tu W Th F Sa
[1545: winter], **1400–1600** Su [1545: winter]
note– Closed in January and for special services
(e.g. Garter service) Garter Ceremony: ticket attendance.
Application for tickets may be made to: Lord
Chamberlain's Office, St. James's Palace, London SW1
Albert Memorial Chapel: 1000–1300 &
1400–1545 M Tu W Th F Sa –
The Curfew Tower: 1100–1300 &
1400–1600 – Tu W Th F Sa –
Queen Mary's Dolls' House: 1030–1700 [–1500 winter]
M Tu W Th F Sa –
Exhibiton of Old Master Drawings: [ibid]
note– Dolls' House & Exhibition are closed on Garter Day
& at short notice
Exhibition of The Queen's Presents:} ibid
Royal Carriages, Royal Mews:
Ceremony of the Changing of the Guard:
1100 hours, Dly Mon–Sat, beside the Castle entrance
ROYAL WINDSOR HORSE SHOW: Advance booking by
written application to: Shows Box Office, 54 Brooksby's
Walk, London E9 6DA General information: T.0753–860633
note– useful to specify tickets (approx. £45 for two, with
parking) *for* Members, reserved seats and Members
Admission.
HOUSEHOLD CAVALRY MUSEUM, Combermere
Barracks, St. Leonards Road, South Windsor: Daily
Mon–Fri, & Sundays in summer months; *comprehensive
collection of military hardware.*
ROYALTY & EMPIRE EXHIBITION Windsor & Eton
Central Station: Daily **0930–1730**
WINDSOR GREAT PARK: Daily **1000–1800** [–to dusk, in
winter]
ETON COLLEGE, Windsor, Berkshire: Enquiries: The
Custodian: T.(0753) 863593
Eton College Chapel: **1130–1230, 1430–1700** Mon–Sat
[closed Sundays]
Museum of Eton Life: **1400–1700 Mon–Sat** in termtime, and
1030–1700 in school recess.
Precincts, Upper & Lower School: **1130–1700** Daily Tours
[but closed lunchtime **1230–1430**, & Sundays]
RIVERTRIPS: The Promenade, Barry Avenue –
T.0753–862933
Hotels information: Castle Hotel, High Street, Windsor
(reservations: 0753–851011)
Sir Christopher Wren's Old House Hotel, Thames Street,
Windsor (reservations 0753–861354)
The Christopher Hotel, High Street, Eton (reservations:
0753–852359)
Sunday lunch on the river? House on the Bridge, Eton
(reservations – window table – 0753–860914

WIMBLEDON
Places to visit –
(pronounced Wimbuld'n: variously spelt, before settling into the
recognised spelling known to-day –
Wimbledounying [967 A.D.] Anglo-Saxon; Wymbell-ton
[1609]; the latter version may have been taken across the Atlantic
and be the basis of the preferred American pronounciation and
emphasis on the last syllable.

While the destination of Wimbledon, itself standing back and
over its river neighbours of Putney, Richmond and Kingston, is
inland of the Thames, it affords a pleasurable and convenient
detour to the general excursions of London's upstream locations.

WIMBLEDON, General Information, T.543–2222
[London Borough of Merton]
(map)
CECIL MAUSOLEUM see St. Mary's Parish Church
WIMBLEDON LAWN TENNIS MUSEUM Church
Road SW19 T.946–6131
1100–1700 Tues–Sat [Closed Mon]) **1400–700** Sun;
note– Closed during Championships except to spectators;
WIMBLEDON MUSEUM OF LOCAL HISTORY*
26 Lingfield Road SW19 T.946–9398
1430–1700 Sat (only) Admission Free;
WIMBLEDON WINDMILL MUSEUM Wimbledon
Common SW19 T.788–7655
1400–1700 Sat & Sun (Easter thru October including
Bank Holidays;
ST. MARY'S PARISH CHURCH Church Road SW19
1100–1800 Daily [except Sundays and Services]
Admission Free;
SOUTHSIDE HOUSE Wimbledon Common (South
Side) SW19
Guided Tours @ **1400, 1500, 1600 & 1700 hours on
Tues, Thurs, & Sat** (October thru May), else, visits by
prior appointment in writing to The Curator;

access – From Wimbledon Sation (BR, Tube) take bus 80
or 93 to The Rose and Crown Pub, Wimbledon
Village, then 10 minutes' walk along southern
border of the Common [South Side] gates
opposite Hand in Hand, Crooked Billet Pubs;
CANNIZARO PARK West Side, Wimbledon Common
Thirty-five acres of mature parkland, Open dawn to
dusk, Admission Free;
CANNIZARO HOUSE HOTEL South Side,
Wimbledon Common SW19 bookings – T.879–1464
Telex: 9413837 Telefax: T.879–7338;
*Recently restored mansion now converted into a lavishly-
appointed hotel and restaurant;*

WIMBLEDON 'PUBS' INCLUDE –
CROOKED BILLET Crooked Billet Lane SW19 T.946–5898
HAND IN HAND Crooked Billet Lane SW19 T.946–5720
FOX AND GRAPES Camp Road SW19 T.946–5599

SPECTATOR SPORTS: *Tennis* Information about tickets:
T.946–2244; *Greyhound racing* Information about fixtures and
dinner reservations: T.946–5361; EVENING EVENTS:
1915 Fri & Sat at The Stadium, Plough Lane SW19; *Football:*
Wimbledon's prestigious Football Club – 1988 F.A. Cup
Winners – is closed during the summer

SIGHTS IN THE VICINITY OF WINDSOR
DORNEY COURT (Tudor Manor House), Dorney,
nr. Windsor T.062–864638 *(home-made cream teas)*
ROYAL HOLLOWAY & NEW BEDFORD COLLEGE,
Englefield Green (3 miles) T.07843–34455 (no answer: 1988
attempts suggest write)
(Victorian paintings, admission by prior arrangement)
SAVILL GARDEN, Wick Lane, Englefield Green,
T.0753–860222
(noted for rhododendrons display)
Windsor Great Park
**Unusual note: Great Fosters Hotel, Stroude Rd,
Egham (5 miles), T.0784–33822** (*16thC mansion, Tithe Barn
restaurant,* 1450 A.D.)
ROYAL MAUSOLEUM, Frogmore, Windsor Home Park:
Open May (3 days) T.0753–852010

INFORMATION

Leisureline for main events of the day in London – T.246–8041 (English); T.246–8043 (French); T.246–8045 (German).
LONDON TOURIST BOARD (T.730–3488)
The LONDON TOURIST BOARD offers every visitor to London a complete service of information (including *What to do, How, When & Where to do it*):

Information Centres –
VICTORIA STATION FORECOURT SW1 Hours: 0900–2030 (& 0800–2200 July–August)
HARRODS Department Store Knightsbridge SW1 0900–1700 Mon–Sat (& –1900 Wed, –1800 Sat)
SELFRIDGES Department Store Oxford Street W1 0930–1730 Mon–Sat (& –1900 Thurs)
      THE BRITISH TRAVEL CENTRE 12 Lower Regent Street W1 0900–1830 M Tu W Th F Sa, 1000–1600 Su
      The **British Travel Centre**, right in the heart of London, operates a booking service for all types of accommodation throughout Britain, including London and combines the expertise of BTA, British Rail, American Express and Roomcentre and will book rail, air, and car travel, reserve accommodation, sightseeing tours and theatre tickets, change currency and provide information in many languages on all parts of the United Kingdom. There is also a book shop and gift shop within the Centre.

TAKE A GUIDE LTD

PERSONALISED SIGHTSEEING TOURS

Among the many tour operators who offer a wide range of services to the visitor in London, experts in the field include –

    "TAKE-A-GUIDE LTD offer a personal sightseeing service by private car with qualified Driver-Guide. They will plan any itinerary to suit clients' interests and have unrivalled knowledge of charming inns, manor houses and castles for overnight tours in the Thames Valley and the countryside of Britain. Established in 1960 they have their own USA sales office in New York staffed by qualified guides."

TAKE-A-GUIDE LTD

63 East 79th Street   11 Uxbridge Street, Kensington
New York, NY 10021   London, W8. England
1–800–223–6450/212–628–4823   01–221–5475 (24–hours).

LONDON FROM THE AIR?

From on high, the many aspects of the river take on new dimensions; the collections of buildings and places as described in this book may now be seen in a fresh light; a truly unforgettable experience for everyone; and ideal from the point of view of photographers!
    By Helicopter: (01) 221–5475
    (*Remember*: "Wings" come once in a lifetime, albeit not cheaply).

For a railway journey of a lifetime, the **Orient-Express** is hard to beat. Further details from Venice Simplon-Orient-Express Ltd. T.928–6000.

– A CHECKLIST FOR CHILDREN IN LONDON –

Children who wish to show off London to their friends and family may like to consider including a visit to one or other of the places listed below, and might be suitably combined with an excursion to other places listed in the Appendix.

RIVERTRIP:
recorded information T.730–4812
Thames Line catamarans T.941–5454
Charing Cross Pier T.930–0970, Westminster Pier
T.930–4097

EAST LONDON –
Bermondsey –
Old Operating Theatre and Herb Garret, Guy's
Hospital T.407–7600
Space Adventure, Tooley Street T.378–1405
London Dungeons, Tooley Street T.403–0606
City –
Children's Cinema Club, Barbican T.628–8795
Brass Rubbing Centre, All Hallows, Tower Hill
T.481–2928
Museum of London, Barbican T.638–8891
HMS Belfast, access via ferry, Tower Pier, Tower
Hill T.407–6434
Docklands Light Railwayride, Tower Hill
T.538–0311
Historic Ship Collection & St. Katherine's Dock,
Tower
The Monument steps, Bank T.626–2717
Royal Britain Exhibition, Barbican T.588–0588
Whitbread Shirehorse Stables, Clerkenwell
T.606–4455 x2534
Tower Bridge, City T.407–0922
Tower of London, City T.709–0765
* *eating out:* The Fish Inn, 110 Old Street, City
T.251–3937
Ravello's, 46 Old Street, City
T.253–6279/251–3620
Islington –
Little Angel Marionette Theatre, T.222–1767
Jo Grimaldi Memorial Park,
East End –
Bethnal Green Museum of Childhood T.980–2415
Geffrye Museum T.980–4315
Greenwich –
CS Cutty Sark & Gipsy Moth IV T.858–3445
National Maritime Museum
Woolwich –
North Woolwich Old Station Museum T.474–7244
Thames Barrier T.854–1373

CENTRAL LONDON
Bayswater –
Pollock's Toy & Model Museum T.636–3452
Bathurst Riding Stables T.723–2813 Riding in
Hyde Park:
Chelsea –
National Army Museum T.730–0717
[Battersea Park, summer events]
Covent Garden –
Buskers' entertainment.
London Transport Museum T.379–6344
* *eating out:* Diana's Diner, 39 Endell Street
T.240–0272
Kensington –
Boating on the Serpentine, Hyde Park.
Geological Museum T.589–3444
Natural History Museum T.589–6323
Peter Pan statue, Kensington Gardens [*Telephone
Wendy, and explain request to British Telecom
Operator*]!
Science Museum
Scout Association, Cromwell Road T.584–7030
* *eating out:* Mario's Cafe in Holland Park (near the
Orangery) T.602–2216
Knightsbridge –
Harrods Pet Shop [4th floor] T.730–1234
Harrods New England Ice Cream Parlour [Ground
floor]
Regent's Street –
Hamleys Toy Shop T.734–3161
Regent's Park –
London Zoo T.722–3333
Boating on the Lake
Marylebone –
Madame Tussaud's Waxworks T.935–6861,
& Planetarium
Regent's Canal –
Barge trips (information centre): T.482–0523
Piccadilly –
Guinness World of Records T.439–7331
Hard Rock Cafe 7, Piccadilly, Hyde Park Corner
[T-shirts; shop, 7 Old Park Lane]
Brass rubbing: St. James's Church Hall T.437–6023
* *eating out:* Smollensky's Balloon, 1 Dover Street
T.491–1199

Soho –
* *eating out:* Chuen Cheng Ku, 17 Wardour Street
T.437–1398
Westminster –
Changing the Guard at Buckingham Palace.
Royal Mews, Buckingham Palace.
Brass rubbing: St. Martin-in-the-Fields, Trafalgar
Square T.437–6023

WEST LONDON
Kew
Kew Bridge Engines Trust
Kew Gardens
Hampton Court Maze
Richmond –
Ice Rink skating T.892–3646
Waterslide Complex (all-weather "Wild Waters")
T.948–8853
Boat-hire on the Thames.
* *eating out:* – Maids of Honour Teas
– Mrs. Beetons, 58 Hill Rise T.940–9561
Wimbledon –
Lawn Tennis Museum
Polka Children's Theatre T.543–4888 & 0363
Windmill
Village stables (riding on the Common)
T.946–8579

WINDSOR
Windsor Castle –
Boat trip or boat-hire
Queen Mary's Dolls' House
Royalty & Railways Exhibition
Safari Park
(Runnymede: Magna Carta Memorial)

Escort service for Children: Universal Aunts, 250
King's Road SW3 T.351–5767
* Eating establishments that claim to cater to
children and young adults

The way to see London is from the top of a bus – from the top of a bus, gentlemen.

Remark attributed to W.E. Gladstone, advising some American tourists.

19thC.

Sightseers may find bus routes confusing, but those wishing to follow the late Prime Minister's example should telephone London Transport (01) 222–1234 to obtain assistance in planning their schedules.

SUNDAYS IN AND AROUND LONDON

Some of the nation's many Galleries, Museums and Historic Places are closed on Sunday mornings, if not all day. It is worse still during the winter months, as anyone who has wasted a journey to the Tower of London on a Sunday will remember. Presumably this state of affairs will change in the cultural Capital of Europe. Despite this insularity, there are plenty of things to do and places to visit. Weather permitting, a boat trip might be combined with a visit to one or other place on land.

The following short-list, which should be read in conjunction with the information pages provided in the Appendix, may aid the traveller who seeks to spend Sunday out and about.

Piers abbreviations: Cadogan Pier [CP] – Charing Cross Pier [ChXP] – Festival Hall Pier [FHP] – London Bridge City Pier [LBCP] – Richmond Pier [RP] – St. Helen's Pier [St.HP] – Swan Lane Pier [SLP] – Tower Pier [TP] – Westminster Pier [WP].

Places open on Sundays, include –
– times given are for summer and should be checked –

LOCATION AND PLACE	MORNING -	AFTERNOON
– West End –		
Piers: Charing Cross Pier, Westminister Pier		
APSLEY HOUSE (Hyde Park Corner)		1430 – 1800
BANQUETING HOUSE (Whitehall) *[WP]*		1400 – 1800
BRITISH MUSEUM (Bloomsbury)		1430 – 1800
CABINET WAR ROOMS (Whitehall) *[WP]*	1000	– 1750
COURTAULD INSTITUTE (Bloomsbury)		1400 – 1700
JEWISH MUSEUM (Bloomsbury)	1000 – 1245	
KENSINGTON PALACE (Kensington)		1300 – 1700
LONDON TOY & MODEL Museum (Bayswater)	1100	– 1700
LONDON ZOO (Regent's Park)	0900	– 1900
MADAME TUSSAUD's (Baker Street)	1000	– 1730
NATIONAL GALLERY (Trafalgar Square) *[ChXP]*		1400 – 1800
NATIONAL PORTRAIT GALLERY *[ChXP]*		1400 – 1800
NATURAL HISTORY MUSEUM (S.Kensington)		1430 – 1800
QUEEN's GALLERY (Buckingham Palace)		1400 – 1700
ROYAL ACADEMY (Piccadilly)	1000	– 1800
SCIENCE MUSEUM (S.Kensington)		1430 – 1800
Speakers' Corner, (Marble Arch)		1400 – 1600
VICTORIA & ALBERT MUSEUM (S.Kensington)		1430 – 1750
WALLACE COLLECTION (Marylebone)		1400 – 1700
– City & East End –		
Piers: Swan Lane Pier, Tower Pier		
BETHNAL GREEN MUSEUM Of Childhood		1430 – 1800
GEFFRYE MUSEUM (Whitechapel)		1400 – 1700
Market: PETTICOAT LANE (Aldgate)	1000 – 1300	
MUSEUM OF LONDON (Barbican) *[SLP]*		1400 – 1800
ROYAL BRITAIN MUSEUM (Barbican)	1000	– 1700
ST. BARTHOLOMEW THE GREAT	0900	– 1630
ST. PAUL's CATHEDRAL *[SLP]*	0730	– 1830
TOWER BRIDGE WALKWAY (Tower Hill) *[TP]*	1000	– 1745
TOWER OF LONDON (Tower Hill) *[TP]*		1400 – 1745
– South Bank –		
Piers: Lambeth Pier, festival Hall Pier, London Bridge City Pier		
BEAR GARDENS MUSEUM (Bankside)		1400 – 1800
HMS BELFAST (London Bridge) *[TP]*	1100	– 1630
HAYWARD GALLERY (Southwark)	1200	– 1800
IMPERIAL WAR MUSEUM (Lambeth)		1400 – 1750
SOSEKI NATSUME MUSEUM (Clapham)		1400 – 1700
SOUTHWARK CATHEDRAL *[LBCP]*	1000	– 1700

– Chelsea & Battersea –
Piers: Cadogan Pier, Chelsea Harbour

CARLYLE's HOUSE *[CP]*		1400 – 1700
CHELSEA PHYSIC GARDEN *[CP]*		1400 – 1700
CHELSEA OLD CHURCH *[CP]*	1100 – 1300 &	1400 – 1700
CROSBY HALL *[CP]*	1000 – 1200 &	1415 – 1700
NATIONAL ARMY MUSEUM *[CP]*		1400 – 1730
ROYAL HOSPITAL *[CP]*		1400 – 1600
ST. MARY's CHURCH (Battersea)	1130 –	1700
TATE GALLERY & CLORE GALLERY		1400 – 1750

– Hampstead & Highgate –

BURGH HOUSE [Local History Museum]	1200	1200 – 1700
FENTON HOUSE	1100 –	1700
HIGHGATE CEMETERY (Guided Tours)	1000 –	1700
KEATS HOUSE		1400 – 1700
KENWOOD HOUSE & PARK	1000 –	1700
SIGMUND FREUD's HOUSE	1200 –	1700

– 'Scenic' London –

HAM HOUSE *Twickenham ferry*		1400 – 1800
HAMPTON COURT PALACE *Royal Pier*	1100 –	1800
KEW GARDENS *Kew Pier*	1000 –	1800
MARBLE HILL HOUSE *[RP]*	1000 –	1700
MUSEUM OF RICHMOND *[RP, St.HP]*		1300 – 1600
ORLEANS HOUSE GALLERY *[RP]*		1400 – 1630
Richmond Park	1000 –	1800
Riverside Walks & Pubs *[RP]*		
Twickenham Riverside Walks & Pubs *[RP]*		
WIMBLEDON LAWN TENNIS MUSEUM		1400 – 1700
WIMBLEDON WINDMILL MUSEUM		1400 – 1700

– Windsor & Eton –
Riverside, walks and Pubs, Promenade Pier

Runnymede	1000 –	1800
Savill Gardens	1000 –	1800
WINDSOR CASTLE [*See* information, Appendix]	1030 –	1900
Windsor Great Park	1000 –	1800

STATEMENT BY THE PUBLISHER

This work, LONDON ON THAMES – UPSTREAM – is the first of what we hope will become a series of travelbooks about interesting cities and places as seen through the eyes of the author.

Readers are invited to inform us of their preferred haunts and to submit their first-hand experiences of any anecdotes that, if included in future works, will be attributed and acknowledged, personally. Establishments that consider they should be included in any future edition of this book are invited to submit their details to our editorial department.

Any member of the public who finds difficulty in obtaining a copy of this book from a retail outlet or wishes to commend a prospective outlet is invited to contact our publishing division at the address given below.

for and on behalf of
THIRD MILLENNIUM LEISURE LIMITED
The Courtyard, Chobham High Street, Surrey GU24 8AF.

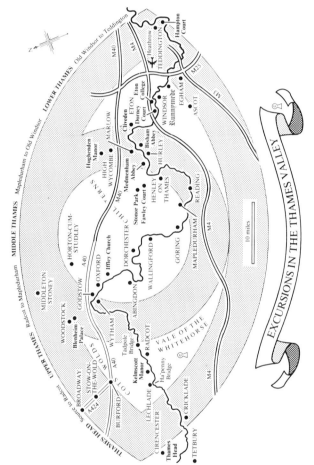

EXCURSIONS IN THE THAMES VALLEY

Those wishing to explore the English countryside of the Thames Valley: there are many hotels and places to stay to choose from, stretching between London and Lechlade, near the source of the Thames, and Shakespeare's Stratford-on-Avon, and the beauty of the Cotswolds. The following list of establishments welcome enquiries from visitors who should enquire of occupancy and restaurant charges before their arrival.

Note. The Publishers have prepared this information for the benefit of the traveller. No responsibility attaches to any adverse experience; however, the Publishers would be most grateful to learn of readers' opinions – good and bad.

At Heathrow (nearly on Thames), there is a selection of large hotels that are conveniently placed for excursions in the Thames Valley and represent good value compared with expensive Central London hotels, hence are included for consideration by the traveller. Most of the hotels at Heathrow offer courtesy shuttle coaches to Heathrow underground station and bus stations.

N.B. [$] Not to be indulged with a weak dollar.   [$$] Out of this world?

244

Hotels Pubs/Inns		Tel.	Telex	Telefax
Abingdon				
THE UPPER REACHES Thames Street Oxon		0235–22311	847707	0235–555182
OLD ANCHOR St. Helen's Wharf		0235–21726		
Ascot				
THE BERYSTEDE Bagshot Road Sunninghill Berks	$$	0990–23311	847707	0990–872301
THE ROYAL BERKSHIRE London Road Sunninghill Berks	$$	0990–23322	847280	0990–27100
Banbury				
WHATELY HALL Banbury Cross Oxon	$	0295–3451	837149	0295–271736
Bisney-on-Thames				
PERCH		0865–240386		
Bray				
MONKEY ISLAND Monkey Island Lane		0628–23400	846589	0628–784732
WATERSIDE INN Ferry Road	$$	0628–20691	–	0628–784710
HIND's HEAD High Street		0628–26151	–	–
Broadway				
BUCKLAND MANOR Buckland Broadway Worcs	$	0386–852626		
LYGON ARMS Broadway Worcs	$$	0386–852255	338260	0386–858611
CROWN & TRUMPET Snowshill Road				
Burford				
BAY TREE	$	0386–853202		
HIGHWAY HOTEL		099382–3137 / 099382–2136	838736	–
Burnham				
BURNHAM BEECHES HOTEL Grove Road		06286–3333		06286–3994
Clanfield				
THE PLOUGH		036781–222	437334	
Datchet				
MORNING STAR The Green		0753–41844		
Dorchester-on-Thames				
THE GEORGE High Street		0865–340404		
SIX BELLS (cricket green) Warborough		06732–8265		
Egham				
GREAT FOSTERS HOTEL Stroude Road	$	0784–33822	944441	
Eton				
BOATERS		0753–863597		
THE HOUSE ON THE BRIDGE 71 High Street		0753–860914	849462	
Godstow-on-Thames				
TROUT INN Godstow Bridge, near Oxford		0865–54485		
Hampton Court				
THE MITRE		979–2264		
BELL, Hampton		979–1444		
KING's ARMS		977–1729		
Heathrow				
ARIEL Bath Road Hayes		759–2552	21777	564–9265
HEATHROW PARK HOTEL Bath Road Longford West Drayton		759–2400	934093	759–5278
EXCELSIOR Bath Road West Drayton		759–6611	24525	759–3421
HEATHROW PENTA Bath Road Houndslow		897–6363	934660	897–1113
HOLIDAY INN Stockley Road West Drayton		0895–445555	934518	0895–445122
POST HOUSE Sipson Road West Drayton		759–2323	934280	897–8659
SHERATON HEATHROW Colnbrook by-pass West Drayton		759–2424	934331	759–2091
SHERATON SKYLINE Bath Road Harlington Hayes		759–2535	934254	750–9150
SKYWAY 140 Bath Road Hayes		759–6311	23935	759–4559
Henley-on-Thames				
LITTLE WHITE HART Riverside		0491–574145	–	–

Hotels Pubs/Inns		Tel.	Telex	Telefax
Horton-cum-Studley				
STUDLEY PRIORY	$	086735–203/254	23152 SPHO	086735–613
Hurley				
OLDE BELL Hurley near Henley	$	06882–5881	847035 BELL HRG	06882–5939
Kingston-upon-Thames				
KINGSTON LODGE Kingston Hill		547–4481	936034	547–1013
Lechlade				
HA'PENNY BRIDGE Lechlade		036785–205		
SWAN INN, Southrop				
TROUT INN St. John's Bridge Farmgdon		0367–52313		
Maidenhead				
SHIRE HORSE Maidenhead Thicket		06882–5335		
Marlow				
THE COMPLEAT ANGLER Marlow Bridge	$$	06284–4444 / 06284–4360	848644	06284–6388
SHIP West Street			–	–
Middleton Stony				
THE JERSEY ARMS		086989–234		
Moreton-in-Marsh				
WHITE HART ROYAL High Street		0608–50731		–
Oxford				
THE RANDOLPH Beaumont Street		0865–247481	83446	
ISIS TAVERN Iffley Lock near Oxford (S ½ mile)		0865–247006		
TURF TAVERN 10 St. Helen's Passage [off Holywell Street]		0865–243235		
THE ROSE REVIVED New Bridge Standlake		086731–221		
Pangbourne				
THE COPPER INN		07357–2244		
Runnymede				
RUNNYMEDE Windsor Road Egham		0784–36171	934900	0784–36340
Sonning-on-Thames				
THE FRENCH HORN	$	0734–692204		
THE BULL INN		0734–693901		
Staines				
THAMES LODGE Thames Street		0784–44435/5	8812552	0784–54858
SHIP The Causeway		0784–52610	–	
Stow-on-the-Wold				
WYCK HILL HOUSE		0451–31936	43611	0451–32243
Streatley-on-Thames				
THE SWAN		0491–873737	848259	0491–872554
MILLER OF MANSFIELD High Street, Goring		0491–872829	–	
Taplow				
CLIVEDEN	$$	06286–64246	846562	06286–61837
THE FEATHERS INN Taplow Common		06286–2929		
Tetbury				
CALCOT MANOR near Tetbury	$	066689–355	437105	0869–50901
THE SNOOTY FOX Market Place	$	066652–436	–	–
Weston-on-the-Green				
WESTON MANOR near Oxford	$	0869–50621	83409	0865–726753 FEATHERS
Woodstock				
THE FEATHERS Market Street		0993–812291	83138 TELKAY G	879–7338
Wimbledon				
CANNIZARO HOUSE South Side Wimbledon Common	$	879–1464	9413837	879–7338
Windsor				
OAKLEY COURT Windsor Road near Windsor (& nr. Maidenhead)	$	0628–74141	849958	0628–37011
CASTLE High Street		0753–851011	849220	0753–830244
WREN's HOUSE HOTEL Thames Street		0753–861354		
ROYAL OAK Datchet Road		0753–865179	847938	
BELLS OF OUZELEY Old Windsor		0753–861526		
Wytham				
WHITE HART Wytham near Oxford (1m.S)		0865–244372		

LONDON ON THAMES
A SIGNED AND INSCRIBED COPY OF THIS FIRST EDITION
OF LONDON ON THAMES – FOR YOU? FOR A FRIEND?

If, in the words of Mr. Noel Picarda Kemp's Introduction –

> LONDON ON THAMES is exactly the sort of book one is
> delighted to give, or, better still, to receive as a present . . .

You may wish to acquire a unique possession and the Publishers have
arranged for the author to inscribe copies of LONDON ON THAMES
to **members of the public who donate £10 to the charity of their
choice**.

Please follow these instructions carefully:

---

1. Order LONDON ON THAMES and pay £6.45* per copy (by
cheque, etc.) from: Third Millennium Leisure Limited,
    The Courtyard, Chobham High Street, Surrey GU24 8AF.

2. Enclose a separate payment (cheque, banker's draft, money
order, traveller's cheque, **but not** cash notes) to the value of £10
sterling **made payable to a designated charity.**

3. With your order and separate payments, enclose the following
personal information, if you wish. *Remember to write clearly.*

Name of person (recipient of book) e.g. *To Emma (Hamilton)*

Special message? e.g. *England expects but you mustn't*

Name of giver (you?) e.g. *From Horatio*

The Publishers reserve the right, in their sole discretion, to withhold inappropriate
requests from the author's attention.

[* £4.95 + £1.50 p. & p.]

If you have no preferred charity, the Publishers commend:

NATIONAL ART-COLLECTIONS FUND   *Patron:* Her Majesty The Queen
(registered charity no. 209174) 20, John Islip Street, London SW1P 4JX
– Preserving the nation's works of art by voluntary subscription from individuals
such as **You**, the reader.

NATIONAL LIBRARY FOR THE BLIND   *Patron:* Her Majesty The Queen
(registered charity no. 213212) 17, Southampton Place, London WC1A 2EH
–This charity provides a lending library of books in *Braille*, and, *Moon* to blind
people, among many other useful causes.

246

RIVER THAMES SOCIETY *President*: Lord Camoys
(registered charity no. 288380) Side House, Middle Assendon, Henley-on-Thames
RG9 6AP
– This charity furthers the protection of the River Thames for the enjoyment of the
public. Its voice is heard and heeded on all matters that affect planning, recreation
and conservation.

The Publishers will forward your donation direct to your designated charity
from whom you will receive due acknowledgement. Please allow 28 days for the
despatch by mail of your inscribed copy of LONDON ON THAMES. You may
order as many copies as you like, by following the above instructions; subject to
stocks of the First Edition being available. If you prefer to have an inscribed copy
solely for your own use you can pass your existing copy to a friend, having sent
off for your own personally inscribed copy, by following the above instructions.

Note – Have you remembered to include your name and address in your order?

LIMITED EDITION PRINTS

A limited edition of a set of illustrations appearing in this book are to be released.
The prints will be individually numbered, 1–500 only, and signed by the artist.
The prints will be printed on the finest paper in the world and will be mounted
ready for framing. Single prints will cost twenty pounds each, and the complete
set seven hundred and fifty pounds; (for office walls, or dull corridors?)

Any person who is desirous of advance information should write his or her
enquiry to the Publishers.

Other Publications to be commended to the attention of the Reader –

> *London exists because of the Thames . . .*

(p.96) **Louise Nicholson: LONDON: Louise Nicholson's Definitive Guide [1988];**
The Bodley Head Limited; 382 pages; £9.95 (hardback)

> *If you want to see London's history in an hour or so – just so you can say you've seen it – and
> then get on with the shopping and the eating and the clubbing, take a river trip. The best way
> to pick up a potted history of London is to take an hour's cruise – upstream or downstream,
> doesn't matter – on a river boat.*

(p.37) **A Time Out Guide: LONDON FOR VISITORS [1988]**
Time Out Publications Limited; 162 pages; £3.25 (magazine)

> *London is seen at its best from the river . . .*

(p.72) **The Mitchell Beazley Traveller's Guides to Art: Britain & Ireland,** *by* Michael
Jacobs & Paul Simon [1984]
Mitchell Beazley Publishers; 304 pages, hardback, £8.95

> *Great Britain's most famous river, the Thames, is a natural water highway through the heart
> of southern England, full of variety and interest and a natural magnet for visitors . . .*

(p.3) **NICHOLSON: The Ordnance Survey Guide to the River Thames [1988]**
Robert Nicholson Publications Ltd; 160 pages; (softcover) £4.95

CRUISING DOWN THE RIVER

Cruis - ing down the riv - er,_____ on a Sun - day af - ter - noon,_____

If you will go a-long with me, we'll tra-vel with the tide.
And I will al-ways keep you, on the shel-tered side.
How-ev-er rough the way may be, the wa-ters dark and low,
Thro' all the storm-y wea-ther I will al-ways steer you home.

Cruis-ing down the riv-er, on a Sun-day af-ter-noon,
With one you love, the sun a-bove wait-ing for the moon.
The old ac-cord-ion play-ing a-sent-i-ment-al tune.
Cruis-ing down the riv-er, on a Sun-day af-ter-noon,
The birds a-bove all sing of love, a gent-le sweet re-frain.
The winds a-round all make a sound like soft-ly fall-ing rain.

Just two of us to-gether, we'll plan a hon-ey-moon
Cruis-ing down the riv-er, on a Sun-day af-ter-noon.

The lyrics and song were written by two middle-aged ladies of Clapham who entered for a "Write a Tune for £1,000" contest at the Hammersmith Palais: Lou Praeger, bandleader, was convinced it would become a hit but found none of the musical publishers – to whom he played it – showed any interest . . . until the representative of Campbell Connelly returned to the auditorium, not for the song – as Lou thought – but to retrieve his overcoat. Thereupon Lou offered to indemnify the publishers' costs against printing it. The rest is history. (Reproduced by courtesy of Cinephonic Music Co. Ltd: 8/9 Frith Street London W1 Copyright) © 1945. Used by permission. All rights reserved.

ANNOUNCING
— LONDON ON THAMES — DOWNSTREAM

LONDON ON THAMES – DOWNSTREAM – will be published shortly.

This book is designed to be a companion volume to LONDON ON THAMES and carries a Foreword by The Rt. Hon. The Lord Mayor of London, Sir Greville Spratt, G.B.E. which is reproduced, by his gracious permission.

This volume by the same author covers the rich scenic heritage of London where the Upstream volume leaves off, at King's Reach near London Bridge. The path of the River is charted in pen and brush from the City of London wending through the reviving Docklands in London's East End, passing Greenwich and the Thames Barrier at Woolwich, to Tilbury and Gravesend, (twenty six miles *below bridge*). Many more illustrations are included.

THE RIGHT HONOURABLE THE LORD MAYOR
SIR GREVILLE SPRATT GBE TD DL DLitt

THE MANSION HOUSE LONDON

Joseph Conrad referred to the River Thames as having the tranquil dignity of a waterway leading to the uttermost ends of the earth, where the tidal current runs to and fro in its increasing service, crowded with memories of men and ships it had borne whose names are like jewels flashing in the night of time.

Certainly the Royal Thames, queen of rivers; mirror of history; artery of commerce; sanctuary of wild life; place of work; source of recreation and stretching some 230 miles from the Cotswolds to the sea, is important above all others.

This importance is searched for and discovered by the author Tim Daniell in this cornucopia of a guide book "London on Thames - Downstream" which, with its elegant prose and delicate illustrations, provides a much needed compass for the explorer of London's river, its history and fascination.

The River Thames is a great natural asset. Yet it is underused aesthetically, socially and economically, and it is not long since we were abusing it rather than using it. Happily we are now more enlightened, and Mr. Daniell's delightful guide will play a useful part in that enlightenment, as well as giving much joy and profit to his readers.

Greville Spratt .

Lord Mayor

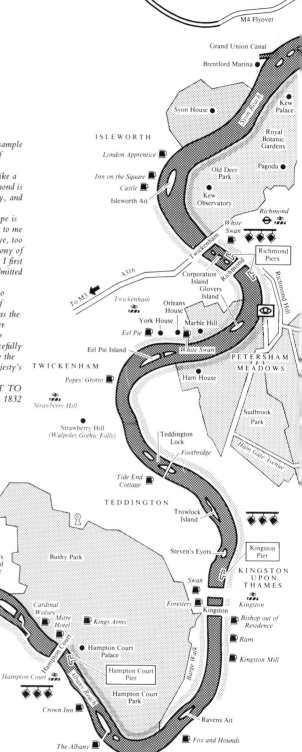

With foreigners it passes pretty generally for a sample (the only one they see) of the rural villages of England; and yet it is no more like the real untrimmed genuine country than a garden is like a field. I do not say this in disparagement. Richmond is Nature in a Court dress, but still Nature – ay, and very lovely Nature too.

The principal charm of this smiling landscape is the river, the beautiful river, for the hill seems to me overrated. That celebrated prospect is, to my eye, too woody, too leafy, too green. There is a monotony of vegetation, a heaviness. The view was finer as I first saw it in February, when the bare branches admitted frequent glimpses of houses and villages.

But the river, the beautiful river, there is no overrating that. Brimming to its very banks of meadow, or of garden, clean, pure, and calm as the bright summer day, which is reflected in clearer brightness from its bosom; no praise can be too enthusiastic for that glorious stream. How gracefully it glides through the graceful bridge! Certainly the Thames is the pleasantest highway in his Majesty's dominions.

Mary Russell Mitford. A VISIT TO RICHMOND, 1832

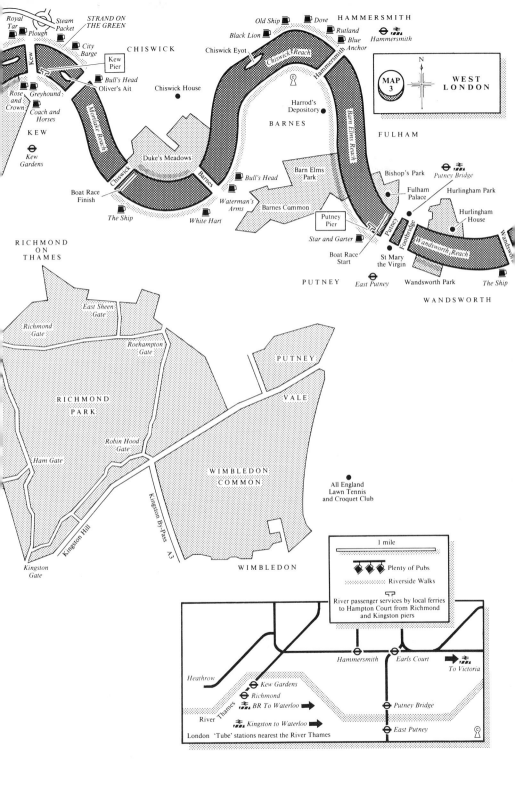

Cover Illustration
– LONDON ON THAMES – UPSTREAM –

THERE IS MORE to this cover illustration than at first meets the eye. It is intended to be a puzzle, a subtle allegory and a gentle polemic against slavish modernism.

The pageantry is a mixture of fact and fiction, of royal pomp and City circumstance. The coach, although enjoying a royal escort, is the Lord Mayor's crossing a 14thC bridge that never spanned the Thames. It is nevertheless fewer than thirty miles from Windsor and its exact location is to be the object of a competition, the details of which are to be announced in due course.

The barge appearing beneath the bridge is royal, the figurehead of the crowned lion shows this. Whoever is aboard has just received a royal salute, at the present, from the idle guardsman on the far side of the bridge whose legs are still "at ease". They are armed, as can be seen from the ordered arm of the nearer man, with the old Lee-Enfield rifle (which should be retained for public ceremonial duties: it being as nonsensical to insist that ceremonial drill is carried out with modern combat weaponry as it would be to insist on the Guards campaigning in scarlet tunics).

The guardsman depicted in the foreground belongs to no known regiment. The easy way to tell which regiment is which is to count the groups of buttons.

The numbers signify:

one button	–	Grenadier
two buttons	–	Coldstream
three buttons	–	Scots
four buttons	–	Irish
five buttons	–	Welsh

Thus the guardsman on this side of the bridge would be a Coldstream if one button was removed from the top row, or a Scots if an additional button was sewn onto his tunic in the rows beneath. In any event, unless he wakes his ideas up he's going to miss the chance of saluting whoever the royal personage is in the barge.

The swans represent the dual powers of monarch and the City of London, through the Dyers' and Vintners' Companies, in their joint monopoly of ownership of all swans on the river Thames. They were purposely painted plump to remind readers of the days when these graceful birds were presented as one of the main dishes at royal and City banquets.

The ostrich feathers which trim the hats of the coachman and the liveried footmen, and the horsehair on the helmets of the Household Cavalrymen, are a tribute to the eagerness with which the English grab whatever they can from the backside of an animal and put it on their heads.

The Cavalrymen are in fact the Life Guards who, together with the Blues and Royals (blue tunics, red helmet plumes, for those readers who attend the Changing of the Guard in Horse Guards Parade, Whitehall), make up the Household Cavalry. They and the five Foot Guards regiments comprise the Household Division which has the privilege of protecting the Sovereign.

The artist posed a challenge to the printers to reproduce a balmy English summer's day such as when overcast hazy blue-greyness in the sky can change in a trice to bursts of sunlight and back to outbreaks of sudden showers (note the guardsman and swan cast no shadows). The printers got their own back by obscuring (with the ISBN code on the back cover) a portrayal of extra cruising celebrities: Toad (of Toad Hall) and his friends the Water Rat and the Mole. Readers may enjoy a sight of them in the postcard-version of the cover on sale where this book was purchased.